Plate 1, Portrait of St. Francis Xavier, 61.0 x 48.7cm, discovered in 1920. (Photo: Kobe City Museum/DNPartcom)

Plate 2, Cover of *Atarashii Nihon no rekishi* (New History of Japan), Ikuhōsha Publishing, 2016.

Plate 3, Cover of *Atarashii shakai rekishi* (New Social Studies: History), Tokyo Shoseki, 2011.

Plate 4, Monument commemorating Xavier's landing on Kagoshima.

Plate 5, Two sculptures, Xavier and Angero (who holds a book), at the Xavier Park in Kagoshima city.

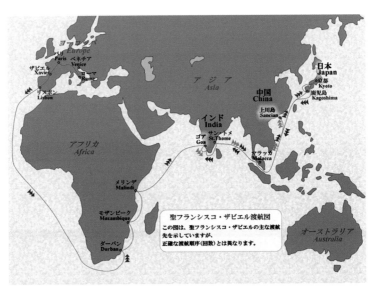

Plate 6, The route of Xavier's voyage to Japan (from the HP of Catholic Bishops' Conference of Japan).

Plate 7, Folding fan featuring Nanbanji by Kanō Sōshū (1551-1601), upper length 50.6cm x lower length 21.2cm x width 19.7cm. (Photo: Kobe City Museum/DNPartcom)

Plate 8, Detail of Nanbanji from a Nanban screen, ca. late sixteenth century-early seventeenth century, artist unknown, Gallery Nanban.

Plate 9, The altar of St. Xavier Church build in 1890, Meijimura Historical Park.

Plate 10, St. Xavier Church built in 1890, Meijimura Historical Park.

Plate 11, Xavier's monument at the site of Daidōji, present-day Xavier Memorial Park, Yamaguchi city.

Plate 12, Villion's statue in Xavier Memorial Park.

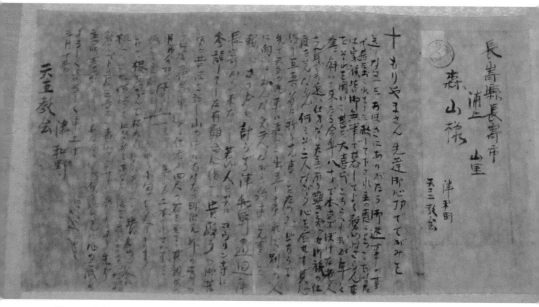

Plate 13, Villion's letter to Moriyama Jinzaburō dated 13 March 1922, Tsuwano Catholic Church.

Plate 14, Stone monument "Light of Faith" at Kōrinji.

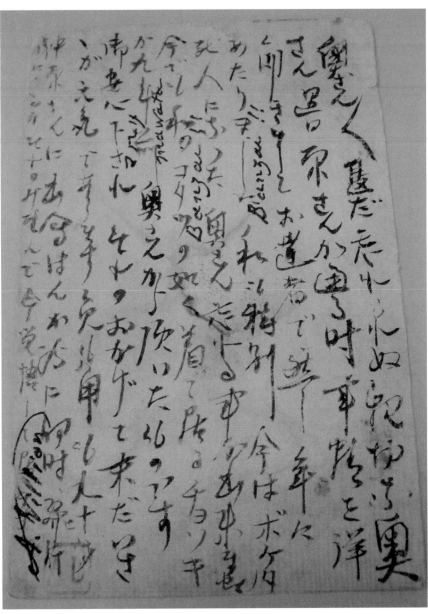

奥さんく、甚だ遠々如く乳母汁の奥
さん昌原さんが迎る時事態を洋
前きく〉とお達者で前々年に
めたり半分〈 令はボケ々
北人にふ〈〉Benzai
今く〉〈のコタ別り如く Benzai
かん〉〉〉奥さん忘とる中々〉〉〉〉
〉〉〉奥さんが頂いた化のアリ
〉〉に下され そしおなゲて来だ〉
が元気でするそも兄北〉申も人十〉
中原さくに弁々ばんが〉にト十〉
神々おりて十少け〉んで今〉〉前
〉〉署名〉

Plate 15, Villion's postcard to Nakahara Koma dated 15 January 1932 written in Nara. Nakahara Chūya Memorial Museum.

Plate 16, Hattori Cemetery, Osaka city.

Plate 17, Villion's death mask at Nara Catholic Church.

Plate 18, Villion's bag. Photograph by the author with the permission of Yoneda Yasuko.

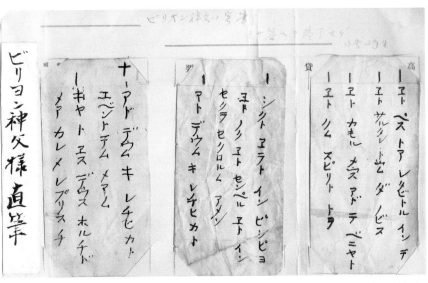

Plate 19, Villion's handwritten Latin prayers in katakana. Photograph by the author with the permission of Yoneda Yasuko.

AMATUS VILLION
Miss-Aposti

1843-1932
R.I.P.

墓之父霊ンヨリビ

Plate 20, Villion's grave and tombstone at Hattori Cemetery.

Plate 21, Graves of Candau and other priests, including G. Neyrand, at Catholic Fuchū Cemetery.

Plate 22, Kulturheim Chapel at Sophia University, where Heuvers saw Villion pray.

Plate 23, DVD cover for the opera *Hosokawa Grazia* composed by
Vincenzo Cimatti, released in 2017.

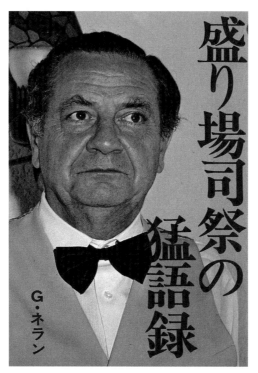

Plate 24, Photo of Georges Neyrand, from the cover of his book *Sakariba shisai no mōgoroku* (Korube Shuppansha, 1980).

Plate 25, Cover of Neyrand's book *Obaka-san no jijoden hanbun: Seisho katate ni Nippon 40 nenkan,* Kōdansha, 1992.

Making Xavier's Dream Real

Vernacular Writings of Catholic Missionaries in Modern Japan

JAPAN LIBRARY

Making Xavier's Dream Real

Vernacular Writings of Catholic Missionaries in Modern Japan

NANYAN GUO

Japan Publishing Industry Foundation for Culture

EDITORIAL NOTES:
This book follows the Hepburn system of romanization. Long vowels are indicated by macrons. Japanese names are given in the customary order, surname first.

Making Xavier's Dream Real:
Vernacular Writings of Catholic Missionaries in Modern Japan
Nanyan Guo

Published by Japan Publishing Industry Foundation for Culture (JPIC)
2-2-30 Kanda-Jinbocho, Chiyoda-ku, Tokyo 101-0051, Japan

First English edition: March 2020

This book is a translation of *Zabieru no yume o tsumugu: Kindai senkyōshitachi no Nihongo Bungaku* (Tokyo: Heibonsha Limited, Publishers, 2018).
English publishing rights arranged with Heibonsha Limited, Publishers,Tokyo.

Cover design: Nagata Toshinobu

Printed in Japan
ISBN 978-4-86658-134-7
https://japanlibrary.jpic.or.jp/

CONTENTS

PREFACE

One wintry Sunday morning late in 2001, I attended a Catholic Mass while visiting Hirosaki, a city in Aomori prefecture in northeastern Japan. As I entered the church a Canadian priest from Quebec was delivering his homily, and I was amazed by the perfect fluency of his Japanese speech. Never before had I encountered such a high-level proficiency by a non-Japanese. He not only incorporated elegant written expressions into spoken Japanese, but also made his philosophical messages on life, love, and forgiveness convincing and easy to understand.

As I listened, I began to wonder how foreign missionaries acquired mastery of a language that is famously difficult for non-native speakers and how they obtained, along with linguistic facility, profound knowledge of the culture of Japan. From that day I eagerly began to collect books written in Japanese by missionaries themselves as sole authors or in collaboration with Japanese assistants.

I myself acquired Japanese as a second language, and as I endeavored to study Japanese literature and culture, I have constantly paid close attention to other foreigners' proficiency. It is these missionaries who impress me most. Their books reveal their painstaking efforts to compose in Japanese, to accommodate Japanese viewpoints, to arrange their messages to be readily understandable, and to convey Christian thoughts to the Japanese people.

In addition to being awed by their deep and acute observations of Japan, I have been astonished by their enthusiasm and relentless energy for evangelization. What attracted these missionaries to this country was Francis Xavier's evaluation of the people and his critique of the customs he encountered when he visited in the mid-sixteenth century. What kept them in Japan for much of their lifetimes was their religious commitment and the gratification gained from their first-hand experience of living among its people, an experience full of pleasure, but also of hardship and often agony.

When I consider the small quantity written in Chinese by European and American modern missionaries, the large quantity of their writings for Japanese readers is truly admirable. Ironically, the majority of Japanese people know little about these books, nor are they aware of the existence of the missionaries. I find the stark contrast between these missionaries' devotion to Japan and ordinary people's indifference to their writings both intriguing and baffling.

Fortunately, some Japanese intellectuals did notice these books, even if the general public did not, and they even incorporated religious and philosophical ideas from the missionaries into their own writings. Through their mediation, missionaries have contributed importantly to modern Japanese culture.

These facts prompted me to establish a new research field that I call "Missionary Literature in the Japanese Language." The reason for grouping these vernacular writings under the title "literature" is that the authors employ literary and rhetoric devices in the same manner as the Holy Bible, the greatest masterpiece of literature in human history. The exploration of this research field has only just begun, and there is a long way to go before we can fully understand the impact of this literature on Japanese culture.

This book, originally written in Japanese, intends to shed new light on how Christianity has been received and absorbed into the soil of Japan. Published by Heibonsha in March 2018, *Zabieru no yume o tsumugu: Kindai senkyōshitachi no Nihongo Bungaku* was immediately reviewed in several major newspapers. Reviewers and readers were amazed to discover just how extensive the communication between these missionaries and Japanese intellectuals was.

This book leads readers on a journey to discover how Japan was woven into Xavier's grand dream of propagating the Christian faith in Asia, and how that dream enchanted and inspired four Catholic missionaries whose writings in Japanese represent the Christian influence that penetrated into the daily life of the country they came to know and love so well.

It is a great honor that my book was selected by the Japan Publishing Industry Foundation for Culture (JPIC) to be translated into English and published in the Japan Library Series. I decided to translate it into English by myself, as I wished to incorporate new research, to correct errors in the original version, and to scrutinize the contents one more time. The JPIC editor Ozaki Izumi gently and persistently guided me through the entire translation process by carefully reading my manuscript.

While I was in the process of translating this volume, two books written in Japanese by Takashi Shogimen were published in Japan: *Aikoku no kyōkasho* (Textbook for the Japanese Nation, Hyakumannen Shobō, 2019) and *Aikoku no kōzō* (The Structure of Patriotism, Iwanami Shoten, 2019). What fascinated me was Prof. Shogimen's analysis of "loving gaze" (a term coined by Iris Murdoch, who was inspired by Simone Weil), an open-eyed attitude toward a country's positive and negative aspects which he contrasts with the "blind love" commonly seen in contemporary "patriotism."

Missionary authors' writings reveal the practice of such a "loving gaze." They not only see the good nature of people, but also their weak points. Their highly affirmative evaluation of the Japanese people should not be taken as "unconditional praise," but rather a sign of strong commitment to improving the people's spiritual lives. If Japan was already a "heaven," these missionaries would have left immediately after their arrival. They realized it was not, but they believed that it was a place where a Christian voice could be heard and understood, and Christian morality could be embraced and passed along.

I am extremely fortunate that two former colleagues from the International Research Center for Japanese Studies (IRCJS) agreed to work with me on this project. James Baxter polished and refined my English style, and Patricia Fister painstakingly edited the manuscript and offered various suggestions. In addition, Kevin Doak of Georgetown University gave me invaluable comments on Catholic terms and expressions, and art historian Sylvie Morishita carefully checked the French, Latin, and Portuguese texts quoted in this book.

I would also like to express my gratitude to Yoneda Yasuko, who permitted me to view and study various items used by the French missionary Aimé Villion during his lifetime, and to Ishihara Tsutomu for providing photos taken by his family members with Villion. Yasukawa Shunsuke of Kyoto Seizan College guided me to Villion's grave at the Hattori Cemetery on a scorching summer afternoon, and Araki Shin'ichirō of Nagasaki Junshin Catholic University gave me a copy of a letter handwritten by Sauveur Candau.

This English version was made possible by the encouragement and inspiration from many people, including journalist Chino Keiko, Numano

Mitsuyoshi and Nakao Masami of the University of Tokyo, art historian Mia Mochizuki, Inoue Shōichi and John Breen of IRCJS, Irmela Hijiya-Kirschnereit of Freie Universität Berlin, Miyata Kazuo of the Twenty-Six Martyrs Museum, Takashi Shogimen of the University of Otago, Yokota Fuyuhiko and Sano Mayuko of Kyoto University, Wakao Masaki of Hitotsubashi University, Kanisawa Itaru of Heibonsha, and Akahane Takaki of Studio Fonte. The Catholic priest Patrick Maloney and my close friend Cecylia Klobukowski in New Zealand have been waiting to see this book since 2016.

Finally I would like to thank my husband Marek, who supports and prioritizes my research and teaching by assisting in every way possible. This English version is dedicated to Marek, my mother-in-law Alicja, and the entire Tamoszkiewicz family.

INTRODUCTION

St. Francis Xavier's Gift to Japan

Christian missionaries in Japan have had a strong impact on many Japanese intellectuals. An outstanding example is Shiba Ryōtarō (1923–1996), one of the most influential novelists in modern Japan, whose historical novels have largely shaped Japanese people's perception of world history.[1]

In order to understand what Japan is and what states and civilizations should be, Shiba traveled extensively inside and outside Japan. His travel journals, *Kaidō o yuku* (Walking the Streets), published in forty-three volumes over twenty-five years (1971 to 1996), documented both local histories and his first-hand observations of various regions in Japan as well as a dozen countries in Asia, Europe, and North America.

Two volumes of Shiba's journals are devoted to his trips to France, Portugal, and Spain. In them he displayed great admiration for two Catholic missionaries, Francis Xavier (1506–1552) and Sauveur Candau (1897–1955). He visited the places where they were born, the colleges they attended, and the churches they served, and contemplated their influence on the Japanese people.

Soon after Shiba's death in 1996, NHK (Japan Broadcasting Corporation) reporters and producers revisited many places described in his travel jour-

---

1 Isoda, *"Shiba Ryōtarō" de manabu Nihonshi*, 16–17.

nals. Eventually they put together twelve TV documentaries (653 minutes in total), which were broadcast from 1997 to 1998. While travelling to the birthplaces of Xavier and Candau in the Basque country, the border region of France and Spain along the west coast, the reporters wrote, "If Xavier, Candau, and other missionaries born in the Basque region had not come to Japan, our country might have taken a very different path."[2] These words echoed Shiba's opinion, who paid high respect to the two missionaries for the footprints they left on contemporary Japan.

If we carefully observe modern Japan, we can see that Christianity has permeated every corner of Japanese society, from kindergartens to universities, from ordinary people's life to the imperial household, and from popular culture to elite writings.[3] This book will investigate how Christian missionaries viewed Japan and communicated with the Japanese people by first looking into how they mastered the Japanese language.

The first missionary to Japan was Francis Xavier of the Society of Jesus (Societas Jesu, or S. J.), who arrived in Kagoshima on 15 August 1549. His letters sent to the Society from Japan show the painstaking efforts he made to learn the language. There were extremely few Japanese who understood European languages, so it was especially important for the missionaries to be able to speak in Japanese. Later, more missionaries came to Japan and managed to master the language so that they could evangelize by communicating with the people. Being able to speak directly to the populace remains the most important task for all missionaries.

Toward the end of the Edo period, on 12 January 1862, a Catholic church, "Yokohama Tenshudō," was completed by the Paris Foreign Missions Society (Société des Missions Etrangères de Paris, or M. E. P.).[4] Its purpose—for this was a decade before the shogunate's two-centuries-long ban on Christianity was lifted—was to serve foreign residents in the town. However, the ceremony of its official opening attracted many Japanese viewers.

According to a letter written by Fr. Prudence-Séraphin-Barthélemy Girard (1821–1867) in charge of the construction, the Japanese were curious by

---

2 NHK Kaidō o Yuku Purojekuto, *Shiba Ryōtarō no fūkei 3: Kita no mahoroba, Nanban no michi*, 208–209.

3 Inoue, Guo/Kaku, Kawamura, *Misshion sukūru ni naze bijin ga ōi no ka: Nihon joshi to Kirisutokyō*, 87–160.

4 Established in 1658, this missionary order has concentrated on evangelizing Asian countries.

nature and were drawn to the church by the beautiful golden cross standing on the roof and the mixture of European gothic architecture and Buddhist temple style. Over about ten days, more than ten thousand Japanese, including commoners, Buddhist monks, and samurai, rushed to the church, where they attentively listened to the priests' sermons. A month later, the Edo government cracked down on those who displayed interest in Christianity and arrested fifty-five Japanese visitors. The missionaries negotiated release of those taken into cusrody, but they had to agree to obey the government's order "Don't preach in Japanese in public!"[5] This reveals how the missionaries' capability to use Japanese was feared by authorities.

In Japan today, almost everyone is familiar with the fact that Francis Xavier brought Christianity along with Western civilization to Japan, and that his arrival can be interpreted as the beginning of a wave of cultural exchange between East and West that took place in the sixteenth century. In 1920, a portrait of him (Plate 1) was discovered in a closed chest among the belongings of a deceased hidden Christian (*senpuku Kirishitan*, i.e., those who had maintained their faith in secret through two hundred years of persecution), a member of a farming family in the mountainous area of Ibaraki village in Osaka prefecture. The color portrait was probably produced in the first half of the seventeenth century at an arts workshop established by the Jesuits. It is presumed to have been created after the news of Xavier's 1622 canonization reached Japan in 1623, as the title of the saint was included in the painting.

This portrait of St. Francis Xavier has become a household image ever since its discovery. Today it is used as a cover illustration not only for books on Christianity in Japan for academic and general audiences, but also for history textbooks widely adopted in junior high schools. The portrait is usually positioned at the center of the images (for example, Plate 2 and Plate 3), conveying the impression that Xavier's visit to Japan was of great significance.

Awareness of "foreign language" is of course deeply embedded in the Judeo-Christian tradition. In the Old Testament's Chapter Eleven of Genesis, the story of the "Tower of Babel" tells how the people of the world shared a common language until they moved to a plain in Babylonia and started to build a city with a tower so high that they could climb it to reach heaven.

---

5 Marnas, *La «Religion de Jésus» (Iaso ja-kyo) ressuscitée au Japon dans la seconde moitié du XIXe siècle*, vol. 1, 391–99; Marunasu and Kuno, *Nihon Kirisutokyō fukkatsu shi*, 196–99.

God was displeased by their vainglory and decided to mix up (or diversify) their language and scatter them over the earth so that they would not understand each other, nor would they be able to build the tower together.

However, New Testament stories relate how foreign languages can be overcome if faith in the Lord is kept. For instance, after his resurrection Jesus commanded his disciples, "Go throughout the whole world and preach the gospel to all people…Believers will be given the power to perform miracles: they will drive out demons in my name; they will speak in strange tongues; if they pick up snakes or drink any poison, they will not be harmed; they will place their hands on sick people, and they will get well." (Mark 16: 15–18) In other words, Jesus guaranteed that his disciples would not face language barriers while preaching in the world and that new believers would be given the ability to speak foreign languages.

Another story tells of Pentecost, the descent of the Holy Spirit, witnessed by the disciples, who "saw what looked like tongues of fire which spread out and touched each person there. They were all filled with the Holy Spirit and began to talk in other languages, as the Spirit enabled them to speak." The Jews coming from different countries wondered, "all of us hear them speaking in our own languages about the great things that God has done!… What does this mean?" (Act 1: 3–12)

In the Old Testament, the language barrier created by God was a punishment to the human race, while in the New Testament, the ability to use foreign languages was a sign of receiving the Holy Spirit and a reward from God. Paradoxically speaking, the translation of the Bible into numerous languages is the greatest achievement in overcoming the "strange tongues" created by God. The Old Testament was translated from the original Hebrew into Greek in the third century BC. The translation of both the New Testament and the Old Testament into Latin in the fourth century helped to Christianize the Roman Empire.

As of October 2018, according to a survey conducted by Wycliff Bible Translators, the New Testament and some portions of the Old Testament are available in more than 1,500 languages, and there are complete translations of the Bible in more than 650 languages.[6] The Bible is the most widely read book in the world.

---

6 Wycliff Bible Translators, https://www.wycliffe.org/about/why/

With the aim of propagating Christianity worldwide, Ignatius of Loyola (1491–1556), Francis Xavier, and five other members established the Society of Jesus in 1534. Before long their endeavors in the religious sphere engaged them in linguistic exchanges on a global scale. In 1542 when Xavier started to preach at Cape Comorin, the southernmost point of the Indian subcontinent, he noticed that local Christians "know nothing of the precepts and mysteries of our holy religion."[7] He felt keenly the necessity of understanding the local language, and started to learn Malabar (Tamil) with all his might. Soon he was able to teach Christian principles and to listen to parishioners' confessions without the assistance of an interpreter.

Xavier was a pioneer of Asian language learning. After his arrival in Japan in 1549, he repeatedly emphasized the importance of learning the Japanese language in his letters. His effort to study the local languages and to understand local cultures became a role model for missionaries for nearly five centuries.

Here let us examine how the Japanese language was perceived by the Jesuit missionaries of that time. The Visitor, Alessandro Valignano (1539–1606), who supervised Jesuit missions in Japan, China, and other Asian regions from 1573 to 1603 and who spent three periods (1579–1582, 1590–1592, and 1598–1603) in Japan, conveyed his impression of the language in his 1592 report to the Superior General of the Society of Jesus (*Adiciones del Sumario de Japón*, Additions to the Summary of Japan).

> They have but one language and it is the best, the most elegant and the most copious tongue in the known world; it is more abundant than Latin and expresses concepts better. As well as possessing a great variety of synonyms, it also has a kind of natural elegance and dignity; and so you may not use the same nouns and verbs when talking with different people and about diverse topics, but you must employ polite or common words, honorific or depreciative phrases in accordance with the rank of the person and the subject of the conversation. The written and spoken languages are very different, and men and women also differ in their way of speaking. There is no less diversity in their

---

7 Xavier's letter on 31 December 1543 from Cochin, India to the Jesuits in Rome, in Coleridge, *The Life and Letters of St. Francis Xavier*, vol. 1, 151; Xavier/Zabieru and Kōno, *Sei Furanshisuko Zabieru zenshokan*, vol. 1, 178–79.

way of writing; they write their letters, for example, in one style but their books in another. Finally, it takes a long time to learn the language because it is so elegant and copious.[8]

Many of the missionaries who followed in Xavier's footsteps made great efforts to study the language and mastered it splendidly. One of the most prominent was the Portuguese Jesuit João Rodrigues (1563?–1633), who came to Japan as a teenager in 1577. He became an interpreter for Valignano and had close contacts with the powerful rulers Toyotomi Hideyoshi (1537–1598) and Tokugawa Ieyasu (1543–1616). He came to be popularly known as "Tsūji" (translator); in fact that sobriquet was used more commonly in Japan than his birth name. Two books that he compiled, *Arte da Lingoa de Iapam* (1604–1608, Large Japanese Grammar) and *Arte Breve da Lingoa Iapoa* (1620, Short Japanese Grammar), are recognized as "the first comprehensive grammars of Japanese in any language."[9]

In *Arte Breve da Lingoa Iapoa*, Rodrigues described the language proficiency expected of missionaries: "[M]astery of the language will enable them to preach to the Gentiles and refute their errors and superstitions in debates and in writing, defending the Faith against its adversaries."[10] His attentiveness to the differentiation of spoken and written Japanese reveals the high competency he himself had gained.

Another excellent speaker was an Italian Jesuit—Pietro Paolo Navarro (1560–1622)—who came to Japan in 1588 and spent thirty-four years living there until dying as a martyr. It seems that his Japanese was of a high standard, as he managed to write books in Japanese. Before his death, he was granted a meeting with the lord of the Shimabara domain, Matsukura Shigemasa (1574–1630). He gave the lord a booklet on the Christian faith he had written. The lord "asked his servant to read aloud for him, and was very impressed," Navarro reported in a letter to his director in Nagasaki.[11] We can imagine that this booklet, which piqued the lord's interest in

---

8 Valignano, *Adiciones del Sumario de Japón*, 54; English trans. by Cooper, *They Came to Japan: An Anthology of European Reports on Japan, 1543–1640*, 171.

9 Moran, "The Well of Japanese Undefiled, Joan Rodrigues' Advice on How to Study Japanese," 277; Rodrigues/Rodorigesu and Ikegami, *Nihon shōbunten*, 35.

10 Ibid., 35.

11 Villion/Biriyon and Kako, *Fukusha Pōro Naboro oyobi tsure no chimei*, 314–15; Anesaki, *Zesusu-kai no jinbutsu, Nihonbun no tassha Nabaruro to so no jūsha sūnin*, 54–55.

Christianity, must have been well written. Unfortunately it no longer exists.

Another good example of mastery of the language is that of a Dominican missionary from Spain, Diego Collado (1589?–1638), who studied Japanese for eleven years (eight in Manila before coming to Japan and an additional three while serving near Nagasaki).[12] In 1632, ten years after his departure from Japan, Collado published three books in Rome: *Ars Grammaticae Japonicae Lingvae* (On Japanese Grammar), *Niffon no Cotōbani yô confesion* (Confessions Made in Japanese), and *Dictionarivm; sive Thesavri lingvæ iaponicæ compendivm* (A Dictionary of Latin, Spanish, and Japanese).

In the preface to *Niffon no Cotōbani yô confesion*, Collado proudly stated, "I have retained this language to the extent that I am capable of not only compiling a grammar book and a dictionary in which thousands of words are listed, but also to complete Japanese texts for the sacrament of confession and profession of faith without depending on other sources, thanks to the Lord's Power."[13] This book, written to help missionaries understand confessions made in Japanese, is regarded as "an excellent piece of *Kirishitan Bungaku* (Christian literature)" because of its rich "poetic professions of faith and realistic confessions."[14] The term "Kirishitan" is a Japanese translation of the Portuguese word Cristaõ (Christian). In this book, this term is used as an adjective, as well as a singular or plural noun, to indicate Catholic practices in early modern Japan.

Missionaries were able to systematically analyze the Japanese language by applying Latin grammar. They published several dictionaries, among them *Dictionarivm Latino Lvsitanicvm, ac Iaponicum* (1595, A Dictionary of Latin, Portuguese, and Japanese), *Racvyoxv* (1598, A Dictionary of Kanji), *Vocabvlario da lingoa de Iapam* (1604, the famous *Nippo jisho*, a Dictionary of Japanese and Portuguese), and Rodrigues' *Arte da Lingoa de Iapam* (1604–1608) and *Arte Breve da Lingoa Iapoa* (1620), which are regarded as the pinnacle of Japanese-language acquisition by non-Japanese.[15]

Rodrigues' *Arte de Lingoa de Iapam* cited a great number of expressions from Japanese classical literature and stated the necessity of mastering such

---

12 Kojima Yukie, "Koryādo no akusento: *Seinichi jisho* no jihitsu kōbon o megutte," 44.

13 Hino, *Koryādo Zangeroku*, 110.

14 Irie, "Koryādo kan *Zangeroku* zakkō (No. 2)," 57.

15 Sugimoto, *Kirishitan to Nihongo kenkyū*, 50–51.

elegant idioms.[16] This dictionary documented the Japanese language of the medieval era in careful detail, and it is regarded as a great treasure to modern Japan.[17] Rodrigues drew particular attention to the variety of combinations of nouns and verbs:

> Such combinations express succinctly and forcefully objects and actions which cannot be well expressed in our languages, or at least not without much verbiage. Its large number of adverbs, for example, describe objects and actions with great accuracy. What we for the most part express with gestures and movements of the hands, the Japanese can describe with these combinations and adverbs.[18]

Rodrigues' statement is accurate and no less fresh today than when he wrote it.

Linguist Sugimoto Tsutomu aptly observes, "It is surprising to see how the missionaries enthusiastically and loyally followed the teaching of God and the Bible, and made such great efforts to master the Japanese language in medieval times. Their insatiable thirst for language acquisition (*gengo shūtoku tamashii*) was inherited by the missionaries who came to Japan from the end of the Edo period till the beginning of the Meiji era."[19] Santō Isao, a scholar of Christianity in Japan, says that the missionaries observed the Japanese language precisely and made two discoveries: one an "external discovery" as they scrutinized it from the perspective of foreign languages, and the other an "internal discovery" since Japanese provided them with the opportunity to reflect on their own languages.[20]

Works by missionaries and their Japanese collaborators of the late sixteenth and early seventeenth centuries constitute a genre called *Kirishitan Bungaku* (Christian literature). It includes books on doctrines, prayers, rituals, and meditations, notably *Doctrina Christam* (Christian Doctrines, 1592); *Salvator Mundi* (Savior of the World, 1598); *Guia do Pecador* (Guide for

---

16 Rodrigues/Rodorigesu and Doi Tadao, *Nihon daibunten*, 4.

17 Kanai, "Kirishitan senkyōshi no Nihongo kenkyū," 4.

18 Rodrigues/Rodorigesu and Doi, *Nihon daibunten*, 5–6. English trans. by Cooper, *They Came to Japan: An Anthology of European Reports on Japan, 1543–1640*, 172–73.

19 Sugimoto, *Kirishitan to Nihongo kenkyū*, 50.

20 Santō, *Nihongo no kansatsusha tachi: Senkyōshi kara oyatoi gaikokujin made*, 39–41.

Sinners, 1599); *Manvale ad Sacramenta Ecclesiae Ministranda* (Manual to Administer Church Sacraments, 1605); and *Contemptus Mundi* (Contempt of the World, 1610). There are also partial translations of Bible stories, Western classics (*Aesop's Fables*), and an adaptation of the Japanese classic *The Tale of the Heike*. These books were written either in romanized Japanese or kana-kanji.[21] Researchers have studied this genre for 150 years, since the Meiji era, from the perspectives of linguistics, religion, history, philosophy, literature, printing, publishing, and education.

The Edo government's persecution of Christians lasted more than two centuries. In the nineteenth century, missionaries from Europe and the United States commenced serious study of the Japanese language while awaiting permission to propagate the faith freely in Japan. An English man from the London Missionary Society, Walter Henry Medhurst (1796–1857), learned the language from Japanese castaways in Southeast Asia, and in 1830 published *An English and Japanese, and Japanese and English Vocabulary, Compiled from Native Works* in a lithograph edition printed in Batavia (present-day Jakarta). This pioneering work started the trend of compiling dictionaries of Japanese-European languages. It contributed not only to missionaries' learning of Japanese, but also to Japanese people's study of English in the nineteenth century.[22]

For instance, a Hungarian-born medical missionary dispatched by the Loochoo Naval Mission to the Ryūkyū Islands in 1846, Bernard Jean Bettelheim (1811–1870) lived in Naha for nine years and completed his *English-Loochooan Dictionary* in 1851. John Liggins (1829–1912), an English-born missionary of the Protestant Episcopal Church of the United States of America, came to Nagasaki in 1859 and published *Familiar Phrases in English and Romanized Japanese* in Shanghai in 1860. Samuel Robbins Brown (1810–1880) of the Dutch Reformed Church in America came to Yokohama in 1859 and four years later published *Colloquial Japanese* in 1863 in Shanghai too. Eugène-Emmanuel Mermet de Cachon (1828–1871) of M. E. P. arrived in Naha in 1855 and published *Dictionnarie français-anglais-japonais* in 1866 in Paris. Medical missionary James Curtis Hepburn (1815–1911) of the Presbyterian Church in the United States came

---

21 Ebisawa, *Kirishitan Nanban bungaku nyūmon*, 28–29; Obara, "Kirishitan jidai no Iezusukai kyōiku: Zabieru no shukugan 'Miyako ni daigaku o'," 22–23.

22 Kawamoto, "Medohāsuto no *Eiwa Waei goishū*: Sono riyō no sarekata," 13–27.

to Yokohama in 1859 and published *A Japanese and English Dictionary*, the first of this kind of dictionary in Japan (printed in Shanghai) in 1867.

Meanwhile, missionaries exerted great effort to translate the Bible into Japanese. For instance, Prussian-born missionary Karl Friedrich August Gützlaff (1803–1851) translated the Gospel According to John in 1837; Samuel Wells Williams (1812–1884) of the American Board of Commissioners for Foreign Missions translated the Gospel According to Mathew in 1839; and Bettelheim translated the Gospel According to Luke in 1847 and the other three Gospels in 1851. These missionaries from Europe and the United States were well prepared for their future evangelizing efforts in Japan.[23]

After a Treaty of Amity and Commerce between France and Japan was signed in 1858, priests sent by the Paris Foreign Missions Society started to arrive in Japan. They completed the building of a Kirishitan church in the Ōura village of Nagasaki in December 1864. Only three months later, on 17 March 1865, a group of people who identified themselves as Kirishitan presented themselves at this church after two centuries of persecution. This was regarded as a "miracle" of the East, although remarkably it had been predicted by Xavier three hundred years earlier in a letter from Cochin, India on 29 January 1552 to Ignatius of Loyola, the first Superior General of the Society of Jesus, in Rome.

> As far as I know, the Japanese nation is the single and only nation of them all which seems likely to preserve unshaken and for ever the profession of Christian holiness if once it embraces it; but this will doubtless not be without great sufferings and heroic conflicts on the part of the preachers of the Gospel.[24]

Xavier's prophecy became a strong encouragement for future missionaries to come to Japan.

In 1873, when Japan's longstanding prohibition of Christianity was lifted by the regime that had replaced the Tokugawa shogunate in 1868, missionaries arrived in Japan one after another, evangelizing, establishing schools and hospitals, and saving people from poverty, among other

---

23 Nihon Kirisutokyō Rekishi Daijiten Henshū Iinkai, *Nihon Kirisutokyō rekishi daijiten*.
24 Coleridge, *The Life and Letters of St. Francis Xavier*, vol. 2, 372–73; Xavier/Zabieru and Kōno, *Sei Furanshisuko Zabieru zenshokan*, vol. 3, 218.

endeavors. Many of them mastered the Japanese language and started to pen articles and books. Since then tens of thousands of missionaries have come to Japan, and among them about three hundred missionaries have used the Japanese language to write and publish books.[25]

How did they write in Japanese? There were three ways. One was co-authoring with native speakers, for example, by having their speeches, sermons, or talks in Japanese transcribed and re-arranged by a Japanese. Another was by having their romanized Japanese writings transliterated into the kana-kanji form by a native. And the final way was by composing in kana-kanji from the beginning themselves. While there are other non-native speakers who wrote in Japanese, there is probably no one among them who could write as quickly, abundantly, and continuously as the missionaries have done during the last century and half.

The contents of their writings can be classified as follows: Bible translations, doctrinal exegesis and commentaries, prayers, church rituals, meditations, stories about saints, dictionaries, essays, letters, dialogues, speeches, diaries, songs, travel journals, academic research, children's illustrated books, and miscellanies.

A comparison with the vernacular writings by missionaries in China and Korea provides an illuminating context. From the nineteenth century to the mid-twentieth century, there were about 430 books written in the Chinese language by missionaries in China.[26] The figure did not increase after 1949 due to the establishment of the communist government, which viewed Christianity as opposed to the government's ideology and expelled foreign missionaries from the continent. On the Korean peninsula, the number of books written in the Korean language by missionaries has been limited[27] because government persecution made them unable to pen anything, and later the successful training of Korean clergy replaced foreign missionaries.

In contrast to the situations in China and Korea, there have been about three thousand books written in Japanese since 1860s, either single-authored,

---

25 The number of foreign missionaries currently living in Japan in 2017 is 1,945 (1,545 male and 400 female). In comparison, the number of missionaries in 2007 was 2,895, about 1.5 times the current figure, according to the survey conducted by Bunkachō, *Shūkyō chōsa tōkei*, online.

26 Song, *Chuanjiaoshi hanwen xiaoshuo yanjiu*.

27 Rausch, "Hanguru ni yoru Katorikku no shomotsu;" Lee, "Gaikokujin senkyōshi no Hantō dendō to chojutsu katsudō;" Choe, "Gaikokujin josei senkyōshi no bunkateki eikyō."

co-authored, or edited by missionaries. This is a result of several factors, such as Japanese people's curiosity about Christianity; the shortage of local clergy, which results in a continuing need for foreign missionaries to work in Japan; and the presumption that missionary books would gain acceptance by Japanese readers once published.

The writing system of the Japanese language (a mixture of hiragana, katakana, and kanji) is much more complex than that of Chinese (only kanji) and of Korean (mainly Hangul, some kanji). Missionaries in Japan must have struggled with the writing system while being fully engaged in evangelization, social welfare, education, and other work. The three thousand books in Japanese constitute a major cultural achievement by missionaries in East Asia.

While propagating the Gospels and introducing Western cosmology, ethics, history, literature, and thought, missionary books also display insightful understanding of Japanese language and culture. However, so far these books have been studied by only a few scholars.[28] During the last thirty years, a new academic discipline termed "Nihongo Bungaku" has been established. Scholars in this field study literary works by foreign writers, Japan-born Korean writers, writers from Japan's colonies, and Japanese immigrants overseas.[29] Up to now, the so-called "Nihongo Bungaku" has often been thought to have started in the twentieth century, and it has not included the works by missionaries. Strictly speaking, "Nihongo Bungaku" originated in *Kirishitan Bungaku* of the sixteenth century, and has had a history of more than four centuries.

Unlike *Kirishitan Bungaku* of which most literary texts were lost due to the persecution, modern missionary books form a large body of "Japanese literature by missionaries." This corpus of work merits being examined systematically in order to recognize its significance to Japanese culture.

---

28 For instance, Kōno, *Kagoshima ni okeru Seisho hon'yaku: Rage shinpu to Daishichi Kōtōgakkō Zōshikan kyōju tachi*; Mochizuki, *Hebon no shōgai to Nihongo*; Yamanashi, "Pari Gaikoku Senkyōkai no shuppanbutsu to kindai Nihon no bungakusha," "Kindai Nihon ni okeru Rigyōru shinpu no shuppan katsudō to sono hankyō," "Sōvūru Kandō shinpu to Nihon no chishikijin"; Taniguchi, "Nihongo no kakite to shite no Hoiverusu"; Guo/Kaku, "Hoiverusu kyakuhon *Hosokawa Garashia Fujin*"; Guo, "Internationalization of the Japanese Language in Interwar Period Japan (1920–1940): Foreign Missionaries and Writers."

29 The term "Nihongo Bungaku" 日本語文学 started to be used in the 1990s in the following books: Hayashi Kōji, *Zainichi Chōsenjin Nihongo Bungaku ron*; Tarumi, *Taiwan no Nihongo Bungaku*. Since the twenty-first century, this term has become conventional. See Hosokawa, *Nikkei Burajiru imin bungaku*; Hibi, *Japanīzu Amerika: Imin bungaku, shuppan bunka, shūyōjo*; Guo/Kaku, *Bairingaru na Nihongo Bungaku*.

This book will focus on how Xavier's dream of evangelizing Asia has been made a reality in modern Japan. Chapter 1 examines the existing documents on how Xavier emphasized the necessity of direct communication with the Japanese people, how he devoted himself to studying the language, and what level of proficiency he might have reached. It challenges the prevailing view of Xavier's Japanese-language capability as very low.

Chapter 2 will discuss how Xavier's prediction that Japanese people would hold strongly to the Christian faith attracted countless missionaries to Japan, and how his affection for Japan was inherited and further developed. This chapter also periodizes missionaries' writing into four stages: the starting period (1860s–1900s), the active period (1910s–1942), the prolific period (1946–1990), and the computer-using period (1990s–2010s).

In the subsequent four chapters, the lives and writings of four Catholic priests (A. Villion, S. Candau, H. Heuvers, and G. Neyrand) will be explored in some depth because of their significant influence on modern Japan. Responding to Xavier's call, they learned from his loving attitude toward the people and eagerly absorbed Japanese culture while bringing Christianity into Japanese hearts, helping the religion to take root in Japan.

Chapter 3 centers on Aimé Villion (1843–1932), M. E. P. who is one of the most renowned missionaries of modern times and is called the "Second Xavier." He came to Japan in 1868 and lived in various places, including Nagasaki, Kyoto, Kobe, Tsuwano, Hagi, and Nara. He used the ten years he spent living in Kyoto to study Buddhism and its major sects. His book *Yamato hijiri chishio no kakioki* (Japanese Martyrs' Testament in Blood, 1887) made the history of Christian persecution widely known to Japanese intellectuals. It has been adapted for films and dramas, and it is still being used by writers of historical novels. Villion had limited time for writing, as he was fully engaged in evangelizing and welfare activities. It was his longtime companion, the Japanese preacher Kako Giichi, who played the major role in turning Villion's oral teaching into publications.

Chapter 4 investigates the achievements of Sauveur Candau (1897–1955), M. E. P., who was born in the same area as Xavier—the Basque region. After arriving in Yokohama in 1925, he immediately noticed the similarity between the Japanese language and his mother tongue (Basque). He quickly mastered the language, employing a talent for kanji usage that was nothing short of amazing. He spent twenty-one years in Japan, writing essays and giving public lectures while devoting himself to church, social, and educational activities. From his writings we can appreciate his insightful observations on Japan and his enlightening advice to the Japanese people.

Chapter 5 analyzes the literature of the Jesuit missionary Hermann Heuvers (1890–1977) who was born in Westfalen, Germany. He studied the Japanese classical poetry anthology *Manyōshū* and the lyrics of noh drama music before coming to Japan. He arrived in Japan just before the Great Kantō Earthquake occurred (1 September 1923), and later became the second president of Sophia University in Tokyo. Heuvers' *Jinsei no aki ni: Heruman Hoiverusu zuisōshū* (In the Autumn of Life: A Collection of Hermann Heuvers' Essays) became well known recently in Japan when a poem included in this book was repeatedly recited in the film *Tsunagu* (To Connect, 2012). His poetic works have enriched modern Japanese literature.

Finally, Chapter 6 will present the story of a French missionary, Georges Neyrand (1920–2011) who came to Nagasaki in 1952 and quickly mastered the local dialect and kanji. A unique figure in many respects, he wrote prolifically in Japanese without much assistance, and became famous as the model for the protagonist in Endō Shūsaku's *Obaka-san* (*Wonderful Fool: A Novel*). His style of preaching the Gospels was unconventional. For instance, he opened a "mission bar" in the Shinjuku district of Tokyo to introduce Christianity to company employees who otherwise would have no chance to go to church. He taught them Christianity while serving them alcohol. His respect for Japanese people's Buddhist sentiments and his well-balanced understanding of Japanese culture deserve to be properly evaluated.

These four missionaries all lived in Japan for long periods, had excellent Japanese language skills, and managed to interpret Japanese culture profoundly. It is difficult to commit oneself to a different language and culture if one does not have an affection for it. These missionaries chose to live in Japan and to serve the Japanese people until their final days because of their deep commitment to the people. Their affection, however, was not "blind." They were aware of the weak points of the Japanese as human beings and tried to improve their spiritual world by introducing them to Christianity.

Missionary writings in Japanese have been overlooked by most scholars primarily for three reasons. First is that the missionaries' Japanese ability has been underestimated, and therefore their works in Japanese have received little attention, apart from religious curiosity. Second is that for the most part, missionary books are circulated among the faithful, rather than being aimed at the general public, and many of them have gone out of print. Third is that the considerable cultural and artistic values of the books have been unheeded, as they have tended to be regarded simply as religious propaganda.

By investigating missionary contributions to Japanese culture, this book shall reveal the significance of Xavier's visit to Japan, which not only internationalized the country during the turbulent sixteenth century (at the beginning of what academic historians call the early modern period), but also provided the soil for missionary writings in Japanese to grow and mature in modern times.

I

Francis Xavier's Passion for Japan

1. A Summons from Japan

The Society of Jesus was founded on 15 August (the feast day of Our Lady's Assumption) 1534 by Ignatius of Loyola, Francis Xavier, and five others. On the hill of Montmartre of Paris, where they were university students, the seven professed vows of poverty, chastity, and obedience to the pope. The Society was formally approved by Pope Paul III in 1540.

This Roman Catholic order of priests and brothers is renowned for its members' extensive education. Aiming to propagate Christian faith worldwide, the Jesuits have believed that success largely depends on their ability to manifest God's existence by explaining everything in the universe—"finding God in all things."

One of the best exemplars of the Society's advancement of knowledge is the Belgian Jesuit, mathematician, and astronomer Georges Lemaître (1894–1966) who proposed a theory for the origin of the universe that he termed "Fireworks Universe," a theory better known today as the Big Bang. He argued for a definite origin of the universe, that is, "the beginning of the world happened a little before the beginning of space and time."[1] His theory, supported by astronomical observations of receding galaxies and cosmic microwave background,[2]

---

1 Lemaître, "The Beginning of the World from the Point of View of Quantum Theory," 706.
2 Ewart, "The Physical Sciences and Natural Theology," 420.

has gained widespread acceptance,[3] although when Lemaître first proposed it, the notion was criticized for being similar to the image of God's creation of the universe described in the Old Testament.

Francis Xavier arrived in Asia in May 1542. Before making his way to Japan in 1549, he taught in Goa, the Fishery Coast, Cape Comorin, Cochin, Malacca, and the Moluccas Islands. He died on the Shangchuan (or Sancian) Island of China in 1552 and posthumously was called "the Apostle of the East."

What brought Xavier to Japan was the enthusiasm for learning of a Kagoshima-born Japanese fugitive (referred to by the name Han-Siro, or Anger), whom he met at Malacca in December 1547. Only one month after their initial encounter, Xavier was so impressed by this man's intelligence and diligence that he wrote,

FRANCISCVS XAVERIVS SOCI-
ESV INDIARVM APOSTOLVS.

Fig. 1, Portrait of Francis Xavier, *Lettres du B. pere Saint Francois Xavier, de la Compagnie de Iesus, apostre du Iapon* (Paris: Che Sebastien Cramoisy, 1628).

"If the rest of the Japanese have the same ardour for gaining knowledge that Anger has, then they surpass in genius all nations anywhere found."[4] After baptizing Anger, Xavier christened him Paul of the Holy Faith (his Japanese name was written Han-Siro). Xavier's assessment of Paul is astonishing:

> In the College at Goa, which is called the College of Santa Fè, we have three Japanese students who came thither with me last year from Malacca. They tell us wonderful things about Japan. They are youths of very good virtue and extremely sharp wit; Paul in particular, who is

3 Roy, *Unveiling Galaxies: The Role of Images in Astronomical Discovery*, 129.

4 Xavier's letter to the Society in Rome from Cochin on 21 January 1548, in Coleridge, *The Life and Letters of St. Francis Xavier*, vol. 1, 417.

sending you a letter of very good length. In the space of eight months he has learnt perfectly to read, write, and speak Portuguese...by God's help there will be a large number made Christians in Japan.[5]

Paul's language proficiency and eagerness to learn accorded with the Society's expectations for its members' education. What impressed Xavier most was probably Paul's introduction to Japan through their conversations. Xavier felt a summons from Japan, and wanted to go there by all means, writing, "So great is the hope of propagating the Christian religion which has arisen in me from what Paul the Japanese tells me, or rather from what God Himself puts in my heart."[6]

Using documents preserved at the Jesuit College of Coimbra, let us look at how Paul introduced Japan to Xavier.[7] Paul talked about religious practice in Japan such as belief in "one Supreme God, Creator of all things," the existence of "Purgatory, Paradise, and Hell," and Xaqua (that is, Sakyamuni [Jp. Shaka], the historical Buddha) who prohibited followers from killing, stealing, committing adultery, being attached to worldly matters, and withholding forgiveness. Paul also told Xavier that "all the Japanese will become Christians, because...they expect a more perfect law than their own, and... cannot imagine one more perfect than ours."[8] Henry James Coleridge, who translated this document, pointed out that it must have been a religious person at the College at Goa who transcribed the words "from the lips of Han-Siro," employing expressions colored by a desire "to discover as many resemblances to Christianity as possible in the religion of the country to which so much attention was then drawn."[9]

Xavier was no doubt greatly encouraged by Paul's words when contemplating his mission to Japan. After a preparation of less than one and a half years, Xavier embarked for Japan on 15 April 1549. Accompanying him were Paul, two other young Japanese men, Jesuit priest Cosme de Tor-

---

5 Xavier's letter from Cochin to Rome, on 14 January 1549, in Coleridge, *The Life and Letters of St. Francis Xavier*, vol. 2, 71–72.

6 Ibid.

7 "Account of Japan sent to Father Ignatius Loyola in Rome, drawn from the statement of Anger (Han-Siro), the Japanese Convert," in Coleridge, *The Life and Letters of St. Francis Xavier*, vol. 2, 208–15, 222.

8 Ibid., 210–13.

9 Ibid., 222.

res (1510–1570), brother Juan Fernandez (1526–1567), both from Spain, Manuel of China, and Amador of Malabar, India.

After a perilous journey lasting four months, Xavier and his companions landed at Kagoshima on 15 August, the feast day of Our Lady's Assumption and the fifteenth anniversary of the founding of the Society of Jesus. Xavier spent the following two years and three months evangelizing in Japan, traveling to Kagoshima, Hirado, Yamaguchi, Kyoto, Sakai, and Funai (present-day Ōita prefecture) to sow the seeds of Christianity on Japanese soil.

Xavier's mission would not have been successful if he had not been able to communicate with the Japanese people directly. However, his Japanese language proficiency was estimated to be low by the prominent Jesuit scholar Georg Schurhammer (1882–1971),[10] whose research has not been challenged. This chapter will examine Xavier's proficiency from a different perspective, showing how in fact he could be regarded as a role model for learning the Japanese language.

2. A Pioneer of Asian Language Study

Christian priests had been active in India before the Jesuits arrived. However, it is said that they were not keen to learn the local language, but rather more interested in conducting business and accumulating wealth during their three-year assignments.[11] In contrast, during his seven years in India, Malay, and Indonesia, Xavier mastered the local languages, showed great interest in local cultures, and devoted himself completely to evangelization.

Apart from his mother tongue Basque, Xavier was fluent in Latin, French, Spanish, Portuguese, and Italian. But the Tamil and Malay languages were not easy for him to learn. After arriving at Cape Comorin in October 1542, he immediately started studying the Tamil (Malabar) language, continuing for about eleven months. Later, in Malacca, he quickly mastered the Malay language. He also preached on the Moluccas Islands where the Malay language was spoken. Let us look at how Xavier himself described his language learning.

---

10 Schurhammer, *Das kirchliche Sprachproblem in der japanischen Jesuitenmission des 16. und 17. Jahrhunderts; ein Stück Ritenfrage in Japan*; Doi, *Kirishitan ronkō*, 19–22.
11 Kishino, *Zabieru to Higashi Ajia*, 132; Neill, *A History of Christianity in India: The Beginnings to AD 1707*, 126–27.

At Cape Comorin, Xavier was faced with a language barrier. He first gathered those who not only understood Portuguese, but also had good knowledge of their own language, and then taught them intensively for several days, showing them how to make the sign of the cross and how to profess faith in the Trinity. He asked them to translate the Latin text of Apostles' Creed, Ten Commandments, Lord's Prayer, Hail Mary, Hail Holy Queen, and Act of Contrition into Tamil, requesting that they write down their translations in romanized form. He memorized these quickly, and then assembled all the children and as many adults as possible to teach them step by step for one month. Xavier managed to convert so many people to Christianity that his hands became sore from the repeated act of baptizing them. Using the Tamil language to explain the concepts of faith, heaven, hell, and who will go to heaven and who to hell, he exhausted himself so thoroughly that he became unable to open his mouth.[12]

Xavier thus not only memorized the prayers in Tamil, but also developed the capacity to explain Christian doctrines. He remarked on the difficulties of learning the language in a letter to the Jesuits in Rome. "In order to communicate with the local people by their language which is so hard to memorize, I have had to take great pains physically and mentally."[13]

Xavier's method was to learn the language himself without depending on local interpreters. He also encouraged other Jesuits to learn the local language. One of them was Anrique Anriquez (1520–1600), who had acquired very little Tamil between his arrival in Goa in 1546 and Xavier's appearance in February 1548. Stimulated by Xavier's encouragement, Anriquez studied the Tamil language so diligently that he managed to master it within six months.[14] Xavier praised him in his letter to Rome: Anriquez "writes and speaks the Malabar tongue very well indeed; and he alone works with great profit as if he were a great many. His sermons and private conversations have made him a marvelous object of love and veneration to the native

---

12 Xavier's letter to the Jesuits in Rome from Cochin on 15 January 1544; Xavier/Zabieru and Kōno, *Sei Furanshisuko Zabieru zenshokan*, vol. 1, 179, 186–87.

13 Xavier's letter to Ignatius in Rome, from Cochin on 12 January 1549; Xavier/Zabieru and Kōno, *Sei Furanshisuko Zabieru zenshokan*, vol. 2, 197.

14 According to Anriquez's letter to Ignatius on 31 October 1548, quoted from Kishino, *Zabieru to Nihon*, 48.

Christians."[15] Xavier had experienced the huge difference between direct communication and talking through interpreters, as he was keenly aware of translators' limited knowledge of local religions and Christian doctrines.[16]

Anriquez wrote that Xavier commissioned him to "make a perfect grammar and vocabulary of the Malabar tongue, and thus at once to elevate, fix, and preserve it, and make it more useful as a means of communication among the tribes of different dialects."[17] Xavier's idea of recording and preserving local languages was far-sighted, and was implemented by later Jesuit missionaries to Asia who compiled numerous grammar books and dictionaries of Asian languages. Some of them, such as *Nippo jisho* (*Vocabvlario da lingoa de Iapam*) published in 1603–1604, are still being used today.

Xavier went to Malacca in September 1545, and observing that it was "very troublesome to be absolutely ignorant of the language of those one is living among,"[18] immediately started to learn the Malay (Macazar) language. He wished to translate the Catechism from Latin into Malay, and after mastering the language, he was able to preach, to hear confessions, to teach Christian doctrines to new converts (especially children), and to foster "reconciliations among the soldiers and the inhabitants who had quarrels and feuds one with another."[19]

In February 1546, Xavier arrived in the Moluccas Islands, where again he could use Malay. He "taught the children and the converts the explanation of the Creed in the common native tongue of the country, so that everybody might understand it," and successfully laid "in their minds the foundations of the Christian religion."[20] His achievements in mastering two Asian languages must have given him the confidence and skills to begin

---

15 Xavier's letter to Ignatius in Rome from Cochin on 14 January 1549, in Coleridge, *The Life and Letters of St. Francis Xavier*, vol. 2, 73; Xavier's letter to Ignatius in Rome from Cochin on 12 January 1549, in Xavier/Zabieru and Kōno, *Sei Furanshisuko Zabieru zenshokan*, vol. 2, 207.

16 Kishino, *Zabieru to Higashi Ajia*, 192.

17 Coleridge, *The Life and Letters of St. Francis Xavier*, vol. 2, 33; according to Anriquez's letter to Ignatius on 31 October 1548, quoted from Kishino, *Zabieru to Higashi Ajia*, p. 48.

18 Xavier's letter to the Society in Portugal from Malacca, dated 10 November 1545, in Coleridge, *The Life and Letters of St. Francis Xavier*, vol. 1, 354.

19 Xavier's letter to the Society in Rome from Amboyna (on the Moluccas Islands of Indonesia) in May 1546, in Coleridge, *The Life and Letters of St. Francis Xavier*, vol. 1, 375.

20 Xavier's letter to the Society at Rome from Cochin, on 21 January 1548, in Coleridge, *The Life and Letters of St. Francis Xavier*, vol. 1, 391.

learning the Japanese language before his journey to Japan.

3. Studying the Japanese Language

Xavier learned to write Japanese characters from Paul before departing for Japan. In his letter to Ignatius, he included examples of the characters "beginning at the top of the page and writing straight downwards to the bottom" and described a conversation he had with Paul. Why, Xavier had inquired, did Japanese not write as Europeans did. Paul responded, "[Why] do not you write as we do? The head of a man is at the top and his feet at the bottom, and so it is proper that when men write it should be straight down from top to bottom." This witty answer seems to have pleased Xavier.[21]

In the same letter, Xavier said that after arriving in Japan, "When I am there I will write you an account of what their books contain, for I cannot get at this from Paul, who was a layman, and so never had any acquaintance with the literary monuments of Japan, which are in a sort of different language, like books written in Latin among ourselves."[22] Here we can see Xavier's confidence in his ability to master the Japanese oral and written language. This confidence came from his skills in the Tamil and Malay languages, and also from his determination to communicate with the Japanese people.

Three months after arriving at Kagoshima, Xavier described the Japanese people in a letter to the Jesuits in Goa: "There can be none that has more natural goodness than the Japanese. They are of a kindly disposition, not at all given to cheating, wonderfully desirous of honour and rank. Honour with them is placed above everything else. There are a great many poor among them, but poverty is not a disgrace to any one...They are wonderfully inclined to all that is good and honest, and have an extreme eagerness to learn."[23] It seems that Xavier fell in love with Japan at first sight.

He continued, "[T]his island is well fitted and prepared to receive the Gospel....If we all knew the language, I do not doubt but that a great many

---

21 Xavier's letter to Ignatius in Rome from Cochin, on 14 January 1549, in Coleridge, *The Life and Letters of St. Francis Xavier*, vol. 2, 78–79.

22 Ibid., 79.

23 Xavier's letter to the Society at Goa from Kagoshima on 11 November 1549, in Coleridge, *The Life and Letters of St. Francis Xavier*, vol. 2, 237–38.

Japanese would become Christians. God grant that we may soon acquire it well!"[24] Xavier and his companions advanced rapidly in their language study, for he reported, "In these six weeks, by God's favour, we have got so far that we already give explanations in Japanese of the Ten Commandments."[25]

They must have made a great progress because explaining abstract concepts like the Ten Commandments requires proper pronunciation, vocabulary, and grammatical structure. It would have been out of character for Xavier, a man who practiced "humility and lowliness," to exaggerate his language proficiency at that stage.

However, Japanese was not easy to learn, and the first several months proved to be particularly hard for them. "May God grant that in order to explain His divine truths we may master the language as soon as possible... At present we are like so many dumb statues in the midst of the people. They talk about us and discuss us a good deal among themselves, and we are able to say nothing all the time, not knowing their language. We are making ourselves children over again in learning the elements of it. Would that we may match the simplicity and candour of children! At all events we are at present making ourselves like them, both in learning the tongue of the country and in meditating on their simplicity."[26] From these words, we can see the great efforts Xavier expended to learn the language. He was determined to master it so that he could carry out missionary work successfully in Japan.

Paul was placed in charge of translating Christian prayers into Japanese. A notable example of his service was with Kantei, the mother of Shimazu Takashisa, lord of the Satsuma domain. To her Paul showed "a very fine picture of Our Lady with the Child Jesus sitting in her lap, which we brought from India." She was filled with "wonderful admiration and delight" and wanted to know "the chief points of the Christian religion" in writing. Paul immediately worked on this for several days, and "wrote out in his own native language a great many things concerning Christian mysteries and laws," including a translation of the Creed and Catechism into Japanese.[27] Xavier praised him highly. "Our good Paul," Xavier said, "will

---

24 Ibid., 241–42.
25 Ibid., 242.
26 Ibid., 251–52.
27 Ibid., 233, 251.

most faithfully render into his native language all that may seem necessary for salvation."[28] There is a record that Paul left his translations of the prayer against the Seven Sins, the Litany of the Saints, other prayers, explanations of baptism, and a calendar of feast days to the Kirishitan of Ichiku, a small domain located about thirty kilometers away from Kagoshima.[29]

Xavier did not explicitly discuss his level of Japanese proficiency in his letters. But other documents, such as the writings on Japan by Jesuit missionary Luís Fróis (1532–1597), suggest that Xavier gained considerable facility. Fróis spent a year on the Takushima Island (present-day Hirado city, Nagasaki prefecture) with Juan Fernandez, who had closely accompanied Xavier throughout his Japan mission and possessed first-hand knowledge of his personality and language competency. Therefore we can assume that Fróis learned a great deal about Xavier from Fernandez.

Fróis wrote that Xavier and his companions "spent most of daytime talking to people living nearby, and at night prayed and studied elementary Japanese until late. After understanding a bit of the language, Master Francis and Brother Fernandez took whole days to answer the questions raised by the pagans."[30] This indicates that from the early stage of their days in Japan, both Xavier and Fernandez were able to use the Japanese language for abstract discussions.

Xavier himself wrote that they spent much time "in instructing our converts, in learning Japanese, and in translating into that tongue the chief heads of the Christian faith…we translated diligently all the great mysteries of the life of Christ until His Ascension into heaven, and also the account of the Last Judgement. We have now translated this book, for such it was, into Japanese with great labour, and have written it in our own characters. Out of this we read what I have mentioned to those who came to the faith of Christ, that the converts may know how to worship God and Jesus Christ with piety and to their souls' health."[31] The translation of the New Testament into Japanese, transcribed into the Roman alphabet, would have enabled Xavier himself to read directly to a Japanese audience.

---

28 Ibid., 259.

29 Xavier/Zabieru and Kōno, *Sei Furanshisuko Zabieru zenshokan*, vol. 3, 142.

30 Fróis/Furoisu, *Nihonshi 6, Bungo hen 1*, 42.

31 Xavier's letter to the Society at Goa from Yamaguchi in July 1551, in Coleridge, *The Life and Letters of St. Francis Xavier*, vol. 2, 296.

After spending one year in Kago-shima, Xavier and his companions went to Hirado and Yamaguchi. In Yamaguchi, they preached twice a day on the streets and crossroads, "reading out parts of our book, and then speaking to the people about the Christian religion."[32] That they not only read aloud from the translation, but also used their own words to explain the Catechism shows that Xavier and Fernandez had acquired some sophistication in the language.

Based on the information from Fernandez, Fróis wrote that in Yamaguchi, Xavier used all the knowledge of Japanese he had gained to teach Buddhist monks about Christian concepts and the Holy Trinity.[33] Xavier's teaching was highly abstract, and even though his Japanese may have been limited, his proficiency was evidently adequate to enable him to speak logically and philosophically.

Fig. 2, Painting of Xavier's (lower left corner) preaching to the lord of Bungo (center), from Cornelius Hazart, *Kerckelycke historie van de gheheele wereldt* (Antwerp: Cnobbaert, 1667).

Fróis also observed that Xavier stopped using "Dainichi" (Japanese name for the celestial buddha Mahāvairocana) to refer to the Christian God, and decided to use instead the Portuguese word "Deus."[34] However this term was ridiculed by the Japanese as it sounded like "diusa" [sic] ("Dai-uso," the great lie).[35] According to the Japanese scholar of Christianity Kishino Hisashi, Xavier was prudent about using Buddhist terms to explain Christianity even before he came to Japan. His purpose of using "Dainichi" to

32 Ibid., 297.

33 Fróis/Furoisu, *Nihonshi 6, Bungo hen 1*, 62.

34 Ibid., 62–63.

35 Xavier's letter to the Society in Europe from Cochin on 29 January 1552, in Coleridge, *The Life and Letters of St. Francis Xavier*, vol. 2, 342.

render "God" was to bridge Christianity and Buddhism, not, as commonly believed, a result of being misled by Paul's "ignorance."[36]

After spending two years and three months in Japan, Xavier returned to India. There he wrote of Japan and its language, "Japan is a very large empire entirely composed of islands. One language is spoken throughout, not very difficult to learn."[37] These words clearly convey that Xavier did not feel the language was very difficult to master, and they served to encourage new missionaries who would be dispatched to Japan in the future.

However, Xavier's Japanese language proficiency was not as high as that of Fernandez. He wrote, "Cosmo (Cosme de Torres) writes the sermons in our language, and Fernandez, who knows that of the country well enough, translates them into Japanese. Through their labours the Christians are advancing greatly in piety."[38] Without mentioning his own role, Xavier hinted that he did not attain Fernandez's level.

Influenced by Xavier's enthusiasm for learning the Japanese language, Cosme de Torres recommended that all Jesuits in Japan speak only Japanese among themselves for daily conversations. Fernandez rigidly followed this suggestion to the extent that he even talked in Japanese with the priests and brothers who just arrived in Japan from India.[39]

Xavier expected Jesuit priests not only to learn the language, but also to "acquaint themselves with the doctrines and rules of the different sects."[40] Having knowledge of Buddhist practice thus seemed to him to be essential to understanding Japanese culture.

Xavier quickly realized the convenience of Chinese characters used by both Chinese and Japanese, reporting to Ignatius in his letter, "We have written a book in the Japanese language explaining the origin of the world, and all the mysteries of the life of Jesus Christ. We have transcribed this book into Chinese characters, and intend to carry this copy with us when we go into China, so that while we are learning the language of the country

---

36 Kishino, *Seiōjin no Nihon hakken, Zabieru rainichizen Nihon jōhō no kenkyū*, 201–205; Kishino, "Furanshisuko Zabieru to 'Dainichi'," 81–85.

37 Xavier's letter to the Society in Europe, from Cochin on 29 January 1552, in Coleridge, *The Life and Letters of St. Francis Xavier*, vol. 2, 331.

38 Ibid., 346.

39 Fróis/Furoisu, *Nihonshi 9, Nishi Kyūshū hen 1*, 298–99.

40 Xavier's letter to the Society in Europe from Cochin on 29 January 1552, in Coleridge, *The Life and Letters of St. Francis Xavier*, vol. 2, 346.

we may be able to show the Chinese a sample of the truths we bring to them written in characters which they know."[41] These words demonstrate Xavier's approach to learning a new language and preaching in it, such as he did with Tamil, Malay, and Japanese. For him, mastering the Japanese language was also a step toward laying a foundation for his future mission in China.

4. Accurate Observations of Japan

While Xavier was preaching at Yamaguchi in 1551, the domain lord Ōuchi Yoshitaka (1507–1551) warmly received him and provided an old temple—Daidōji—for him to use. "A great many used to come to this place for the sake of hearing about the new religion. We used to preach twice a day, and after the sermon there was always a good long dispute concerning religion. Thus we were continually occupied either in preaching or in answering questions... After disputes and questionings for many days, they at last began to give in and betake themselves to the faith of Christ."[42] Despite his linguistic limitations, what Xavier achieved is amazing.

During his frequent interactions with the Japanese people, he carefully observed their ways of thinking and behavior. They "are led by reason in everything more than any other people, and in general they are all so insatiable for information and so importunate in their questions, that there is no end either to their arguments with us, or to their talking over our answers among themselves. They did not know that the world is round, they knew nothing of the course of the sun and stars, so that when they asked us and we explained to them these and other like things, such as the causes of comets, of the lightning, and of rain, they listened to us most eagerly, and appeared delighted to hear us, regarding us with profound respect as extremely learned persons. This idea of our great knowledge opened the way for sowing the seed of religion in their minds."[43] Their knowledge of natural sciences thus helped Xavier and his companions to propagate Christianity, and within

---

41 Ibid., 374.

42 Xavier's letter to the Society at Goa from Yamaguchi in July 1551, in Coleridge, *The Life and Letters of St. Francis Xavier*, vol. 2, 299.

43 Xavier's letter to the Society in Europe from Cochin on 29 January 1552, in Coleridge, *The Life and Letters of St. Francis Xavier*, vol. 2, 337–38.

two months they had baptized five hundred people in Yamaguchi.[44]

Xavier not only taught the Japanese people, but also learned much from them. They made him reflect on himself deeply. "No words can express all that I owe to the Japanese. It is by their means alone that our Lord, by an interior illumination, has penetrated me with a knowledge of my countless sins."[45] Xavier's testimony reveals that at that moment, in his mind, there was real two-way communication between the Japanese people and him, and between East and West.

Xavier prophesied the future of Christianity in Japan, saying, "As far as I know, the Japanese nation is the single and only nation of them all which seems likely to preserve unshaken and for ever the profession of Christian holiness if once it embraces it; but this will doubtless not be without great sufferings and heroic conflicts on the part of the preachers of the Gospel."[46] His prediction proved to be accurate. After horrendous persecutions by Japanese rulers for two hundred and fifty years from the early seventeenth century, Kirishitan in the Nagasaki area who had kept their religious beliefs secret from the authorities surfaced on 17 March 1865 at the newly-built Ōura Church, where they proclaimed their Christian faith to Bernard-Thadée Petitjean (1829–1884) of the Paris Foreign Missions Society (M. E. P.). The world was shocked by this "miracle." It seemed impossible that any Christian would have survived the centuries of systematic oppression. But the Japanese people's "unshaken" faith had been foretold by Xavier three hundred years earlier, based on his insightful understanding of their language and religious practices.

5. Competency in Japanese

What was the level of Xavier's Japanese language proficiency? Georg Schurhammer's reading of various primary sources led him to conclude that it was very limited. Although Xavier wrote that the Japanese language was

---

44 Ibid, 338.

45 Xavier's letter to Ignatius in Rome from Cochin on 29 January 1552, in Coleridge, *The Life and Letters of St. Francis Xavier*, vol. 2, 366.

46 Ibid., 372–73.

"not very difficult to learn,"[47] Schurhammer interpreted this statement as an indication of Fernandez's Japanese level, not of Xavier's own.[48] So far there is no new evidence to overturn Schurhammer's assertion, but in this section I would like to reexamine this issue by carefully reviewing extant documents and Xavier's language background.

From the above-mentioned letters written by Xavier, we know that Xavier was able to speak Japanese. There are other facts we need to consider to determine his proficiency. First, he was born in Navarre of the Basque country (present-day Spain) and his native tongue was Basque, which differs from Spanish and has no close relation with other European languages.[49] Most Basque-born missionaries to Japan have quickly noticed a similarity between Basque and Japanese, and have usually found learning Japanese easy. For example, Sauveur Candau (1897–1955) of the M. E. P. stated that because of his mother tongue, "it is much easier for me to learn Japanese than most French do as there are a lot of similarities between the two languages." The Japanese verb *da* だ (to be) is similar to the *da* in Basque, and "both Basque and Japanese have the same word order, therefore I did not find Japanese to be unfamiliar, and this helped me a lot."[50]

Other missionaries from the Basque country felt similarly after their arrival in Japan. The second Archbishop of the Tokyo Archdiocese, Pierre Mugabure (1874–1910) of the M. E. P., was surprised, when he arrived at Yokohama, to be addressed by a Japanese man who was taking care of his baggage with the words "kore bakari da" (This is all). Mugabure was struck by the expression, because the pronunciation and meaning were very close to what they were in the Basque language.

When Candau arrived at Yokohama, he too found that Japanese pronunciations sounded like Basque. Later he said, "I have been studying Japanese, and have never thought that it is difficult to learn." He mentioned another Basque-born missionary, Jean Lissarrague (1876–1937), who felt the Japanese language sounded very familiar as if he had already heard it before. Candau

---

47 Xavier's letter to the Society in Europe from Cochin on 29 January 1552, in Coleridge, *The Life and Letters of St. Francis Xavier*, vol. 2, 331.

48 Schurhammer, *Das kirchliche Sprachproblem in der japanischen Jesuitenmission des 16. und 17. Jahrhunderts; ein Stück Ritenfrage in Japan*; Doi, *Kirishitan ronkō*, 21.

49 Yoshida, "Basuku go," 272–82.

50 Candau/Kandō and Shishi, "Nihon are kore 'Shishi Bunroku-shi to no taidan," 146–47.

said that there are countless Japanese and Basque words that share similar pronunciations and meanings, and made a list to support his point of view.

There are also similar idiomatic expressions too, according to Candau. For instance, "a shower while the sun shines" is referred to in Japanese as "a fox's wedding" (*kitsune no yomeiri*); Basque has the same expression. The Japanese believe Japan is blessed by the spirit of the language (*kotodama*), and similarly Basque people take it for granted that Basque is the best language in the world, citing that it was used by Adam and Eve in the Garden of Eden.[51]

Candau's perception of the similarity between the two languages is based on his deep linguistic knowledge which enabled him to compile a Latin-Japanese dictionary, *Rawa jiten*, published in 1934. On numerous occasions he related that the Basque language has the same word order and sentence structure as Japanese. He pointed out similar grammatical functions, such as *taezu* (continually, without a break) and *kangaezu* (thoughtlessly, without thinking). Another example is the attaching of the verbs "go" and "come" to other verbs to indicate the direction of the actions, as in *motte kuru* (to bring here), *motte iku* (to take there), *oite mairimashita* (to have left it behind before coming), and *mite kimashita* (to have seen before coming). These structures do not exist in English and French, he said—only in Basque and Japanese.

Candau further noted, "Both Basque and Japanese are agglutinative languages. This means that the meaning of a word differs depending on the prefix or suffix attached to its stem." He continued, "In the Japanese language, different forms of a verb are chosen in accordance with the rank of the people of the conversation. For instance, the meaning of 'That's it' can be expressed by 'sō da (intimate),' 'sō desu (polite),' 'sō dearimasu (formal),' and 'sō degozaimasu (more polite)' to reflect different degrees of honorifics. The Basque language has the same device." Moreover, the two languages have very similar pronunciations, and "all the Japanese consonants and vowels, including the important distinction between the long ones and the short, can be found in Basque too."[52]

Because of these similarities, Candau found the Japanese language easy to learn. In fact, his proficiency has been highly praised by many. The scholar

51 Candau/Kandō, "Nihonjin to Basukujin," 30–32.
52 Ibid., 32.

of French literature, Tatsuno Yutaka (1888–1964), for example, stated, "He used the Japanese language completely effortlessly. We are constantly impressed by his faith gushing out from full-fledged European philosophical beliefs."[53] Candau "does not have a foreign accent when speaking in Japanese, and the words he used are suitable for the educated class. He uses expressions with rich nuance...His eloquence amazed many as he skillfully used *kango* (words of Chinese origins), idioms, and lines from kabuki plays, as well as proper expressions for students, women, workers, and farmers."[54]

French missionary Georges Neyrand, who came to Japan in the 1950s and noted that among European tongues, only the Basque language has the same structure as the Japanese, asserted that "the Japanese language certainly is easy for Basque people to learn."[55] Tobe Miyuki, a scholar of linguistics who has good knowledge of at least seventy languages including Basque, is of the view that it is suitable for Japanese to conduct research on the Basque language because its grammar is close to that of Japanese.[56] Novelist Inukai Michiko (1921–2017) saw the similarity in sentence structures between the two languages and judged that relative pronouns in Basque are "very much Oriental."[57]

When the Basque-born missionary Vincent Mugica (1920–2006, M. E. P.) journeyed to Japan in 1949, on his ship were several more missionaries from his region. Mugica said that the Basque people like to learn different customs and languages, and are adventurous and highly adaptable. His own spoken Japanese, as noted by reporters from the Japan Broadcasting Corporation (NHK), was "fluent with dramatic intonation."[58] While talking with Mugica, the novelist Shiba Ryōtarō felt that listening to him was like "reading a highly refined poem."[59]

In sum, Basque-born missionaries have tended to master the Japanese language very well. Japanese Catholic priest Kohira Takubo said, "The sim-

---

53 Tatsuno, "Basuku no hoshi," 2.

54 Diarusu, *Jinrui ai no shito*, 143–44.

55 Neyrand/Neran, *Obaka-san no jijoden hanbun, Seisho katate ni Nippon 36 nenkan*, 202–203.

56 Tobe, *Basukugo jiten: Basukugo, Eigo, Nihongo*, 8.

57 Inukai, *Seiō no kao o motomete*, 250–51.

58 NHK Kaidō o Yuku Purojekuto, *Shiba Ryōtarō no fūkei 3: Kita no mahoroba, Nanban no michi*, 131–32.

59 Shiba, *Shiba Ryōtarō zenshū 59: Kaidō o yuku 8, Nanban no michi*, 122.

ilarity between Basque and Japanese enables the missionaries from Basque to make remarkable progress in learning Japanese, as is widely known."[60] Scholar of French literature Shinoda Kōichirō also wrote, "It is a fact that among the Catholic priests who came to Japan after World War II, those who are best at using the Japanese language are from the Basque region."[61] Jacques Candau (1920–1990), Sauver Candau's nephew, believed that Basque and Japanese descended from a common ancestral language.[62]

Although Sauver Candau's perception of the similarity between the two languages has not been theorized linguistically, it seems that the sense of affinity toward a new language is much more important than knowledge and theory when studying it. Linguist Wada Yūichi observes, "When we face a new language and try to grasp its general character, the first thing we attempt is to find its similarity with the language we know of. If we are familiar with more languages, we naturally categorize similarities into groups." Wada noticed that foreign students learn Japanese more quickly if their mother tongues are Tamil, Turkish, or Basque. "It is a renowned phenomenon that Basque-born priests are masters of the Japanese language, such as today's Fr. Candau and Francis Xavier of the medieval age."[63] Wada thus evidently believed that Xavier must have excelled in Japanese.

Johannes Laures (1891–1959), a Jesuit missionary and founder of the Kirishitan Bunko archives at Sophia University, harbored a similar belief. In his book on Xavier's life, Laures described his fervent prayers shortly before his death: "Sometimes he lost consciousness, and his spirit became delirious with fever. He was praying loudly. Which language did he use, Tamil, Malay, Japanese, or Basque, his mother Tongue?"[64] It is unlikely that a language in which one is not proficient would come forth unconsciously. According to Laures, the Japanese language is certainly among those that Xavier had mastered.

One expert of the Basque language, Shimomiya Tadao, disagrees with the view that emphasizes the similarity of Basque and Japanese, noting that "Anyone who has studied a bit of linguistics would realize that this kind of

60 Kohira, *Kagoshima ni kita Zabieru*, 53.

61 Shinoda, *Shura to chinkon: Nihon bunka shiron*, 181.

62 Ibid.

63 Wada, "Tōji ruikei ron: Nihongo no ichizuke ni tsuite," 3–4, 20.

64 Laures, *Sei Furanshisuko Zabieru no shōgai*, 387–88.

coincidence can be found all over the world."[65] In fact, not all the missionaries from Basque learned Japanese quickly. For instance, Laurent Labarthe (1924–2001), born in the Basque region of southern France, had difficulty in learning the language after coming to Japan in 1954. "It is not true that I was able to speak Japanese better than the Japanese people, nor was I already an expert of Japanese history when I arrived at the Yokohama Port. In fact, I knew nothing about Japan. I prayed the rosary to divert my anxiety, and rushed to the Tokyo Archdiocess of the Paris Foreign Missions Society for help... After two years of intensive study of Japanese, I started to work as an assistant priest at the Kawagoe Church." Labarthe obviously struggled with Japanese. Once he said that if he would be allowed by God to live again, he would choose to become a priest, and hopefully he would improve his Japanese.[66] From his book *Senkyōshi no jigazō* (Self-Portrait of a Missionary), we can see that Labarthe did eventually reach a high level of colloquial Japanese after putting painstaking efforts into language study.

Another Basque-born missionary, Pedro Arrupe (1907–1991), who became the twenty-eighth Superior General of the Society of Jesus, likewise felt that learning Japanese was particularly difficult. According to his book *Este Japón Increíble* (The Incredible Japan), he spent a great deal of time studying the language.[67] His hard work paid off, and by the late 1930s, less than two years after his arrival in Japan, Arrupe seems to have mastered the Japanese language.[68]

According to Vincent Mugica, there were thirty to forty Basque-origin missionaries and nuns in Japan in the early 1980s.[69] When the NHK television reporters visited the main office of the Paris Foreign Missions Society in 1997, they were told that the total number of missionaries sent to Japan by the Mission was 149, among whom twelve were Basque.[70] The online archives of the Mission shows that at least seventeen priests from Basque

---

65 Shimomiya, *Basukugo nyūmon: Gengo, minzoku, bunka*, 30.

66 Labarthe/Rabaruto, *Senkyōshi no jigazō*, 38–39.

67 Arrupe, *Este Japon Increible*, 47–48. His endeavors impressed another Basque-born Jesuit Tomas Eceizabarrena (1923–2015), according to Besineau/Bejino and Echizen, *Tsukaeru tameni: Iezusu kaishi no ayumi*, 322.

68 Catret/Katoretto, *Pedoro Arupe: Kibō o motarasu hito*, 37, 40.

69 Shiba, *Shiba Ryōtarō zenshū 59: Kaidō o yuku 8, Nanban no michi*, 125.

70 NHK Kaidō o Yuku Purojekuto, *Shiba Ryōtarō no fūkei 3: Kita no mahoroba, Nanban no michi*, 142–43.

had been sent to Japan by October 2017.[71] Mugica noted that if Basque-born missionaries from other mission orders are counted, then the number presumably would rise significantly.

Although the similarity between Basque and Japanese that Candau identified in the 1930s may not have been sensed completely the same by Xavier, it is easy to assume that in the mid-sixteenth century, when there were no dictionaries or textbooks for learning Japanese, Xavier made maximum use of the similitude between Japanese and his mother tongue. And his Basque background may well have disposed him to regard Japanese as "not very difficult to learn."[72]

We also need to pay attention to the fact that Xavier had mastered the Tamil and Malay languages before coming to Japan, and Tamil grammar is said to be similar to Japanese grammar.[73] Xavier agonized over studying the Tamil language, as he wrote to Ignatius, "In order to communicate with the local people by their language which is so hard to memorize, I have had to take great pains physically and mentally."[74] Through the experience of learning Tamil, he may well have found it easier to learn Japanese.

The renowned Japanese linguist Ōno Susumu has done extensive research on the relation between ancient Tamil and ancient Japanese. He discovered many corresponding words between the two languages, similar grammatical patterns, and the same poetic rhythmic lines of five-seven-five-seven-seven syllables. This led Ōno to publish several books positing that the two languages descended from the same ancestral language.[75] Taking into account Ōno's research, it is quite possible that Xavier used Tamil, in addition to Basque, as a reference to get familiar with the Japanese language.

---

71 They are Jean-Pierre Aïnciart (1923–1987), Pierre Anchen (1879–1967), Justin Balette (1852–1918), Marc Bonnecaze (1893–1991), Jacques Candau (1920–1990), Sauveur Candau (1897–1955), Léon Gracy (1875–1945), Pierre Dominique Harguindeguy (b. 1935), Laurent Labarthe (1924–2001), Manuel Labarta (1926–2015), Joseph Marie Laucaigne (1838–1885), Jean-Baptiste Lissarrague (1876–1937), Paul Jean Louis Marie Lovens (1928–1984), Jean-Marie Martin (1886–1975), Pierre Mounicou (1825–1871), Pierre Xavier Mugabure-Saubaber (1850–1910), and Vincent Mugica (1920–2006).

72 Xavier's letter to the Society in Europe, from Cochin on 29 January 1552, in Coleridge, *The Life and Letters of St. Francis Xavier*, vol. 2, 331.

73 Iemoto, "Tamirugo," 271.

74 Xavier's letter to Ignatius in Rome, from Cochin on 12 January 1549, in Xavier/Zabieru and Kōno, *Sei Furanshisuko Zabieru zenshokan*, vol. 2, 197.

75 Ōno, *Nihongo no kigen* (1957), *Nihongo to Tamirugo* (1981), *Nihongo izen* (1987), and *Nihongo no genryū o motomete* (2007).

In sum, Xavier learned to speak the Japanese language in order to communicate with the Japanese people. Although there are no sources that would enable us to objectively judge his Japanese language proficiency with confidence, my speculation in this chapter is based on the evidence that he wholeheartedly endeavored to learn Asian languages and evangelized in local tongues, successfully sowing the seeds of Christian faith in Asia and laying the foundation for the Jesuit "adaptation" policy which priotizes learning of local languages.

6. Admiration for Xavier among Modern Japanese Intellectuals

Many Japanese intellectuals have expressed their deep admiration for Xavier. In May 1949, memorial services commemorating the 400th anniversary of Xavier's visit to Japan were held, and a relic from the saint's right forearm was brought from Rome to Japan where it was carried in a procession throughout the country. Historical novelist Yoshikawa Eiji (1892–1962) wrote in a newspaper article, "God's Gospel brought by Xavier to Japan during the tumultuous medieval era was of great significance in both world history and Japan's history, next in importance to the founding of Japan. It marked the opening of the page to Japan's early modern era." Yoshikawa continued to say that although no one suffered as much in Japan as Xavier did, no foreigner loved Japan so deeply as Xavier. His great esteem for Xavier's Japan mission is evident in his words, "We Japanese are spoiled by his sincerity and love, aren't we?"[76] Yoshikawa also wrote that Japan is the most fortunate country on the planet because Xavier's visit brought Christianity here.

On the occasion of this 400th anniversary, General Douglas MacArthur, the Supreme Commander of the Allied Powers that occupied Japan from 1945 to 1952, issued a statement praising Xavier's evangelization in Japan as "a great ecclesiastical milestone in the spiritual evolution of mankind." He continued to say, "it was in such humble spirit this man with his soul of serenity brought to the Far East the greatest concept the world has ever known."[77] This statement was published in daily newspapers and surely attracted the attention of Japanese intellectuals.

Shiba Ryōtarō, the famous author of Japanese historical novels, sought

---

76 Yoshikawa, "Sōchō no nokku," 6.
77 MacArthur, "Seijin no kokoro de heiwa o: Ma gensui kinō seimei," 2.

to document Xavier's family background, experiences, and personality by comparing Georg Schurhammer's four-volume biography *Francisco Xavier: His Life, His Times* (1973–82) with other records. Passionate about examining Xavier's devotion to Japan and his influence on the country, Shiba journeyed far and wide, recording his findings in his travel journal (*Nanban no michi*), which was published in 1984 and awarded the Japan Literary Grand Prize in the following year.

Shiba wrote in his journal, "Although Xavier only stayed in Japan a little more than two years, he had a huge impact on Japan, becoming the first serious reporter of Japan to Europe... He even dedicated Japan, without consulting us, to the Archangel Michael. Since then, Michael has been the guardian angel of Japan until today."[78]

Tsurumi Shunsuke (1922–2015), philosopher and critic, concurred with Shiba that Xavier and Candau exerted considerable influence on Japanese culture and they in fact—together with the Japanese people—deserve credit for creating modern Japanese culture. Tsurumi had a sense of affinity for the Basque people because they did not have a concept of "nation state." He learned this from Vincent Mugica and quoted his words, "They did not care much about the Kingdom of Navarre, the Kingdom of Spain, or the Kingdom of France...They lived peacefully and believed they were independent."[79] The lack of commitment to a "nation state" concept might have played a role in the worldwide evangelization conceived by Ignatius and Xavier. At least they did not create an artificial border in their minds.

To the Japanese, in the view of the Japanese translator (Hagio Shō) of Jacques Allières' *Les Basques* (The Basque People, originally published in 1971), what best represents Basque culture are Ignatius, Xavier, Candau, and Picasso's painting "Guernica" (1937).[80]

The four-volume complete translation of Xavier's correspondence by Kōno Yoshinori (*Sei Furanshisuko Zabieru zenshokan*, published by Heibonsha), was awarded the Japan Translation and Publishing Culture Award (Nihon hon'yaku shuppan bunka shō) and the Japan Translation Culture Award (Nihon honyaku bunka shō) in 1986 by the Japan Society of Translators. In addition to recognizing the excellent quality of the translation,

---

78 Shiba, *Shiba Ryōtarō zenshū 59: Kaidō o yuku 8, Nanban no michi*, 13.
79 Tsurumi, "Basuku made kita nagai nagai michi," 394.
80 Allières, *Basukujin*, 258.

these prizes also affirm the historical significance of conveying Xavier's spirit to the Japanese populace.

It seems that all missionaries to Japan had read Xavier's correspondence before coming to this country. Or shall we say that it is very possible that most of them decided to evangelize in Japan *after* reading Xavier's descriptions. Among the various "gifts" Japan received from Xavier are the many later missionaries who inherited and kept alive his passion for Japan.

Chronology of F. Xavier's Life

Year (Age)	Date	Major events
1506 (0)	7 April	Born at Xavier Castle in Navarre, Basque country.
1525 (19)	Summer	Entered College Sainte-Barbe, University of Paris.
1529 (23)	September	Began sharing a room with Ignatius Loyola.
1530 (24)	March	Gained qualification of philosophy professor and taught about Aristotle.
1533 (27)	June	Became enthusiastic about Christianity because of Ignatius' influence.
1534 (28)	15 August	Made vows of poverty, chastity, and obedience on the Hill of Montmartre, along with Ignatius and five other men; established the Society of Jesus.
1536 (30)		Studied theology at the College of Sorbonne, University of Paris.
1537 (31)	3 April	Had audience with Pope Paul III in Rome.
	24 June	Ordained together with the seven founding members of the Society of Jesus.
1540 (34)	June	Worked for King Juan III until leaving for India.
1541 (35)	August	Departed from Lisbon and arrived at Mozambique of Africa, where he devoted his efforts to the sick.
1542 (36)	February	Left Mozambique and arrived at Goa on 6 May. Wrote a book about the Catechism.
	October	Went to the Fishery Coast. Later evangelized at various places including Goa and Cochin.
1545 (39)		Prayed at the St. Thomas Church of Chennai, South India, and determined to go to the East to evangelize.
	September	Arrived at Malacca, where he translated prayers into the Malay language.
1547 (41)	7 December	Met with the Japanese Han-Siro (Paul), and started planning a visit to Japan.
1549 (43)	15 April	Left Goa for Japan, accompanied by Cosme de Torres, Juan Fernandez, Manuel of China, and Amador of Malabar, Paul, and two other Japanese men.
	15 August	Arrived at Kagoshima.
	29 September	Met Shimazu Takashisa, lord of Satsuma domain; gained permission to evangelize.

1550 (44)		With Paul's assistance, translated the Catechism and the Apostles' Creed into Japanese.
	August	Went to Hirado and was welcomed by domain lord Matsuura Takanobu; gained permission to evangelize.
	November	Arrived at Yamaguchi; preached on the streets and met the domain lord Ōuchi Yoshitaka.
	December	Arrived at the port of Sakai.
1551 (45)		Arrived at Kyoto, stayed for eleven days. Gave up his plan to get permission to evangelize from the Japanese emperor.
	March	Returned to Hirado.
	April	Went to Yamaguchi to meet the domain lord again, with letters and gifts from the Governor of India and the bishop. Gained permission to evangelize, and was given permission to use Daidōji temple. Busy with preaching and answering questions, baptized five hundred people within two months.
	September	Arrived at Funai (present-day Ōita) upon the invitation of the lord Ōtomo Yoshishige (Sōrin).
	15 November	Worried about situation in India, so left Japan for India. Passed by the Ryūkyū Islands, arrived at Shangchuan Island of Canton, China. Determined to evangelize China.
	24 December	Arrived at Malacca.
1555 (46)	24 January	Arrived at Cochin, India. Returned to Goa in February. Later returned to Malacca, where he was warmly received by local people.
	August	Returned to Shangchuan Island.
	4 September	Celebrated a Mass at the hilltop. Fell ill on 21 November, lost consciousness on the 26th.
	1 December	Regained consciousness, and continued praying.
	3 December	Died early morning.

CHAPTER
2
Responding to Xavier's Prophecy

1. Deep-Rooted Faith in Japanese Hearts

From the arrival of Xavier in 1549 until 1587, a span of less than four decades, at least 200,000 Japanese, 1 percent of the Japanese population of that time, converted to Christianity.[1] Xavier's descriptions of Japan in his numerous letters to the Jesuits in Europe and India made the land and its people visible on the world stage for the first time. Future missionaries' curiosity about Japan and their admiration for it were greatly stimulated by these letters. Only a few years later, however, Japanese rulers began efforts to eliminate Christianity from the country. Their ruthless persecutions produced thousands of martyrs whose unwavering Christian faith touched countless people overseas.

In 1634 the Tokugawa shogunate banned Christianity entirely, and those missionaries who remained in Japan were eradicated, either by banishment or by execution. However, in 1708 an Italian priest Giovanni Battista Sidoti (1667–1714)[2] entered Japan secretly, fully aware of the possibility of being caught and put to death. He was soon arrested. Interrogated by the scholar

---

1 Crasset, *The History of the Church of Japan*, vol. 2, 439.

2 New research recently established that the surname of the Italian priest was Sidoti, instead of Sidotti which has been used for centuries. See Torcivia, *Giovanni Battista Sidoti: (Palermo, 22 agosto 1667 – Tokyo, 27 novembre 1715) missionario martire in Giappone.*

and shogunal official Arai Hakuseki (1657–1725), Sidoti managed to communicate a substantial amount of information about Christian philosophy and Western science. Arai documented what he learned in two books, *Seiyō kibun* (Information on Foreign Countires) and *Sairan igen* (Knowledge of the World). Though Sidoti died six years later in a jail in Edo, the knowledge that he brought to Japan fueled an underground stream of Christianity during the 250 years of persecution.

Required by the authorities to step on Christian sacred images to demonstrate that they were not believers, the so-called "hidden Christians" disguised themselves as Buddhists and Shinto adherents. Privately, however, they maintained their Christian faith. This strategy enabled them to preserve the Christian tradition uninterrupted.

Meanwhile, the Paris Foreign Missions Society (M. E. P.), established in 1658, concentrated on evangelizing East Asia and Southeast Asia. It was looking for opportunities to send missionaries to Japan as well. At the end of the Edo period, the Missions Society singled out Naha, the capital of the Ryūkyū Kingdom, as a promising site from which they might gain access to mainland Japan. Already the Ryūkyū Islands were being frequented by ships from Europe and the United States. In 1844 the Missions Society dispatched Théodore-Augustin Forcade (1816–1885) to Naha, and in 1855 they sent Eugène-Emmanuel Mermet Cachon (1828–1889), Prudence Seraphin-Barthelemy Girard (1821–1867), and Louis-Theodore Furet (1816–1900) there as well. While waiting for opportunities to enter mainland Japan, these priests were learning the Japanese language.[3]

After a Treaty of Amity and Commerce between France and Japan was signed in 1858, the Missions Society sent more members directly to Japan. The famous priest Bernard-Thadée Petitjean (1829–1884) arrived at Yokohama in 1862 and moved to Nagasaki the following year. As noted above, the Ōura Church built by the Missions Society in Nagasaki witnessed the surfacing of hidden Christians on 17 March 1865.

Around 12:00 noon on that day, according to Fr. Petitjean's letter, a group of twelve to fifteen men, women, and children came to the church. "They stood outside the church door, and it did not look like simply out of curiosity. As the door was closed, I rushed to open it, and then I moved

---

3 Polak, "Nichi-futsu kōryū ryakushi," 50–60.

to the front of the altar. They also followed me." After watching Petitjean pray for a while, a woman in her forties or fifties approached him and said, putting her hand on her chest, "Watashi no mune, anata no mune to onaji" (My mind is like yours), and introduced herself as coming from the Urakami village. Then she asked him, "Sancta Maria go zō wa doko?" (Where is the statue of Our Lady?). Petitjean pointed to the figure of Mother Mary with a baby in her arms. The villagers were overjoyed and shouted, "Indeed, that is Santa Maria! Look, she is holding the holy son Jesus (on ko Djezous sama)!" They also told Petitjean that they celebrated Christmas and Lent before the Passion. Petitjean continued, "They worship the Cross, love the Blessed Mother, and pray. I am not sure what kind of prayers they say, but I shall know more later, including about other matters."[4]

News of the discovery of these hidden Christians soon spread all over the world, and was regarded as a "miracle." However, as noted earlier, that the Japanese people would be steadfast in their deep faith had been predicted by Xavier three hundred years earlier.

Aimé Villion, M. E. P., who reached Japan in 1868, was astonished that these people had been able to keep their faith for over two centuries without any formal contact with the church. "This is a light of God's blessing!" he proclaimed.[5] In his co-authored book written in Japanese, *Yamato hijiri chishio no kakioki* (日本聖人鮮血遺書, Japanese Martyrs' Testament in Blood), Villion described this dramatic historical moment and included a reproduction of a painting (Fig. 3). Later Georges Neyrand also wrote, "There is nothing so marvelous and touching like this in the history of Christianity."[6]

How did the Japanese manage to maintain this deep-rooted faith? Renowned novelist Osaragi Jirō (1897–1973) viewed the persecution of Christians as a stain on Japan's history. He recounted their story in his samurai novel *Tennō no seiki 16: Bushi no shiro*: "During the three centuries of samurai rule, most Japanese people developed a subservient personality. But only the farmers of Urakami village were clearly aware of their dignity, and did not yield to oppression. It is Christianity that planted the

---

4 Junshin Joshi Tanki Daigaku Nagasaki Chihō Bunkashi Kenkyūjo, *Puchijan shikyō shokanshū*, 69, 72, 174.

5 Yamazaki, *Idai naru Viriyon shinpu: Viriyon shinpu ni manabite*, 55.

6 Neyrand/Neran, *Obaka-san no jijoden hanbun: Seisho katate ni Nippon 36 nenkan*, 180.

Fig. 3, Illustration of the resurfacing of hidden Christians, with the caption "At the Nagasaki church, descendants of medieval Christians suddenly appeared and talked to the priest on 17 March 1865."[7]

concept of 'human rights' in their hearts. Their resistance is very rare for Japanese people." [8]

The French missionary Georges Neyrand said of the hidden Christians, "They took Christ as an absolute existence. They would not renounce Christ even if it meant risking their life. This achievement is beyond description, a victory of faith won by their indomitable spirit."[9] In fact, it was the strong faith of the Japanese that attracted many missionaries to Japan, including Villion and Neyrand.

For several years after the Meiji Restoration, the new government continued the Tokugawa regime's religious policy, arresting Christians and incarcerating them in locations far from their homes. When the Iwakura

---

7 Villion/Biriyon, *Yamato hijiri chishio no kakioki*, p. 385–86.

8 Osaragi, *Tennō no seiki 16: Bushi no shiro*, 113–22.

9 Neyrand/Neran, *Obaka-san no jijoden hanbun: Seisho katate ni Nippon 36 nenkan*, 181.

Mission visited the United States and Europe between 1871 and 1873, they were constantly subjected to protests against Japan's proscription of Christianity. Responding to overseas reactions, in early 1872 Minister of Finance Inoue Kaoru (1836–1915) proposed liberalization of the treatment of those arrested, although he did not advocate a total lifting of the ban. He urged that Christians who apostatized be released from exile. By a Cabinet Order of 15 March 1872, about eight hundred such persons were permitted to return to Urakami.[10]

The first Japanese ambassador to the United States, Mori Arinori (1847–1889) wrote an essay titled "Religious Freedom in Japan" in November 1872 and submitted it as a petition to Cabinet Chief Sanjō Sanetomi (1837–1891). Arguing that the Christian faith must be respected without being controlled by political authorities, he also enclosed a draft of a "Decree of the Great Empire of Japan Regarding Religion" (Dainippon Teikoku shūkyō rei) that he himself had authored.[11]

Itō Hirobumi (1841–1909), one of the members of the Iwakura Mission, appealed to the government in 1873: "Wherever I go, I encounter bitter complaints about Japan's persecution of Christians and restriction of religious freedom. If we do not immediately release the former, and show our tolerance to the latter, we cannot expect any friendship from foreign countries."[12]

On 21 February 1873, Iwakura Tomomi (1825–1883) sent a telegraph from Berlin to the Japanese government, warning that "If the Christians are not immediately released, we will gain nothing from this visit."[13] The pressure from foreign governments was crucial, forcing the Meiji government to abandon its policy of religious intolerance. Three days later, on 24 February, the widely used noticeboards prohibiting Christianity were removed from Japan's streets, and by the spring of 1873 the government had adopted a policy of tacitly permitting its citizens to embrace the Christian faith.[14]

---

10 Abe, "From Prohibition to Toleration: Japanese Government Views Regarding Christianity, 1854–1873," 132.

11 Ikeda, *Birion shinpu*, 116.

12 Ibid., 129.

13 Ibid., 130.

14 Abe, "From Prohibition to Toleration: Japanese Government Views Regarding Christianity, 1854–1873," 132.

From that moment forward, regardless of domination, Christian mission-aries rushed to Japan and began working in the spheres of evangelization, education, medical care, and promotion of social welfare and industry.

2. Pioneers of Missionary Writings in Japanese

Five years before the Japanese government lifted its proscription of Christi-anity, the Paris Foreign Missions Society realized the limits of oral preaching, and decided to publish texts in the Japanese language for wider distribution. Marc Maria de Rotz (1840–1914) was summoned to Nagasaki in 1868 to start lithographical printing, which could produce a larger quantity at higher speed than woodblock printing. With the guidance of Bishop Petit-jean, De Rotz mainly used kana syllabary together with a few kanji in the Missions Society's publications to enable illiterate farmers and fishermen to understand Christianity. These publications are named "Petitjean prints"[15] or "De Rotz woodblock prints" after the priests who pioneered modern missionary writings in the Japanese language.[16]

It is said that De Rotz's Japanese proficiency was not very high and his preaching had to depend on his assistant Nakamura Kinzō (1859–1945).[17] Nevertheless, De Rotz kept precise records in Japanese—using Roman let-ters (*rōmaji*) instead of kanji and kana—of daily activities such as farming procedures, financial transactions, management of the Rescue Center (*kyū-join*), and gifts purchased for children.[18] It seems that the Japanese language was part of his life, and he used it at ease.

In a booklet published by De Rotz in 1879, he used the vernacular to explain Christian love for neighbors.

> *Himojiki hito ni wa tabemono o* (ヒモジキ人ニハタベモノヲ)
>   To feed the hungry,

---

15 Kōso, *Putijan-ban shūsei: Honpō Kirishitan fukyō kankei shiryō: Kaisetsu 1865–1873 nen.*

16 Guo/Kaku, "Kindai Nihongo Bungaku no senkusha: Putijan shikyō to Do Ro shinpu," 184.

17 Yano, *Do Ro shinpu sono ai no te*, 46.

18 Yano, *Do Ro shinpu kurokawa no nichinichiroku.*

Kawakitaru hito ni nomimono o (カワキタル人ニノミモノヲ)
　To give water to the thirsty,

Binbō naru hito ni wa kimono oba (ビンボウナル人ニハキモノヲバ)
　To clothe the poor,

Yadonaki hito ni wa yadoya oba (ヤドナキ人ニハヤドヤヲバ)
　To shelter the homeless,

Jiyū naki hito ni wa aganai oba (ジユウナキ人ニハアガナイヲバ)
　To ransom the captive,

Byōnin ni wa kaihō o (ビョウ人ニハカイホウヲ)
　To assist the sick,

Shinishi hito ni sōrei o (死ニシ人ニソウレイヲ)
　To bury the dead.

Kanau hodo atauru wa karada no nanatsu jihi no shosa
(カナフホドアタフルハ カラダノ七ツジヒノショサ)
　The more you gain, the more you offer. These are the seven corporal
　works of mercy.[19]

Writing mostly with kana is reminiscent of the style of Japanese children's
literature. In fact, missionary writings in Japanese tend to use easy-to-under-
stand expressions and vocabulary. Paris Foreign Missions Society members
left many works written in Japanese. Among them, six priests in particular were especially prolific. Aimé Villion (1843–1932) published six books,
François-Alfred-Désiré Ligneul (1847–1922) seventy, Lucien Drouart de
Lezey (1849–1930) twenty, Emile Raguet (1854–1929) fifteen, including
a complete translation of the Bible, Julien Sylvain Bousquet (1877–1943)
twelve, and Clément-Joseph Lemoine (1869–1941) eleven. Most of these
books were "narrated" (述) or "consulted" (閲) by the missionaries, and
"recorded" (記), "authored" (著), "translated" (訳), or "edited" (編) by
their Japanese assistants. Works so designated were products of collaboration between the missionaries and the Japanese people.

---

19 Kataoka, *Aru Meiji no fukushizō: Do Ro shinpu no shōgai*, 61–62.

3. Sharing Xavier's Joy

What is common among missionaries is their admiration for Francis Xavier, their love for Japan, and their endeavors to promulgate Christianity in Japan. After spending years in Nagasaki, Kobe, and Kyoto, Aimé Villion moved to Yamaguchi, where he traced Xavier's footsteps and located the site of Daidōji, the temple given to Xavier by the domain lord Ōuchi Yoshitaka. Villion was very familiar with Xavier's activities in Japan, and he often quoted Xavier's words praising the Japanese people. The versions of Xavier's correspondence Villion had read are Léon Pagès' French translation (1855), Henry Coleridge's English translation (1871), and Asai Torahachirō's Japanese translation (1891).

A postcard (Fig. 4) Villion sent to a parishioner, Yamazaki Tadao, features a huge monument at the Daidōji temple site commemorating Xavier's evangelization. Villion wrote in rōmaji, quoting Xavier's words from

a letter written on 29 January 1552 from Cochin, India, soon after his return from Japan: "I know not how to end when I am writing to my dearest fathers and brothers, and about <u>my joys in Japan</u> too, the greatness of which I could never express, however much I might wish to do so."[20] The underlined part was translated into Japanese by Asai as "warera no yukaikoku to naseru Nihonkoku" (我等の愉快国となせる日本国).[21]

Fig. 4, Villion's postcard to Yamazaki Tadao, from Yamazaki's *Idai naru Viriyon shinpu: Viriyon shinpu ni manabite.*

---

20 Coleridge, *The Life and Letters of St. Francis Xavier*, vol. 2, 349.

21 Xavier/Zaberiyo, *Sei Furanshisuko Zabiriyo shokanki*, vol. 3, 277–78.

Villion rendered it in the postcard as follows:

Waga cocoro no yukwai no tanoshimi Nihon no Kuni nari
Xaverio
Indo-Cochin
29 janv 1552
Tenbun 20 nen, 12 gwats[22]

Villion added "cocoro" (Jp. *kokoro*; heart) to emphasize the joy that filled Xavier's heart. In Asai's translation, there is a portrait of Xavier accompanied by this sentence at its bottom (Fig. 5). Asai's Japanese translation was based on Henry Coleridge's (1822–1893) English translation.

Similarly, in Léon Pagès' (1814–1886) French translation *Lettres de saint François-Xavier de la Compagnie de Jésus*, based on a Latin translation, the sentence has a similar meaning: "Mais je cesse d'écrire, quoique j'aie regret à le faire, en écrivant à de si chers Pères et Frères, et sur le Japon, mes délices, dont je ne pourrais jamais tout dire, quel qu'en fût mon désir."[23] In other words, the Latin, French, English, and Japanese versions all emphasized the "joy in Japan" experienced by Xavier.

When Xavier was evangelizing at Yamaguchi, he preached fervently, defeated Buddhist believers in debates, and converted many to Christianity. The following passage reveals his satisfaction.

> The labours which are undergone for the conversion of a people so rational, so desirous to know the truth and be saved, result in very sweet fruit to the soul. Even at Amanguchi (Yamaguchi) when the King allowed us to preach the faith and a vast concourse of people gathered round

Fig. 5, Frontispiece of Asai Torahachirō's translation of Xavier's correspondence. The Japanese caption below the image of Xavier reads "我等の愉快国となせる日本国の事に就きては書することも能はざるなり."

22 Yamazaki, *Idai naru Viriyon shinpu: Viriyon shinpu ni manabite*, 148–49.

23 Pagès, *Lettres de saint François-Xavier de la Compagnie de Jésus, apotre des Indes et du Japon: traduites sur l'édition latine de bologne*, vol. 2, 238.

us, <u>I had so much joy and vigour and delight of heart, as I never experienced in my life before</u>…if the world knew and was aware how well the souls of the Japanese are prepared to receive the Gospel, I am sure that many learned men would finish their studies, canons, priests, and prelates even, would abandon their rich livings, to change an existence full of bitterness and anxiety for so sweet and pleasant a life. And to gain this happiness they would not hesitate to set sail even to Japan.[24]

In the French translation of Xavier's letter, the underlined sentence has the same nuance, "que j'ai goûté des fruits de vie plus délicieux qu'en aucun autre temps de mon existence."[25]

Villion was so impressed by Xavier's expressions that he quoted some of them in his own book *Pourquoi j'aime les Japonais?* (Why Do I Love the Japanese?) published in 1929. For instance, when mentioning the devoted love he received from Japanese Christians: "Mes délices, dont je ne pourrai jamais assez dire… J'ai goûté ici des fruits de vie plus délicieux qu'en aucun temps de mon existence"[26] (My delights, which I can never say enough… I have tasted here fruits of life more delicious than at any time of my existence). Villion's words are very similar to Xavier's, as he fully understood Xavier's joy after he had been able to baptize so many and had recieved so much support from the faithful at Yamaguchi, as well as discovering the site of Daidōji.

The Preface for Asai Torahachirō's translation was written by Villion. He concluded by imitating Xavier's letter ending "Amanguchi (July 1551)"[27]: "In the same month and at the same Yamaguchi, our holy master wrote a letter 341 years ago, numbered eighty-four, that described his wholehearted love for Japan. 31 July 1891, missionary A. Villion."[28]

---

24 Xavier's letter to the Society in Europe from Cochin on 29 January 1552, in Coleridge, *The Life and Letters of St. Francis Xavier*, vol. 2, 349.

25 Pagès, *Lettres de saint François-Xavier de la Compagnie de Jésus, apotre des Indes et du Japon: traduites sur l'édition latine de bologne*, vol. 2, 237.

26 Villion, *Pourquoi j'aime les Japonais?*, 7.

27 Xavier's letter to the Society at Goa from Yamaguchi in July 1551, in Coleridge, *The Life and Letters of St. Francis Xavier*, vol. 2, 301.

28 Xavier/Zaberiyo, *Sei Furanshisuko Zabiriyo shokanki*, vol. 1, 4. Villion's original expression in the Preface: 三百四十有一年の昔聖師が山口に於て其日本国に対する至仁至愛の心を以て我等に書遺せし第八十四号の書翰を認したため給ひしと同月に同山口に於て 一千八百九十一年七月三十一日 派遣宣教師 ア、ヴィリヨン

4. Xavier's Voice through "Creative" Translations

The above-quoted famous sentence "I know not how to end when I am writing to my dearest fathers and brothers, and about <u>my joys in Japan</u> too, the greatness of which I could never express, however much I might wish to do so," seems to be a creative translation of Xavier's original Portuguese phrasing.

There are two printed versions of Xavier's letters in Portuguese. One is *Sancti Francisci Xaverii: epistolas aliaque scripta complectens*, published in the eighteenth century, which renders this phrase as, "Com isto acabo, sem poder acabar, escreuemdo a meus Padres e Irmãos tam queridos e amados, e escreuemdo de amigos tam gramdes como são os <u>xpãos</u>, de Japão."[29] The other is a version published in 1944–1945 with Georg Schurhammer's research appended. The only difference between the two is the orthography of the words I have underlined here. In Schurhammer's version "xpãos" is rendered as "cristãos": "e sprevemdo de amigos tão gramdes como são os <u>cristãos</u> de Japão."[30]

This passage means, "I must end now although I am writing to my dearest fathers and brothers, and about <u>the dearest Japanese Christians</u> too, [there is] so much I would like to express." Xavier's original Portuguese sentence does not have the nuance of "my joys in Japan" or "sur le Japon, mes délices." The more recent Japanese translation (1986) by Kōno Yoshinori does not have this either.[31]

Then, what is the reason for this "creative" translation? When Xavier's letters reached Europe, they were usually translated into Latin, Spanish, and Italian to be distributed to all Catholic institutes. The Latin translation (1600) by Orazio Torsellino (1545–1599) was "de Iaponibus meis delitii"[32] (my happiness in Japan), which was already different from its original Portuguese meaning. A later French translation (1628) based on

---

29 *Sancti Francisci Xaverii: epistolas aliaque scripta complectens*, 696–97.

30 Schurhammer and Wicki, *Epistolae S. Francisci Xaverii aliaque eius scripta*, vol. 2, 279.

31 Xavier/Zabieru, *Sei Furanshisuko Zabieru zenshokan*, vol. 3, 206.

32 Xavier, *Francisci Xaverii Epistolarum libri quatuor*, 249: "Itaque finem scribendi, etsi finem facere non possum, cum ad carissimos patres meos, fratresque scribam, & <u>de Iaponibus meis delitiis</u> scriba, de quibus omnia persequi, vt maxime velim, nullo modo possim."

this Latin translation reads "de mes delices, les Iaponnois"[33] (my delights are the Japanese). Two hundred years later, another French translation appeared (1828), with the phrase rendered as "de mes chers Japonois, de l'objet de mes affections et de ma tendresse" (my dear Japanese, the object of my affections and tenderness).[34] This kind of "creative" translation was taken a step further twenty-seven years later by Pagès' French translation (1855), which interprets the phrase as "et sur le Japon, mes délices (Japan, my delights)."[35]

Both Latin and French translations "created" the nuance "my joy" which did not exist in the original Portuguese version. As the original letter was brimming over with the joy Xavier had experienced, saying "I had so much joy and vigour and delight of heart, as I never experienced in my life before,"[36] the translators seem to have been "infected" by this expression and felt compelled to add the expression "Japan, my delights." Neverthe-less, this creative translation still conveys Xavier's true voice, even though the translators did not provide word-for-word equivalence.

It was not only Villion who emphasized the "joy." Other missionaries also presumed Xavier's emotion in a similar manner. For instance, when the Catholic church Yokohama Tenshudō was completed by the Paris For-eign Missions Society in January 1862 and attracted more than ten thou-sand curious Japanese, Prudence-Séraphin-Barthélemy Girard (1821–1867) preached to them for ten days. He recounted his experience in a letter, "nous font comprendre, à présent mieux que jamais, cette parole de saint François Xavier: "O Japon, mes délices!" (This made us understand better

---

33 Xavier and un P. de la mesme compagnie. *Lettres du B. pere Saint Francois Xavier, de la Compagnie de Iesus, apostre du Iapon: divisees en quatre livres*, p. 713: "Ie fais donc fin puis qu'il il faut faire, jaçoit que i'aye bien de la peine de trouuer la fin d'vn fi doux & agreable entretien, auvec vous mes tres-chers Peres & frerea, mefmement quande ie fuis vne fois fur le propos de mes delices, les Iaponnois; defquels ie ne vous pourrois iamais acheuer de dire tout ce qui en eft"

34 Xavier, *Lettres de S. François-Xavier, apôtre des Indes et du Japon*, vol. 2, p. 239: "et je la finirai comme je l'ai commencée, quoiqu'il m'en coûte beaucoup de rompre brusquement un entretien aussi doux avec vous, mes très chers Pères et Frères, quand je parle surtout de mes chers Japonois, de l'objet de mes affections et de ma tendresse sur lequel je ne puis jamais tarir."

35 Pagès, *Lettres de saint François-Xavier de la Compagnie de Jésus, apotre des Indes et du Japon: traduites sur l'édition latine de bologne*, vol. 2, 238.

36 Xavier's letter to the Society in Europe from Cochin on 29 January 1552, in Coleridge, *The Life and Letters of St. Francis Xavier*, vol. 2, 349.

than ever the words of St. Francis Xavier, "Oh Japan, my delights!").[37] Obviously, creative translation was embraced by many of the missionaries who followed Xavier's footsteps to Japan.

5. Reverberation of Xavier's Happiness

A. Villion has been considered one of the most brilliant and enthusiastic Catholic priests in Japan, next to Xavier.[38] Taking Xavier's humility as his model, he once said, "Missionaries are like beggars. All they do is forget about self, leave family behind, and wander around to search for people's souls on behalf of Christ. The total capital they possess is prayer, knowledge, and enthusiasm to save souls…When I read the biography of St. Francis Xavier, what moved me the most is that no matter how much I endeavor, I am no match for the holy master, although I was chosen as one of his successors by God's blessing."[39]

When Villion was a small boy, his babysitter repeatedly told him about Xavier's street preaching in Yamaguchi and enjoined him, "You must do the same when you grow up."[40] Later in his life, at a meeting Villion raised his hand in which he held a translation of Xavier's correspondence and declared to the audience, "It is this book, nothing else but this book, that brought me to Japan."[41]

However, there is another person who played an important role in attracting Villion to Japan—Yoshida Shōin (1830–1859)—the Yamaguchi-born samurai, educator, and thinker whose teaching and example did much to inspire the Meiji Restoration. Villion read a newspaper article about Shōin when he was a fourth-year student in middle school. The article recounted how a young Japanese man was stubbornly refused by Commodore Perry when he wanted to board the American warship. Villion was disturbed by Perry's refusal and admired the young man's bravery.[42] Decades later,

---

37 Marnas, La "Religion de Jésus" (Iaso ja-kyo) ressuscitée au Japon dans la seconde moitié de XIXe siècle, vol. 1, 398.

38 Soden and Fukai, Seibo Maria to Nihon, 155.

39 Ikeda, Birion shinpu, 408.

40 Related by Villion to Ayukawa Yoshisuke (1880–1967), a Yamaguchi-born politician and industrialist. See Tomoda, Ayukawa Yoshisuke jūōdan, 27.

41 Okada Hiroko, Kokyō no shibakusa, 31.

42 Villion and Takenaka, "Yoshida Shōin o omou," vol. 10, 686–87.

Villion stated in a letter to Takada Seiho, a priest of Shōin Shrine in Hagi, Yamaguchi prefecture, that this event was "the major reason" that motivated him to go to Japan.[43]

To Xavier, success in Yamaguchi was the happiest moment in his life. For Villion, "the happiest day of my life overflowing with joy" was 11 February 1889, the day the Meiji Constitution was promulgated and religious freedom was officially guaranteed in Japan.[44]

The places in Japan where Xavier spent most of his time were Kagoshima (Satsuma domain) and Yamaguchi (Chōshū domain). The journalist and political commentator Kaji Ryūichi (1896–1978) went so far as to say, "The fact that the driving force of the Meiji Restoration originated in Satsuma and Chōshū can be explained by the Christian influence left by Francis Xavier. It can also be interpreted as resulting from the unique combination of Saigō Takamori (1828–1877) and Yoshida Shōin's Tendō (ruling by nature) and Jindō (ruling by humans) theories blending with Confucianism and Christianity."[45] This presumption of Xavier's long-lasting influence may sound like an exaggeration, but well reflects Japanese intellectuals' admiration for him.

In comparison with Xavier, modern missionaries spent much longer periods in Japan and therefore had more time to learn the Japanese language and to directly communicate with people. The four missionaries whom I discuss in this book—A. Villion, S. Candau, H. Heuvers, and G. Neyrand— all penned books in the Japanese language which are widely read in Japan.

Villion is reputed to have been a "Second Xavier." Candau is considered to "have carried out most efficiently and properly the evangelization Xavier planned for Japan."[46] Heuvers entered the Society of Jesus, and fulfilled Xavier's passion for missionary work in Japan. Neyrand transformed Xavier's "street preaching" into "bar preaching." What is common among them is their mastery of the Japanese language and their insightful understanding of Japanese culture. They were tolerant and open-minded toward the indigenous people. Even if they did not succeed in converting Buddhists to Christianity, they still cultivated close relationships with those who were devotees of Buddhism.

---

43 Kumura, "Viriyon-san no itsuwa," 20–24.

44 Nagatomi, *Zaberiyo to Yamaguchi*, 122.

45 Kaji, "Dōtokuteki shinsei ni okeru Tōyō to Seiyō," 274–75.

46 Tanaka, *Gendai seikatsu no ronri*, 298.

The missionaries' writings in the vernacular are the product of their adaptation to the Japanese language and culture. They documented their efforts to introduce Christian views of the world to Japan, and by analyzing these writings, we shall be able to discern these men's wide-ranging influence on modern Japan.

CHAPTER
3
Aimé Villion's Dedication to Modern Japan

1. Understanding Japan

During his sixty-four years of evangelization in Japan, Aimé Villion lived in Nagasaki, Kobe, Kyoto, Ise, Yamaguchi, Tokuyama, Shimonoseki, Hagi, Tsuwano, and Nara. His circle of friends encompassed ordinary people, politicians, financiers, religious persons, and military personnel. His influence on Japan is widespread and his mission, in his own words, was "turning hatred and suspicion into love and trust."[1] His patience and effort in bringing "salvation" to Japan can be viewed as a modern version of Xavier's mission.

Villion detailed his Japan mission in his autobiography *Cinquante ans d'apostolat au Japon* (1923, Fifty Years of Apostolate in Japan) and *Pourquoi j'aime les Japonais?* (1929, Why Do I Love the Japanese?). The former has been discussed in three biographies: Kariya Heiji's *Viriyon shinpu no shōgai* (1938, The Life of Fr. Villion), Yamazaki Tadao's *Idai naru Viriyon shinpu* (1965, Great Fr. Villion), and Ikeda Toshio's *Biriyon shinpu: Gendai Nihon Katorikku no chūseki* (1965, Fr. Villion: The Cornerstone of Modern Japan's Catholicism). Ikeda Toshio (1928–2019), a Catholic priest himself, was a researcher of the history of Christianity in modern Japan as

---

1 Ikeda, *Birion shinpu*, 3.

well. Villion's activities, together with records of baptisms he performed, have also been studied by the Jesuit missionary José Palacios, who published his findings in *Ima, Birion shinpu o ou* (2003, Following Fr. Villion: From the End of the Shogunate till the Shōwa Period).

Villion was born on 2 September 1843 in Lyon, France, the son of a judicial officer. His mother died when he was only four years old. Three years later, he found in her notebook a prayer that inspired him to make missionary work his vocation: "My God, please bless my children. Please summon one of them to serve you."[2] In fact, before reading it, he was already thinking about "Going to the country of little Chinese" when he was only five years old and unable to distinguish Japan from China. At the age of seven, on his way to his primary school one day, while crossing the Pierre Bridge over the Saône River, he looked up at the Statue of the Blessed Mother on the Hill of Fourvière and suddenly heard a voice asking, "Little boy, will you be a missionary for me when you grow up?" Ever since, this voice kept coming back to him.[3]

In May 1866, Villion was ordained a priest after graduating from the Seminary of the Rue du Bac, established by the Paris Foreign Missions Society. On 14 June he departed from Marseille for East Asia, knowing that he would never see his father again. After two years of waiting in Hong Kong, he was invited to Japan by Bishop Petitjean who wrote: "Don't judge Japan according to your European ideas. People here do not think in the same categories. Look at the many contradictions one finds in foreign books on Japan. Their authors have not understood the Japanese people."[4] Villion landed in Nagasaki in October 1868, started to serve the Ōura Church, and took charge of the descendents of Kirishitan of Urakami and foreign residents.[5]

Villion was surprised by everything he saw at Nagasaki. Samurai wearing two swords stalked along the streets with dignity and were greeted courteously by townspeople. All ordinary people behaved politely, and their good manners were impressive.[6] One day, four to five local officers came to search

---

2 Yamazaki, *Idai naru Viriyon shinpu: Viriyon shinpu ni manebite*, 1.

3 Ikeda, *Birion shinpu*, 20–21.

4 Verwilghen, "The Buddhist Studies of Father A. Villion," 251–52.

5 Ikeda, "Birion shinpu no nenpu," in *Birion shinpu*.

6 Nagatomi, *Zaberiyo to Yamaguchi*, 117.

his house, as Christianity was still strictly banned. One of them approached Villion quietly and asked for books; he wanted to learn more about Western culture. When he repeated his request, Villion thought, "When this kind of young man takes charge, a new Japan will appear and eventually the current situation will change." Villion offered him several books. The man was Ōkuma Shigenobu (1838–1922), then about thirty years old. Later he became a famous politician and founded Waseda University in Tokyo. His strong desire for Western knowledge must have reminded Villion of Han-siro (Paul)'s strong curiosity that had impressed Xavier and guided him to Japan. After moving to Kobe, Villion met Ōkuma again at the Osaka Mint Bureau,

Fig. 6, Photo of A. Villion, frontispiece of Yamazaki Tadao's *Idai naru Viriyon shinpu* (1965).

where the government had appointed him to the executive position of councilor. The two marveled at Japan's changes and recalled the old days when they first met.[7]

When Villion arrived at Nagasaki in 1868, the Tokugawa shogunate was continuing its policy of persecuting the Kirishitan. The Meiji government left the ban in place after replacing the Tokugawa in 1868. Kirishitan from Urakami were tortured and then deported to Hagi, Tsuwano, Fukuyama, Wakayama, Kanazawa and Nagoya, as well as other locations around Japan. Villion himself was placed under house arrest for two months. Local officials constantly threatened to kill him, but he was indifferent to their menacing remarks, having prepared for persecution in Japan before leaving his homeland.[8] He and other missionaries sheltered the Kirishitan and found ships to carry young ones to Shanghai and to seminaries in South Asia. Villion also managed to send the Missions' lithography printing machines to

---

7 Ibid., 120.
8 Ibid., 118.

Shanghai,[9] which were used later to print books and magazines by another priest, Marc Marie de Rotz.[10]

In Nagasaki, Villion was touched by the strong faith of many Kirishitan who, instead of apostatizing, chose exile and persecution. Their attitudes influenced Villion's Japan mission in the years to come. Two decades later, Villion moved to Yamaguchi, where he traced the sites of Urakami Kirishitan who had died as a result of persecution in Hagi and Tsuwano. He prayed for the martyrs and built monuments to commemorate them.[11] His effort in locating the sites contributed significantly to future research on the history of Christianity in Japan.

In November 1871, Villion moved to the Kobe Catholic Church, where he looked after foreign residents of that port city, and also after the Urakami Kirishitan who were exiled nearby. In order to protect orphans, he managed to convince Catholic sisters—members of the Congrégation des Soeurs de l'Enfant-Jésus de Chauffailles (established in 1859 in Chauffailles, France)—to come to Kobe. The sisters' dedication to the sick and the poor changed many Kobe people's attitudes toward Christianity. When local residents saw the sisters on the street, they gave way to them politely and murmured, "Amazing, they care about the poor!"[12]

In 1878 there was an outbreak of cholera in Kobe, resulting in heavy casualties. Villion and his assistants rushed to help those who were afflicted, looking after them day and night, ignoring the risk of being infected themselves. Their selfless devotion moved the hearts of local people, who praised them with these words: "When the epidemic spread, we saw what the missionaries did. If their faith was not genuine, they would not have done that."[13] In other words, Villion preached Christian love not just by words, but through his actions.

In 1879, he moved to Kyoto to "teach the French language and study ancient Japanese culture."[14] This was ten years before the Meiji Constitution

9 Ikeda, *Birion shinpu*, 82.

10 Guo/Kaku, "Do Ro hanga no zensōkyoku: Sekiban insatsu kara saishiki mokuhanga e," 18–19.

11 Okimoto, *Otome-tōge to Kirishitan*, 157–58; Nagatomi, *Zaberiyo to Yamaguchi*, 119.

12 Ikeda, *Birion shinpu*, 155–60.

13 Ibid., 191–96.

14 Yunesuko Higashi-Ajia Bunka Kenkyū Sentā, *Shiryō oyatoi gaikokujin*, 223.

was promulgated. Villion asked one newly-converted Christian preacher who used to be a Buddhist monk on Mt. Hiei to teach him about Buddhism. In order to understand Japanese thinking, customs, and traditions, he decided to seriously study Buddhism by regularly visiting Chion'in, the head temple of the Jōdo (Pure Land) sect. He sought answers to several questions: "Why does Buddhism take the universe as the Absolute, instead of recognizing God's existence that transcends the universe? If all creatures are controlled by the inevitable fate of reincarnation, being positioned in ceaseless transmigration according to their deeds in previous lives... then humans will have no freedom to take responsibility for whatever they do, and theoretically will lose an ethical foundation in life." Bearing these questions, he visited the temples and shrines of most Buddhist and Shinto sects.[15] The knowledge he gained from Buddhism was very useful for his Christian mission.

Later, he was permitted to propagate the faith and he openly taught Christian doctrine, despite frequent objections from Buddhist monks. He used a large format book (about 90cm x 151cm) with illustrations of Jesus's life on the left, and explanations in Japanese, written in ink with a brush, on the right. These images supplemented his spoken Japanese and made his teaching easy to understand.[16] Gradually he was able to convert and baptize new believers.

The illustrations of the large format book Villion used were likely imitations of ones imported from Shanghai. According to recent findings, the Paris Foreign Missions Society in Japan frequently used woodblock prints produced by the Jesuit Adolphe Henri Vasseur (1828–1899) in cooperation with T'ou-sè-wè Orphanage Art Production in southeast Shanghai, during the period from the 1860s till 1880s. The size of the illustrations Villion used is close to that of Vasseur's prints (67cm × 130 cm, Fig. 7).[17]

During the Christmas season, Villion made a small model of the manger of Bethlehem decorated with statues of baby Jesus, Mary, and Joseph for his little room facing the street. At night, he lighted his crèche and it attracted a large crowd of passers-by. Seeing the people gaze at the little smiling baby with small hands opened, Villion also smiled with satisfaction and started to tell them about the birth of Christ.[18]

---

15 Ikeda, *Birion shinpu*, 206–209.
16 Ibid., 257.
17 Guo/Kaku, "Do Ro hanga no rūtsu: Konsutantsu kara Shanghai, Nagasaki e," 78–79.
18 Ikeda, *Birion shinpu*, 283.

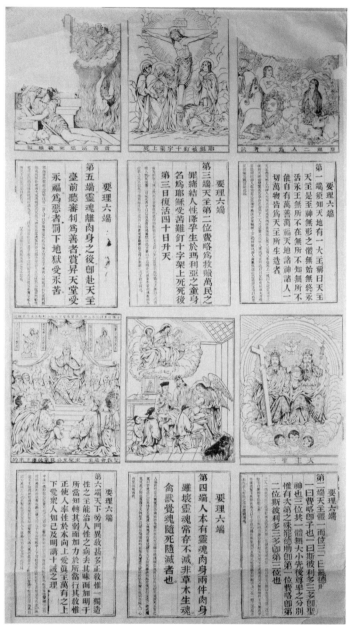

Fig. 7, Copy of a woodblock print produced by A. Vasseur and T'ou-sè-wè Orphanage Art Production, 67cm x 130 cm, Convent of Mary's Annunciation, Nagasaki.

Three hundred years earlier, Xavier tried to obtain permission to propagate in Kyoto, but had to abandon the idea because of the chaos of the civil wars. To mark the twenty-seventh anniversary of Xavier's landing on Kagoshima, the Society of Jesus started to build a church in Kyoto. Consecrated on 15 August 1576 and popularly called Nanbanji, it became a big attraction and was repeatedly featured by artists on fans (Plate 7) and folding screens commonly called "Nanban byōbu" (Plate 8). The church was destroyed pursuant to Toyotomi Hideyoshi's policy of proscribing Christianity, first decreed in 1587. Only the church bell was saved, and it has been preserved at the Zen temple Shunkō-in, located within the Myōshinji complex in Kyoto.

Villion was determined to get a church built in Kyoto to fulfil Xavier's dream of evangelizing the old capital. He managed to purchase a piece of land near the crossroad of Sanjō and Kawaramachi streets in 1888, and a church named "St. Xavier Church" was built in 1890 (Plate 10). The church building is preserved today at the Meijimura Historical Park near Nagoya.

During the early Meiji period, prominent intellectuals in Japan cultivated a keen interest in Christianity. For instance, educator and thinker Fukuzawa Yukichi (1835–1901) was teaching his two sons to respect God and to follow God's will and the Ten Commandments in 1871, even before the ban on Christianity was lifted. He emphasized to his boys that they should be grateful to God because He created everything in the world including their parents.[19] Fukuzawa not only hired an Anglican clergyman from Canada, Alexander C. Shaw (1846–1902), as a private teacher for his children in 1874, but also frequently sought missionaries' help to develop his school Keiō Gijuku, which was established in 1868.[20] He found Christian views and morality to be beneficial to modern Japan.

The Meiji Constitution of 1889 legally permitted religious freedom in Japan. In the same year, Villion moved from Kyoto to Yamaguchi, where Xavier had spent several months propagating the faith.

---

19 Fukuzawa, *Fukuzawa Yukichi zenshū*, vol. 2, 70–74.

20 Shirai, *Fukuzawa Yukichi to senkyōshi tachi: Shirarezaru Meiji-ki no Nichi-Ei kankei*, 305–306.

2. Searching for Xavier's Site

Yamaguchi is the place where Xavier achieved his greatest success in converting Japanese people to Christianity. He used Daidōji, the Buddhist temple given to him by domain lord Ōuchi Yoshitaka, as a chaple to preach, as mentioned in the previous chapter.

Villion described his first days in Yamaguchi humorously to his parishioners, among whom was the young poet and translator, Nakahara Chūya (1907–1937).

> I am approaching Xavier's town! A brightly shining river welcomed me. The river's name Fushino-gawa was in Xavier's book too. A young woman passing by told me that Yamaguchi is on the other side of the river. I spread my arms like a bird, gliding over the river, and landed in the town. I lay down on the ground, calling out "Lord" and "Master Xavier." Then small stones flew over my head, and a voice shouted, "Hey you, Yaso!" "Oh! I am so close to Xavier." I looked around, expecting a rock to follow. All I could see was an old man with his hair in a topknot (*chonmage*), just like in the time of Xavier. I entered Yamaguchi while receiving the glory of being pelted by stones.[21]

ザビエルの町は近い。すると白い川が私を迎えにきた。椹野川だ、その名はザビエルの書物にある。通りすがりの娘さんが、川の向うが山口ですという。私は、両手をひろげ、鳥のように、橋を飛んでザビエルの街に着陸した。大地にうち伏し、主とザビエルの名を呼んでいると、頭の上に石つぶてが飛んできた。ヤソやーいという声がする。有難い有難い、私はザビエルに近づいた。岩のような苦難が飛んでこないかと、辺りを見廻したら、チョンマゲを結った老人がいた。ザビエルの時代そのままです、私は石つぶての栄光をうけながら山口の街に入りました。

This is a witty, but sad description comparing Christ, who was warmly welcomed by palm branches when entering Jerusalem before the crucifixion, with Villion himself, who was greeted by stones. We can see his admiration for Xavier, whose footsteps he would closely follow.

In Yamaguchi, Villion often visited Chūya's grandfather Nakahara

---

21 Nakahara, *Ani Nakahara Chūya to sosen tachi*, 173.

Masakuma, who was baptised by Villion and assisted him in finding the site of Daidōji. According to Chūya's younger brother Shirō, when entering their home Villion usually stretched his black soutane like a bat, shouting "Here comes the ghost!" He often brought the children sweets, biscuits, and sometimes coins. He liked to slip the gifts into their kimono through the neck opening.[22] Chūya was often taken to church by his grandmother, and he developted an attachment to Villion. "Chūya never left the Christian environment in his entire life," Shirō wrote.[23]

Chūya's mother remembered Villion's visits well. "When he left, he just said goodbye without tying his shoe laces, doing so outside the door because he did not want us to wait to see him off." She recalled, "Sometimes children threw stones at him and caused him a lot of trouble. He looked a bit nervous, but he was a very considerate person." Chūya's father disliked Christianity, but was touched by the Bible stories Villion related to him. He admitted, "Fr. Villion is a great person indeed."[24]

Just as in Kyoto, Villion used the big book with illustrations to teach. He told the audience, "Look at the Meiji emperor who granted us religious freedom—his medals are glittering. Aren't they cross-shaped? This is Jesus's cross, a symbol of sacrifice for love. Now it has become a symbol of honor in the world."[25] These words immediately drew the attention of the audience. He used the cross and church edifices to familiarize the audience with Christianity.

After residing in Yamaguchi for four years, in 1893, with the aid of an old map provided by local people, Villion finally discovered the site of Daidōji. He decided to build a monument to commemorate Xavier's teaching of Christianity, but his plan failed as the Sino-Japanese War broke out in 1894. Nevertheless, after the war the entrepreneur and politician Ayukawa Yoshisuke (1880–1967) and his sister Kiyo, who married Kuhara Fusanosuke (1869–1965), also an entrepreneur and politician, donated a big sum to finance the project. Villion was assisted by his former student Hara Takashi (1856–1921), who had been baptized "David" by a Catholic priest in Yokohama in 1873, and later became the nineteenth prime minister of

22 Ibid., 210.
23 Ibid., 210–211.
24 Nakahara Fuku, *Watashi no ue ni furu yuki wa: Waga ko Nakahara Chūya o kataru*, 123–24.
25 Ikeda, *Birion shinpu*, 315–16.

Japan from 1918 till 1921. Villion was impressed by Hara's easy-going manner and welcoming attitude even after becoming Japan's top leader.[26]

Villion went to Tokyo several times to meet with Shibusawa Eiichi (1840–1931), the "father" of capitalism in Japan, and solicited donations. Thanks to Shibusawa's mediation, the Mitsui and Iwasaki corporations also decided to donate funds. Villion sent Shibusawa a letter to express his gratitude.[27] It seems that many men in financial and political circles supported Villion's fundraising for the monument project.

Eventually the monument was erected (Plate 11) and the unveiling ceremony on 10 October 1926 was attended by ambassadors of Spain, Italy, France, and Portugal as well as Japanese government officials. Villion gave a congratulatory speech in Japanese in which he also acknowledged the support of local people.

> I have lived in Japan and served God for more than sixty years. Since I first proposed a monument to commemorate St. Francis Xavier, I have gained support from the two prefectural governors Hayashi and Nakagawa, followed by successive governors and members of the Preservation Association as well as other people who helped out with this project. Now that I can see this monument standing here, I have no regrets in my life.[28]

Admirers of Villion had secretly commissioned a bust of Villion to be placed beside the monument to Xavier and unveiled at the same ceremony. However, Villion was enraged and shouted, "I am not worthy of tying his shoe laces. It is outrageous to put me next to him. Remove it right now!" His vehemence embarrassed the Prefectural Governor Ōmori Kichigorō and others. Only after much cajoling did he finally agreed to accept the statue, saying, "Well, keep it covered until I am gone."[29]

Villion was obviously a person indifferent to the honor, power, and wealth of this world. He never tried to impose Western culture on Japan nor exhibited a sense of cultural superiority. His sole wish was to bring

---

26 Nagatomi, *Zaberiyo to Yamaguchi*, 124–25.

27 Ryūmonsha, *Shibusawa Eiichi denki shiryō*, vol. 38, 489–501.

28 Nagatomi, *Zaberiyo to Yamaguchi*, 491.

29 Ikeda, *Birion shinpu*, 486.

Christian salvation to people's souls. What he did in Japan is certainly well remembered by many Japanese.[30]

I visited the Xavier Memorial Park, about 300 square meters in size, in early December 2017. I was overwhelmed by the magnificence of the monument to Xavier. Fifteen meters away, there is a small portrait bust of Villion that was made public after his death (Plate 12). There happened to be three children, pupils of Yamaguchi Shiritsu Ōdono Elementary School, playing in the park. I asked them if they would pose for a photograph. They happily agreed and imitated Xavier's gesture by crossing their hands over their chests. It was a heartwarming moment, with the images of Xavier and Villion shining in the twilight.

3. Evaluation of Villion's Japanese Language Skills

Since there is not much mention of Villion's Japanese language competency in biographies or media profiles, I shall use what I have discovered to deduce the level of his Japanese. In the early days of his stay in Japan, he took part in a debate with the Buddhist monk Ama Tokumon (1826–1908) from the temple Saiyōji of the Kyoto Honganji sect. This debate, according to Ama, revealed Villion's preaching to be a "miserable failure. Villion declared to Ama that he did not want to die in Japan and had already informed the church about this; he asked Ama to give him a Buddhist funeral in France, which Ama planned to visit. But it is hard to ascertain whether Ama's article actually reflects Villion's thoughts. As we already know, when he departed Marseille, Villion had no intention of returning to France, and he repeatedly stated this view throughout his life in Japan. Nevertheless, the dialogue between them may be indicative of Villion's Japanese skills. Villion said to Ama, "I am a French missionary. I came to Japan to evangelize. But I found it extremely hard to understand why Japanese ordinary people and officials distrust and hate God. I asked around for ten years, but no one could tell me the reason…I do not know Japanese well as I only spent ten years learning it."[31] Self-deprecating though his words may be, these sentences reveal that Villion's Japanese was sufficient to communicate with the Buddhist monk.

In fact, there are many people who praised Villion's Japanese. For instance, his student Hagiwara Shinsei (1900–1953), who studied French with him

---

30 Ibid., 499.
31 Ama, *Ikyō taiwa: Ichimei, Inmyōjutsu*, 3, 19.

from 1917 till 1918 when he was preaching at Hagi, was impressed by Villion's "skillful" Japanese when he first met him.[32] Hara Kiku, a parishioner who had known Villion for a long period, recalled that during the unveiling ceremony at the monument to Xavier, "Fr. Villion translated into Japanese the speeches made by the ambassadors of Spain and Portugal and acting ambassadors of Italy and France. He refrained from translating only German and Korean, saying that he did not know those languages. Fr. Villion is indeed a great scholar."[33]

Historian and critic Yokoyama Kendō once happened to sit next to Villion in a train, and chatted with him. "Mr. Villion's Japanese was fluent. He told me about his stay in Kobe, when Itō Hirobumi was governor of Hyōgo prefecture." Yokoyama wrote that Protestant educators Sasao Kumetarō (1871–1941; principal of Doremus School), Wada Rinkuma (1871–1944; president of Doshisha University), and Naruse Jinzō (1858–1919; founder of Japan Women's University), were also influenced by Villion.[34]

When Villion met with Itō Hirobumi for the first time, Itō asked him which language they should use: English, French, or Japanese. Villion responded, "All are fine with me," showing no hesitation in speaking Japanese.[35] He suggested that they speak English, however, as he felt his Japanese at that time was a bit "academic" and not so easy to listen to.[36] Villion had lived in many places and learned local dialects. According to one parishioner, his Japanese was a unique mixture of various dialects, intonations, and expressions.[37]

There are also some people who were more critical of Villion's Japanese language skills. For instance, Kudō Toshiko, daughter of the aforementioned Hara Kiku, wrote, "Although he lived in Japan near seventy years, I cannot say that his Japanese was good...He never had an opportunity to learn 'proper' Japanese systematically. He used regional dialect words and expressions as they popped up in his mind, and his spoken language had a very amusing quality."[38]

---

32 Hagiwara, *Seishun no yume*, 57.
33 Ikeda, *Birion shinpu*, 532–33.
34 Yokoyama, *Chōshū yūranki*, 183.
35 Ikeda, *Birion shinpu*, 548.
36 Yamazaki, *Idai naru Viriyon shinpu: Viriyon shinpu ni manebite*, 66.
37 Ikeda, *Birion shinpu*, 554.
38 Ibid., 535.

Villion's biographer Yamazaki Tadao said, "I cannot praise his Japanese. His preaching was conducted with skillful gestures and passion which touched the audience's hearts and gained their admiration."[39] It seems to have been his personality, rather than his words, that enabled him to convert the Japanese people to Christianity.[40]

Thus, despite the long years he spent in Japan and frequent contact with Japanese people, for some parishioners Villion's Japanese was hard to understand. But they were impressed by "his transcendental lifestyle, like that of the Buddhist monk and poet Ryōkan (1758–1831), his enthusiasm expressed in simple and rustic language, and his sincere attitude toward Christianity." His personality apparently made up for his insufficient Japanese.[41] Villion seldom gave lectures by himself without his assistants. In August 1913, he was invited to talk to the monks of Mt. Kōya. As he recalled later, " I had never done a public lecture by myself. That is because my Japanese is a bit awkward. It was the first time that I had to talk to so many people. I was very nervous the day before and prayed to the blessed Virgin Mary for all the support I needed."[42] So even though not fluent in the language, Villion did communicate with the Japanese people directly, following Xavier's practice. Villion likewise travelled to many places and baptized many converts, succeeding not by his words, but through his personality and sincerity.

There is another case that affords us a sense of the degree of his fluency in Japanese. According to his autobiography *Cinquante ans d'apostolat au Japon*, once Villion gave a lecture at Tsuwano in Shimane prefecture on how the Nagasaki Kirishitan were tortured while in exile at the Tsuwano temple Kōrinji.[43] In the audience were many who had witnessed the persecution. After describing in detail the tortures, Villion introduced one of the victims—Johanna Iwanaga—and then boldly asked for Kanamori Kazumine, who had been in charge of interrogating prisoners at Kōrinji. Tension and excitement gripped the hall. When Villion's speech was over, the audience applauded for a long time. Later, at Villion's request, Kanamori released to the public

---

39 Yamazaki, *Idai naru Viriyon shinpu: Viriyon shinpu ni manebite*, 69.

40 Kariya, *Viriyon shinpu no shōgai*, 166.

41 Ibid., 181.

42 Ibid., 282.

43 Villion, *Cinquante ans d'apostolat au Japon*, 384–85.

the records of torture, which have been invaluable to research on the history of Kirishitan persecution.[44] In sum, even though he was not a fluent speaker and often employed Japanese assistants, when Villion used his own words in Japanese to convey his opinion, it seems to have been quite effective.

4. Letters and Postcards

So far, we have only discussed Villion's spoken Japanese. How about his written Japanese? It seems that Villion was a good writer of letters and postcards. The whereabouts of most of his correspondence is unknown, but some of it has been preserved and can be viewed today. The Tsuwano Catholic Church holds a letter written by Villion addressed to Moriyama Jinzaburō (1846–1932), a famous Kirishitan of Urakami who was deported to Tsuwano and resisted and survived all the tortures (Fig. 8). Villion looked after him after his release, and formed a close friendship.

Fig. 8, Photo of Moriyama Jinzaburō.

The letter, dated 13 March 1922, is illustrated in Plate 13. The handwriting of kanji and hiragana is smooth and elegant, but there are several errors suggesting the author was not a native Japanese. Moreover, it was written colloquially, instead of using the kinds of literary expressions conventionally expected for correspondence, and the kanji for Moriyama 守山 was miswritten as 森山 on the envelope. It appears that this letter was probably written by Villion himself, but even if it was not totally in his own hand, from the colloquial vocabulary and grammar we can assume the level of Villion's Japanese language proficiency was high.

Villion informed Moriyama that he was sending him two tree seedlings which had been taken from near the stone monument in the precincts of Kōrinji. The monument, erected in March 1922, was inscribed with the words "Light of Faith." This temple was the very place where the Urakami Kirishitan had been tortured and thrown into a frozen pond in mid-winter.

---

44 Okimoto, *Otome-tōge to Kirishitan*, 156.

Here I quote the entire letter (followed by its original Japanese text).

† Moriyama-san, thank you so much for your kind letter which I received a while ago. I am very sorry for not replying sooner. Please forgive me. I am very happy to hear that you and your family are all well and are working hard, thanks to God. I am getting older day by day. This year I will be eighty, old and senile, and cannot hear well. I am waiting for God's invitation, and must get prepared for it. Let us pray wholeheartedly for each other. If one of us departs by God's train first, the other must follow. Let us keep this promise. Today I visited Tsuwano and unexpectedly met a young man from Nagasaki at Kōrinji. What a coincidence. I told him about your suffering. A parishioner here helped me to erect a stone monument of 1.2 m in height next to the pond where you were tortured in February 1868. There are tree seedlings growing next to it, like a keepsake of the victims. † Light of Faith. I took two of them and send them to you as a memorial. I wrapped the roots with wet moss. If they reach you without getting dried, please plant them in your garden. Here we often reminisce about you. Jifuku's doctor Peter Hara was asking about you. Please pass my greetings to your family. God bless!

A. Villion, 13 March, at Tsuwano Catholic Church.

†　もりやまさん、先達御心切で、てがみを送りなさった、おほきにありがたう。御返事の事で甚だおくれました、赦して下され。主の恵によって、あなたは家族皆御無事で暮して、よく務めなさらん事を、それを聞いて甚だ大喜び。こちらへも我が年々益々斜いて来たる、今年で八十才で、本当でぼけた老人さん。耳でも遠い、仕方ない。天主の有り難き知らせ、御旅の仕度をせんならん。何うぞ二人ながら心を合せて、其心得で互互の為に、祈りせん事をたのむ。どちらで先で、天主の汽車に乗って出立しますれば、別の人に向ひに出んならん。二人ながら約束せん事を頼む。さて今日、計らず津和野の巡廻の中、長崎から来たりし若い人と共に、コウリン寺に参詣しました。有難き心得で、貴殿方の御苦労の昔話を致し、山の中にあなたの、明治元年の二月のフロ場の記念卑（ママ）の如く、信者が四尺の石を立てて、其親共の片身の如く　†　信仰の光　其所で生じた二本の小さい木を抜いて、貴殿にしるしの如く小包で送ります。こけで根を包んで枯れん様に来たら、貴殿の庭に植えなされ、何時も此処に於て、

あなたの話を忘れません。地福に於てペトロ原医者さん、森山さんの事を尋ねます。先づ主の御聖寵によりて、あなたに家族の皆さんに、心の底よりよろしくよろしく申し上げ。

A. Villion

三月十三日　津和野　天主教会

Moriyama planted the tree seedlings soon after receiving them. One died, but the other grew tall, only to be destroyed by the nuclear bomb dropped on Nagasaki on 9 August 1945.[45] The stone monument (Plate 14) is still standing at Kōrinji representing Villion's mourning for the martyrs.

Villion frequently wrote to Nakahara Chūya's grandparents Masakuma and Koma. In the book authored by Chūya's brother Shirō, Villion's letters and postcards (fifteen in total) are reproduced. Thirteen of them, penned from October 1912 through April 1914, were sent to Masakuma. Twelve of these were written mainly in katakana, and one in kanji and katakana. Two were written to Koma, one in 1930 and the other 1932, both in kanji and katakana. The contents of these letters largely concern the procedure of purchasing the site of Daidōji, as Masakuma was the person helping to facilitate the transaction. The diction in all of these letters and postcards is colloquial. There are a few errors in distingushing long vowels and short ones, and oral consonents and nasal ones, a common problem in Japanese learners.

Let us examine Villion's postcard to Koma (Plate 15).[46] Displaying smoothly written kanji and hiragana, it conveys a very gentle message to Koma, who had been widowed eleven years earlier.

> Thank you for your kindness that I can never forget. Days ago when Hara-san passed by, I heard about the matter in detail. I also heard that you are doing fine but getting older. Long Life!! I myself have gotten old and useless. But I cannot forget about you. I am wearing the cotton jacket you gave me nine years ago like my rosary. Long Life!! Please be assured that I am well. I do not know when I shall board the airplane to the other side to be with your ninety-year-old husband. That is the only thing I look forward to—I am ready to go now.
>
> From Nara, 15 January 1932, Villion.

---

45 Okimoto, *Otome-tōge to Kirishitan*, 164.

46 Nakahara, *Ani Nakahara Chūya to sosen tachi*, 173–92.

奥さん　甚だ忘れられぬ親切な奥さん過日原さんが通る時、事情を詳しく聞きましたお達者で然し年にあたりましたBANZAI!!　私も特別今はボケタ死人になった　奥さん忘れる事が出来ません　今でも私のコタツの如く着て居るチョッキMAWATAが九年前奥さんから頂いたものですBANZAI!!　御安心下され　それのおかげで未だいささか元気であります　　兎も角も九十才中原さんに出会はんが為に何時　飛行機にのるか　それのみ望んで今覚悟して居ます

A. Villion AL

This postcard is presumed to be the last one Villion wrote, just two and a half months before his death on 1 April. His fondness for Masakuma and Koma is clearly shown here, as is his sense of humor, comparing the cotton jacket to his rosary and joking about going by airplane to meet Masakuma in heaven.

If the letter to Moriyama and the postcard to Koma were both written by Villion himself, then the handwriting should be more or less identical, taking into account the fact that Villion was much older when he wrote the latter. After comparing the two, curator Sugawara Mayumi of the Naka-hara Chūya Memorial Museum has suggested that they may have been written by two different hands. It is not easy to ascertain whether Villion really wrote these letters and postcards by himself. However, considering the colloquial language and the errors, the likelihood they were written by an educated Japanese person seems to be slight.

Hara Kiku, who praised Villion's Japanese as mentioned above, also received a letter from him dated 4 December 1931. Responding to Hara's letter, it says, "I was overjoyed by your visit to me. I thank God very much, and believe that it is the Feast Day of St. Francis Xavier that brought me such a happy event. Talking to you, my precious friend, reminded me of the good old days at Jifuku. Please take good care. God bless! A. Villion."[47] This letter was written in colloquial Japanese too.

A parishioner named Nagata Kameko also received a letter from Villion, who was worried about her illness. He wrote, "I heard that you are sick and are suffering a lot. But it is great news that you received baptism by God's blessing. You started to learn the faith several years ago, and kept that in your heart. You are given a special blessing and grace. I pray for your

---

47 Ikeda, *Birion shinpu*, 533.

recovery. A. Villion."[48] This letter, date unknown, employed a mixture of colloquial and literary expressions.

However, the proficiency of Villion's written Japanese seems to have been insufficient for him to author a book entirely by himself. That is why most of his books were co-authored with his assistant Kako Giichi (?–1924). Their collaboration was conducted in the following manner: first Villion voiced the contents orally, next Kako wrote down what Villion had said, and then Kako refined it into a literary form and proceeded to get it published.

5. Villion's Books in Japanese

During his life, Villion published eight books: six in Japanese and two in French. Here is a list of his writings in Japanese.

1) *Yamato hijiri chishio no kakioki* 日本聖人鮮血遺書. Kyoto: Murakami Kanbei, 1887, 400 pages.
2) *Baramon-kyō ron: Bukkyō kigen* 婆羅門教論：仏教起原. Kyoto: Shimizu Kyūjirō, 1889, 501 pages.
3) *Yamaguchi Kōkyōshi* 山口公教史. Kyoto: Kako Giichi, 1897, 381 pages.
4) *Nagato Kōkyōshi* 長門公教史. Hagi: Tenshu Kōkyōkai, 1918, 115 pages.
5) *Yamaguchi Daidōji ato no hakken to saikyojō ni tsuite* 山口大道寺跡の発見と裁許状に就て. Nara: A Villion, 1926, 15 pages; Osaka: Taiyōsha, 1926, 15 pages.
6) Villion's translation of Michael Steichen's book, *Kirishitan daimyō shi* 切支丹大名史. Nara: Villion, 1929; Tokyo: Sansaisha, 393 pages.

Most of these books portray the history of Christianity in Japan, with an emphasis on the Japanese martyrs. His first book, *Yamato hijiri chishio no kakioki* (Japanese Martyrs' Testament in Blood, hereafter *Testament in Blood*), was the most popular, with repeated editions and revisions being published. This book not only portrayed the martyrs from the seventeenth to the eighteenth century based on Léon Pagès' two books on the Japanese

---

48 Ibid., 553.

martyrs and the history of Christianity[49] and Villion's own research, but it also quotes directly from the martyrs' final letters.[50]

This book was so widely read during the Meiji, Taishō, and Shōwa periods that Japanese intellectuals would have been familiar with it. Ebisawa Arimichi pointed out, "The book was read inside and outside Christian circles, and was reprinted the following year, with six editions in the Meiji period. After being revised by Matsuzaki Minoru in the Taishō period, it attracted more attention and was reprinted again. It is a significant contribution to the early study of the history of Kirishitan, along with Jean Crasset's *The History of the Church of Japan*."[51] The book enjoyed a long life in print, from 1887 till 1931, with seven editions in total, apart from the revised edition annotated by Matsuzaki.

Testament in Blood is constructed according to the feast days of the Catholic calendar. Villion included a long description of the early history of Christianity in Japan at the beginning, followed by accounts of martyrs in Japan from a variety of nationalities. The order of the contents is as follows:

The twenty-six Japanese martyrs in Nagasaki on 5 February (1597),
Didacus Carvalho on 22 February (1624),
Kirishitan's profession of faith at Ōura Church on 17 March (1865),
João Baptista Machado and his companions on 22 May (1617),
Alfonso Navarrete and his companions on 1 June (1617),
Francisco Pacheco and his companions on 20 Jun (1626),
Peter Zúñiga and his companions on 19 August (1622),
Miguel Carvalho and his companions on 25 August (1624),
Antonius Ishida and his companions on 3 September (1632),
Thomas Tsuji and Michaël Nakashima on 7 September (1627),
Carlo Spinola, Sebastianus Kimura and their companions on 9 September (1622),
Apolinar and thirty-nine other martyrs on 12 September (1622),
Camillo Constanzo and his companions on 16 September (1622),

---

49 Pagès, *Histoire des vingt-six martyrs japonais* (1862); *Histoire de la religion chrétienne au Japon depuis 1598 jusqu'à 1651* (1869–1870).

50 Although written by Villion and Kako, Villion's input tends to be overlooked, and Kako is sometimes regarded as the sole author; for instance, Orita, "Nihon kankei Yōkosho no wagakuni de no juyō ni tsuite," 3.

51 Ebisawa, "Nihon nijūroku seijin kankei Nihon bunken," 174.

Paolo Navarro and his companions on 5 November (1622),
Leonardus Kimura and his companions on 18 November (1619),
Endō Simon on 4 December (1623),
Eradication of Japanese church and its revival.

The first edition is full of rhetorical descriptions of the martyrs. After several revisions, these rhetorical descriptions gradually decreased. Let us look at the section titled "St. Francis Xavier's Evangelization of Japan" in Chapter 1 to analyze the differences between the different editions.

First (1887) and second (1888) editions:
> It is St. Francis Xavier, missionary of Japan and India, who brought universal Catholicism to Japan and propagated it widely. This holy man is rare in this world. He was rich in moral character and virtue, and good at teaching philanthropy. His preaching was easy to understand, and his voice was far-reaching. Birds would alight on the tree branch above him, and fish would gather in the river closest to him, as though they were learning from him, not to mention humans with sensitive emotions. He could influence the most stubborn men and women and could make them turn over a new leaf.

> 抑も世界の公教たる天主教を大日本国に拡張せられしは日本と天竺の教法師聖フランシスコ、サベリヨと云ふ人なり此人寔に希世の聖師にして胸に徳善の智識を貯へ口に博愛の能辯を有し一度教を説く時は事理分明なるのみならず微妙の音四方に達し為に空飛鳥も翼を垂て樹梢に下り流に遊ぶ魚鱗も鰭を縮めて水涯に集り之を聴かと疑はる況て霊妙不可思議なる感情を備へし人間をや如何なる頑夫愚婦とても其徳善に感化せられ邪を去り正に帰するもの…

Revised sixth edition (1911), Matsuzaki's annotated revision (1926), seventh edition (1931):
> It is Francis Xavier, missionary of Japan and India, who brought universal Catholicism to Japan and propagated it widely. This holy man is rare in this world. Because of his high moral character and great learning, many people have been influenced by him and have turned over a new leaf.

夫れ世界万国の人が一般に守るべき公教を大日本国に伝播せられしは、日本
印度の布教師フランシスコ・ザヴエリヨてふ人なり。此人稀世の聖師にして、
高徳博識絶倫なるより、感化せられて邪を去り正に帰するもの頗る多く……

Here we can see that the figurative expressions used in the first and second editions are captivating and engage the reader's interest, but those expressions disappeared in the revised versions and more "objective" expressions play a central role.

Regarding the first edition, linguistic scholar Shinmura Izuru (1876–1967) highly evaluated its literary expression. "The language is plain and easy to understand, and the passion emanating from the author's faith has the power to touch readers' hearts. Undoubtedly this is the best example of popular literature on martyrdom. After Jean Crasset's (1618–1692) *Histoire de l' Église du Japon* was translated in 1880 by a government agency, there had been no publications on this topic for ten years. Villion's book is a memorable and noteworthy event in the publishing history of the Meiji period."[52] Shinmura categorized this book as "popular literature" because of its literary style.

Matsuzaki Minoru, who changed the book title to *Kirishitan chishio no kakioki* (Kirishitan's Testament in Blood) and revised and annotated it, pointed out the errors in the first edition, saying "This is not a book to be read as a historical document, but rather a popular novel to foster the Christian faith. As it was a record of a foreigner's preaching in awkward Japanese, there are inevitably immature wordings and numerous mistakes in names of places, people, and dates."[53] Obviously Shinmura and Matsuzaki have very different opinions about the first edition. Shinmura paid more attention to its literary quality, while Matsuzaki was more interested in historical facts. Nevertheless, Matsuzaki well understood its literary value and praised it, observing that "it described the author's sincere emotions by using the literary style of the early Meiji period, which is a very attractive aspect of the book."[54]

Matsuzaki also referred to the role played by Villion's assistant Kako Giichi. "When Fr. Villion was living in Kyoto, he talked about Japanese martyrs whenever there was a feast day by using the original books (by

---

52 Shinmura, "Katei Jobun," 3.

53 Villion and Matsuzaki, *Kirishitan chishio no kakioki*, 11–12.

54 Ibid., 20.

Léon Pagès). Kako transcribed his preaching, then showed Villion his notes and edited them into a book to be published later."[55]

Kako first met Villion in Kobe when the priest was learning kanji from Kako's father, a samurai of the Harima domain and a highly cultured person. Villion had studied with the elder Kako since the winter of 1872. After Villion moved to Kyoto, Kako followed him and worked for the Kyōto Shinbun newspaper agency. In 1882 both Kako and his wife were baptized in Kyoto; his Christian name was Joseph.[56] Kako himself was an eloquent preacher who convincingly pointed out discrepancies in Buddhist doctrines, which attracted more and more people. Some of his listeners were later baptized.[57] Consequently Kako quit his job at Kyōto Shinbun and engaged full-time in debating with Buddhist monks who flocked to Villion's place every day. He carried the large-format illustrated book with Villion, and preached in the four wards of Kyoto twice a month.[58] After Villion went to Yamaguchi, Kako became the chief editor of the Catholic magazine Koe.[59] He died in 1924 in Kagoshima at the age of seventy-two.[60] He is viewed as a significant contributor to Villion's writings.[61]

Villion's purpose of writing Testament in Blood was, according to the "Self Introduction" by Kako, "to inform the Japanese people about the Kirishitan martyrs who died in Japan three hundred years ago and have been highly respected in Europe and North America." Because they criticized corrupt bureaucrats and Buddhist monks, they were persecuted by them. The martyrs should be considered as "the originators of human rights" and "the pioneers of civilization" in Japan.[62] Before the first edition of Testament in Blood was published, only Jean Crasset's Histoire de l' Église du Japon (1689) and its Japanese translation, Nihon seikyōshi (1880, based on a 1715 version of this work), were available to readers wanting to know

---

55 Ibid., 10.

56 Ikeda, Birion shinpu, 241–42.

57 Ibid., 266.

58 Ibid., 275–76.

59 Ibid., 241–42.

60 Villion and Matsuzaki, Kirishitan chishio no kakioki, 12.

61 Yamanashi, "Pari Gaikoku Senkyōkai no shuppanbutsu to kindai Nihon no bungakusha," 93.

62 Villion, Yamato hijiri chishio no kakioki, 4–5.

about the early days of Christianity in Japan. Villion's book was crafted as a more literarily colorful version that would appeal to a wide audience.

Villion's second book in Japanese, *Baramonkyō ron: Bukkyō kigen* (1889), explains how Buddhism derived from the ancient Indian religion Brahmanism, and emphasizes the Christian influence on Buddhism. His books *Yamaguchi Kōkyōshi* (1897) and *Nagato Kōkyōshi* (1918) are based on his investigation of the history of Kirishitan in Yamaguchi and Nagato. The booklet *Yamaguchi Daidōji ato no hakken to saikyojō ni tsuite* (1926) details Villion's search for the site of Daidōji which Xavier used for his propagation at Yamaguchi.

Kirishitan daimyō shi is Villion's Japanese translation of Michael Steichen's (1857–1929) book in English, *The Christian Daimyos* (1903), published in 1929. One year later, in 1930, Steichen's French version *Les Daimyô chrétiens* (1904) was translated into Japanese by Yoshida Kogorō. In his Preface to *Kirishitan daimyō shi*, Villion wrote, "This is the final work by Father Steichen which is unskillfully translated by me."[63] The humble expression "unskillfully" indicated the translation was mainly carried out by Villion himself. Let us compare the beginning of Villion's translation (from the English version) and Yoshida's (from the French version).

> Villion's translation: "On 15 August 1549, Francis Xavier came to Kagoshima, Kyūshū, to propagate Christianity in Japan. This is the most memorable day in Japan's religious and political history. At that time, the Japanese people were unknown to Europe and North America. Xavier's arrival provided Japan with an opportunity to start diplomatic relationships with Christian countries."[64]

> Yoshida's translation: "The day of Xavier's arrival in Kagoshima, 15 August 1549, is the most memorable one in Japan's political and religious history. In fact, it is the first day of the plan to bring the mysterious Japanese people, so far surrounded by a deep moat, into the big Christian family."[65]

Compared to Villion's version, which was written in a literary style, Yoshida's

---

63 Steichen and Villion, *Kirishitan daimyō shi*.
64 Ibid., 1–2.
65 Steichen and Yoshida, *Kirishitan daimyō ki*, 1.

oral style was easier to understand.[66] However, Villion's translation contained more information; the three underlined parts did not exist in either the English or French versions, but were added by Villion. Busy as he was in his activities of preaching and social welfare, Villion could not have had much time to write. Therefore this translation was probably a collaboration with a Japanese assistant who came to work with him after Kako Giishi died in 1924. This kind of collaboration was the most reliable (least susceptible to misinterpretation) way of conveying the missionary voices to the Japanese people of that time.

6. Impact on Japanese Culture

Villion's *Testament in Blood* has had a long-lasting impact on modern Japan. Let us first examine how a Kirishitan woman—Hosokawa Gracia (1563–1600)—a figure currently in vogue in Japanese popular culture, was described in Villion's book. This passage recounts how Gracia refused Hideyoshi's summons:

> As the first of God's Ten Commandments prohibits worship of anyone else except God, Hideyoshi was unable to force the Kirishitan population to pay homage to himself. But he did not understand it, and tried to make a young and exceptionally beautiful Kirishitan woman his mistress for his lecherous life. She protected her chastity by sternly refusing his request. Because of this, Hideyoshi started to hate Kirishitan.[67]

> 蓋し天主教十誡の第一に天主の外は何物たりとも拝む事を禁ずとある故に秀吉の望みは到底切支丹に向ひ実施し得ざる事なれども秀吉は之を悟らず曽て切支丹の一人なる嬋妍窈窕たる美女の姿に懸恋し之を引入て妾と為し婬楽を貪らんと欲せしに美女は貞操を守り固く辞して従はざるより秀吉心に切支丹を嫌忌し

Whether Hideyoshi's policy of prohibiting Christianity actually originated from Gracia's refusal cannot be verified. Her courage and faith have been

---

66 Imamiya, "Kirishitan daimyō ki, Shutain cho, Yoshida Kogorō yaku, Ōokayama Shoten hakkō," 165.

67 Villion, *Yamato hijiri chishio no kakioki*, 2.

frequently featured in historical novels and television dramas. In this book's Chapter Twelve, there is another reference to Gracia's readiness to risk her life to resist Hideyoshi's summons.

> Hideyoshi ordered the execution of all missionaries in Kyoto and Osaka. News of the decree quickly spread throughout the region. Not only the missionaries and monastery monks, but also many followers, regardless of status, age, or gender, happily volunteered to die for their faith. They visited each other and shared their resolve. Society was completely galvanized. Worried and heartbroken by the situation, officials were on high alert guarding the town. Takayama Ukon, the Kirishitan daimyō who was exiled ten years earlier, was prepared to die this time. The two sons of Kyoto Governor Ken'i Hōin also made up their minds to sacrifice their lives, and the wife of Tango lord Hosokawa prepared for her final days as well. All Kirishitan bade relatives and friends farewell, proclaiming their faith in Christian teachings, and awaited arrest by the police. Their convictions even touched the hearts of non-believers and made them shed tears.[68]

> （秀吉は）京阪地方に在る切支丹の教師を斬殺すべしと命じたり此事忽地世間に漏れ聞え神父神弟は勿論夥多の信者等教の為に命を捨る事を喜び貴賤貧富の差異なく老若男女の区別なく各自死出の首途を急ぎ西に告げ東に報じ友呼千鳥それならで最も騒がしき形体なれば奉行城代を初め有司の人々窃に胸を痛め万一不測の変をあらんを知れずとて予めかの備を為し非常を警むる程なりしが既に十年以前奉教の為め一度流罪に処せられし高山右近は今度こそと思ひ定め京都奉行玄意法印の二子も致命の決心し丹後田辺の城主細川越中守忠興の夫人も臨終の用意を為し皆な此報の耳に達するや直に親族知音の人を集め今生の離別に天主の教を説き今や縛吏の来るかと待ち受たる態の殊勝さに心なき人々まで孰れも深く感じ入り知らず識らず涙に衿を潤したる

According to this passage, it seems that Hideyoshi's execution order (historically an order of deportation) did not scare the believers, but rather strengthened their faith. From the above-quoted paragraphs, we can also

---

68 Ibid., 39–40.

see the determination of Hosakawa Gracia. She has been described as one of the great beauties in Japanese history in various documents written long after her death. How the discourse of beautifying her first started is unknown, but surely it grew from her refusal to be taken hostage by her husband's rival in 1600. The document closest to her lifetime in which she was mentioned is Luis de Guzman's (1544?–1605) history of the Society of Jesus, *Historia de las missiones que han hecho los religiosos de la Compañia de Iesus* (1601). Guzman did not touch upon her appearance at all, but took note of her intelligence and curiosity about Christianity.[69]

It is Crasset's *Histoire de l'Eglise du Japon* (1689) which described Gracia as an extremely beautiful woman. "C'estoit une Princesse d'une rare beauté, d'un esprit vif, d'un jugement solide, d'un coeur noble & d'un genie au dessu du commun."[70] This sentence was translated into English in 1705 as: "She was a Princess of a rare beauty, of a quick wit, of a sound judgment, and of a Spirit and Genius above the Common."[71] The Japanese translation (1880) conveyed the same nuance.[72] Villion's book also adopted a similar tone by saying she was "a young and exceptionally beautiful Kirishitan woman."

Villion's description of how the world reacted to the revival of the hidden Kirishitan must have surprised Japanese readers. "The Pope was so touched by the news of the continual surfacing of hidden Christians, the offspring of Kirishitan of 300 hundred years ago, that he wept, and told the crowd that such a blessing by God could only happen once in a century. All Catholics of the world thanked God and prayed for the Japanese people's religious freedom and true development of civilization. Newspapers of France and other European countries, as well as the United States, all wrote about this event, and wished for Japan to gain religious freedom and other freedoms."[73] While in the mid-sixteenth century it was Xavier who brought Japan to the world stage, by the mid- and late-nineteenth century it was the hidden Kirishitan's profession of faith that made Japan a center of world attention.

---

69 Guzman, *Historia de las missiones que han hecho los religiosos de la Compañia de Iesus: para predicar el sancto Evangelio en la India oriental, y en los reynos de la China y Iapon,* vol. 2, 383–84.

70 Crasset, *Histoire de l'Église du Japon,* vol. 1, 546.

71 Crasset and N. N., *The History of the Church of Japan,* vol. 1, 453.

72 Crasset and Daijōkan Honyaku Kakari, *Nihon seikyō shi,* vol. 1, 1104.

73 Villion, *Yamato hijiri chishio no kakioki,* 387–88.

The wide-ranging influence of Villion's *Testament in Blood* on modern Japanese culture has been carefully studied by Yamanashi Atsushi, who cites many prominent writers. For instance, the journalist, historian, and philosopher Tokutomi Soho (1863–1957) loved this book and wrote, "It is a great shame that we cannot find a modern Buddhist monk in Japan who is comparable with Fr. Villion." Novelist, translator, and critic Uchida Roan (1868–1929) introduced this book in the *Yomiuri shinbun*, which promoted the book again in the Taisho period, resulting in a demand for more printings. Historian and literary critic Yamaji Aizan (1865–1917) quoted this book extensively when writing about the deportation of Kirishitan from Urakami. Not only the scholar Ōkawa Shūmei (1886–1957), but also poets Kinoshita Mokutarō (1885–1945), Yosano Hiroshi (Tekkan) (1873–1935), and Kitahara Hakushū (1885–1942) drew on Villion's book when writing stories, poem, and essays about Kirishitan. Short story writer Akutagawa Ryūnosuke (1892–1927) came cross Villion's book on the history of Catholicism in Yamaguchi and then hunted for *Testament in Blood* at many used bookstores, seeking material for his own creative writing. Yoshino Sakuzō (1878–1933), scholar of political science and philosopher, mentioned Villion's *Testament in Blood* as well. Novelist Ishikawa Jun was very familiar with the book, and literary figures Miki Rofū (1889–1964), Yoshida Genjirō (1886–1956), Mori Arimasa (1911–1976), and Sakaguchi Ango (1906–1955) all introduced *Testament in Blood* in their writings. Novelist Hori Tatsuo (1904–1953) used this book to write a story about Kirishitan, and Osaragi Jiro (1897–1973) for his historical novel *Tennō no seiki* (serialized in the *Asahi shinbun* 1969–1973) about modern emperors. Kinoshita Mokutarō (1885–1945), a historian of Japanese Christianity, translator, and poet, asserted that one page of Villion's autobiography *Cinquante ans d'apostolat au Japon* is worth 100 pages of a novel because of its wealth of information.[74] Yamanashi's examples make clear beyond a doubt that Villion's book has been widely read in Japan.

Here I would like to add more details not yet mentioned by Yamanashi, in order to give a fuller picture of Villion's influence on modern Japan. Yamaji Aizan, in his book on Christianity in modern Japan (*Gendai Nihon kyōkai shi ron*; 1905), quoted from *Testament in Blood* and appraised

---

74 Yamanashi, "Pari Gaikoku Senkyōkai no shuppanbutsu to kindai Nihon no bungakusha," 89–98.

Villion's work in these words: "Although there is exaggeration and use of imagination, undoubtedly most of the book is based on facts."[75]

As mentioned above, Uchida Roan popularized this book in the Taishō period by his articles in the newspaper *Yomiuri shinbun* (25–26 June 1920). In his opinion, "It is the biggest crime in Japanese history that the Kirishitan were persecuted by such brutal tortures and their relatives were eradicated. I shudder at these atrocities committed by humans...Persecution of Kirishitan showed not only the cruelty that the Japanese were capable of, but also the deep piety and spirit of martyrdom the Japanese [of that time] had." Uchida regarded Villion's *Testament in Blood* and Urakawa Wasaburō's book *Nihon ni okeru Kōkyōkai no fukkatsu* (The Revival of Catholicism in Japan, 1915) as deeply moving. "They touched me more than the Holy Bible... There is probably nothing as beautiful and extraordinary as the Kirishi-tan martyrs in Japanese history. And yet, their beautiful and extraordinary spirit has never been recorded in Japanese documents. I believe the spirit of innocent Kirishitan, who did not submit to the most atrocious punish-ment, is much greater than that of warriors Kusunoki Masashige and Ōishi Yoshio in Japanese history...Can you find any torture in human history that can surpass the persecution of Kirishitan?"[76] Uchida also criticized Japanese history books which did not include any discussion of the Kirishitan faith.[77] He wrote that it is a great pity that both Villion's book and Urakawa's were out of print, and "there was nothing more impressive in Japanese history than their descriptions of Kirishitan resistance that withstood the worst of tortures.[78] Because Uchida's writing brought new attention to *Testament in Blood*, a sixth revised edition was printed in 1926.

Regarding the simultaneous publishing of the sixth revised edition and the annotated revision by Matsuzaki Minoru, Miyake Setsurei (1860–1945), philosopher and critic, pointed out in 1944, "We can see how his book was welcomed by society... Although it is based on Pagès' books about Christianity in Japan and its contents are not that important, the book was written for ordinary people. Its title and illustrations aroused the interest of

75 Yamaji, *Gendai Nihon kyōkai shi ron*, 359–69.

76 Uchida Roan 内田魯庵, "Baku no shita Kirishitan hakugai " 貘の舌 切支丹迫害, *Yomiuri shinbun*, 1920. 6. 25–26.

77 Uchida, *Shimi no jiden*, 433–34.

78 Uchida, "Fujin ni yomasetai yōsho," 214.

many, making them recall the Kirishitan of that long-ago time and understand the difficulty of gaining religious faith. This book, as was the case with the monument to Xavier at Yamaguchi, cannot be easily forgotten."[79]

The journalist and historian Takahashi Kunisuke, a Protestant Christian, has written: "Every page of Villion's *Testament in Blood* is colored by martyrs' holy blood. I can find no other drama that is so cruel and beautiful as this one... In the history of Japanese Buddhism, there were also persecutions. Most Buddhist monks fought back bravely. By contrast, Kirishitan followed the Christian doctrine of nonresistance, and were persecuted tragically and heroically. Without reading Villion's book, we cannot understand the two sides of the religion, and cannot even discuss it."[80]

Yoshino Sakuzō, in his book *Arai Hakuseki to Yowan Shirōte*, wrote about the Italian priest Giovanni Battista Sidoti who entered Japan secretly and was immediately arrested. Drawing on Villion's *Testament in Blood*, Yoshino described the dialogues between Sidoti and the Japanese official Arai Hakuseki, who documented the knowledge Sidoti brought to Japan. Yoshino appreciated Villion's old-fashioned style of story-telling, which made history easy to understand for the populace.[81]

Miki Rofū, poet and writer of children's literature, went to listen to Villion's lecture on martyrs to gain inspiration for his own writing.[82] He taught Japanese literature at Tobetsu Trappist Monastry in Hokkaido from 1916 to 1924. On Easter Sunday of 1922, he and he wife were baptized in the Monastry and became Catholics. Osaragi Jirō carefully read Villion's book and based his own rendering of persecution of Kirishitan before and after the Meiji Restoration on it in his serialized novel *Tennō no seiki 15: Shinsei no fu*. He was impressed by how carefully Villion described the persecution.[83]

The poet Nakahara Chūya went to Yamaguchi Church with his grandparents when he was a small child, but because of his father's dislike of Christianity, he gradually stopped attending church services.[84] Nevertheless he had a deep attachment to Villion, and at the age of twenty-three,

79 Miyake, *Setsurei zeppitsu*, 128–30.
80 Takahashi, "Kirishitan chishio no kakioki o yomu," 20.
81 Yoshino, *Arai Hakuseki to Yowan Shirōte*, 91–92.
82 Miki, "Chishio no kakioki kō," 14–15.
83 Osaragi, *Tennō no seiki 15: Shinsei no fu*, 164–65.
84 Ōoka, "Nakahara Chūya den: Yōran," 19.

went to see him at Nara Church in April 1930.[85] This visit took place right after Nakahara's publication of "A Contaminated Sorrow," a poem that is thought to embrace Catholic sentiments.[86] This visit indicates Nakahara's continuing interest in Catholicism. Critic Kawakami Tetsutarō (1902–1980) believed that Catholicism did not restrict Nakahara's activities, but rather provided him with freedom which made him both "a strict person like those in the Old Testament and a liberated person of the modern times."[87]

Mori Arimasa, philosopher and scholar of French literature, read Villion's book as a junior high school pupil and was shocked by the martyrdom. His school, Gyōsei Chūgakkō, was a Catholic school mainly staffed by French missionaries whom he highly respected. He presumed that "these quiet teachers would become martyrs if persecutions were to happen again." He saw Villion on the campus one day, wearing a black soutane and a broad-brimmed black hat; he looked emaciated as though he were around ninety years old. Mori recognized him immediately from the old priest's small stature and slender feet, which were clad in black shoes. It was as if Villion's external form made visible his strong will and faith, making him stand out from the people around him who were just going along with the current of everyday life.[88] Another writer who made use of *Testament in Blood* was the noted activist and novelist Ishimure Michiko (1927–2018) in her famous novel *Haru no shiro* (A Castle in Spring) about the Kirishitan rebellion at Amakusa (1637–1638).[89]

Although Villion's *Testament in Blood* has won acceptance as a fascinating account of the story of Christian martyrs, it has not been recognized as a historical document. Indicative of this, neither Urakawa Wazaburō, in his book *Nihon ni okeru Kōkyōkai no fukkatsu* (The Revival of Catholicism in Japan), nor Kataoka Yakichi, in his *Nihon Kirishitan junkyō shi* (A History of Kirishitan's Martyrdom in Japan, 1979), quoted *Testament in Blood*. There are also errors in Villion's book. For instance, history scholar Matsuda Kiichi pointed out that Nishinomiya station was not the place, as Villion imagined, where St. Thomas Kozaki (one of the twenty-six martyrs)

---

85 Nakahara, *Nakahara Chūya nōto*, 210–11.
86 Niki, "*Hakuchi gun* to so shūhen ni tsuite," 216.
87 Kawakami, "Nihon no autosaidā," 471.
88 Mori, "Omoide sonota," 161–62.
89 Ishimure, *Ishimure Michiko zenshū: Shiranui*, 541.

wrote his final letter to his mother before his execution.[90] Another historian, Ebisawa Arimichi, described this book as "helping to strengthen the Christian faith" rather than presenting the results of dispassionate historical research, and remarked, "There are obvious errors in dates and names."[91]

In fact, what Villion's *Testament in Blood* was famous for is its literary quality and its descriptions that touched readers' hearts, rather than its presentation of precise research. These features have made this book one of the missionary writings in Japanese that has most influenced modern Japan.

Partially based on Villion's *Testament in Blood*, a feature film about the twenty-six martyrs, *Junkyō ketsushi Nihon 26 Seijin*, was produced in 1931 by Nikkatsu. It was widely screened in Japan to propagate the Christian faith. The screenplay was written by Villion's friend, the Jesuit missionary Hermann Heuvers (1890–1977). This film was funded by Moriyama Jinzaburō's nephew Hirayama Masajū (1880–1958), a successful business man, who also went to the United States and Europe to promote the film.[92] Shortly before his death, Villion gave public lectures about the twenty-six martyrs which was followed by the screening of the film. Thousands of viewers gathered to participate in the event.[93]

7. Villion's Heritage

Villion once questioned the Japanese people, "Although my nationality is French, I feel I am a Japanese, and I love Japan no less than a Japanese does...During the period of less than sixty years, the Japanese people have built up a surprisingly advanced material civilization. But why have they not tried to develop their spiritual world, which remains uncivilized, as they are still worshiping idols, instead of searching for truth?... Civilization is not only about material development, but must be accompanied by spiritual advancement too."[94] It is obvious that Villion not only looked at the posi-

---

90 Matsuda, *Kinsei shoki Nihon kankei Nanban shiryō kenkyū*, 169.

91 Ebisawa, "Kirishitan shi kenkyū kotohajime," 31.

92 Yamanashi, "Eiga *Junkyō ketsushi Nihon 26 Seijin* to Hirayama Masajū: 1930 nendai zenhanki Nihon Katorikku kyōkai no bunka jigyō," 179–217.

93 Kracht/Kurahato and Kracht/Kurahato-Tateno, *Ōgai no Kōtansai (Kurisumasu): Mori-ke o meguru nendaiki*, 331.

94 Nagatomi, *Zaberiyo to Yamaguchi*, 125–26.

Fig. 9, Nara Catholic Church.

tive aspects of Japan, but also at various parts that needed to be improved.

From 1925, Villion spent his final seven years in Nara, calling himself "the guardian of the Daibutsu sama" (referring to the Great Buddha of Tōdaiji) and "a friend of deer" who are treated as sacred creatures and freely wander near the temple. Villion also expended a lot of effort on fund-raising for a Catholic church in Nara and a hall to educate young people. His activities were reported to the Pope Pius XI by Bishop Carlo Salotti (1870–1947), Secretary of the Sacred Congregation for Propagation of the Faith. Salotti told the Pope that in Japan there was a hard-working French missionary nearly eighty years old who had devoted sixty years to the country without ever returning home. As he aged, his enthusiasm for evangelization intensified. He had just sent a letter to the Vatican asking for financial support to build a church and a school in a Japanese city. The Pope was touched by the news and immediately said, "Good! I will provide half of the cost, and the rest will come from the Sacred Congregation for Propagation of the Faith. Please quickly send a telegraphic transfer to him. I wish to make this old missionary happy."[95] The church Villion raised funds for was completed shortly after his death (Fig. 9).

In the early days of Villion's mission, when he was preaching in locations from Kyoto to Ise, a local official from Matsuzaka village questioned why he had come to Japan, when he would return home, and how he could be so lacking in filial piety as to leave his father behind. Villion replied, "If I intended to return, I would not have come. I will die in Japan." The official was amazed and told his wife, "He does not seem to have a mental

---

95 Kotera, "Papa sama to Virion shinpu," 67.

disorder—his religion must be genuine."[96] When he turned eighty, Villion stated that if he were given another eighty years to live, he would happily go to the seminary, come to "my dear Japan," and "devote my whole life to preaching God's love here again."[97]

Three years before his death, he published his book titled *Pourquoi j'aime les Japonais?*. In it he wrote:

> Well! Here, I have emptied my old bag; not to the bottom, of course, because when I speak of my Japanese, I am like St. Francis, my boss, I could never say enough; but this little book is enough to make you understand how and why it has become dear to me. Truly, I say to you, if I love them, that is because I know them.

> (Eh bien! voilà, je vous ai vidé mon vieux sac; pas jusqu'au fond, bien sûr, car quand je parle de mes Japonais, je suis comme S. François, mon patron, jamais je ne pourrais assez en dire; mais ce peu suffit pour vous faire comprendre comment et pourquoi il me sont devenus chers. En vérité, je vous le dis, si je les aime. c'est que je les connais.)[98]

Villion died at the Catholic church Osaka Kawaguchi Tenshudō on 1 April 1932, at the age of eighty-nine. The news of his death was extensively reported by the local newspapers *Ōsaka Asahi shinbun* and *Ōsaka jiji shinpō*, as well as by national newspapers. Articles about him likewise were printed in newspapers and magazines in Europe and the United States. He was buried at the Hattori Cemetery in Osaka city (Plate 16), becoming "Japanese soil" as he wished.[99]

Two days after his death, on 3 April the *Ōsaka Asahi shinbun* printed an obituary with the eye-catching headline "Fr. Villion Rest in Peace, Culminating Ninety Years of Eccentricity, Transcendence, and Faith, as well as Preaching to Japanese Notables." The article reported:

> As a little boy, Villion saw a painting of the Japanese martyrs' execution

---

96 Kariya, *Viriyon shinpu no shōgai*, 11–12.
97 Ikeda, *Birion shinpu*, 3–4.
98 Villion, *Pourquoi i'aime les Japonais?*, 32.
99 Ikeda, *Birion shinpu*, 506–19.

and decided that in the future he would go to Japan. Sixty-six years ago, he departed from Lyon and came to Nagasaki. He preached all over the country, including Hagi, Kobe, Kyoto, and Nara, without ever returning home…His transcendence resembles that of Japanese Zen masters.

He talked about interesting things, never disparaging anyone or harshly criticizing Japanese society. He would jokingly say, 'I would like to go to heaven by airplane,' as if making a serious decision. He never cared about death… He often preached on the streets, gathering children and teaching them Christian doctrine with pictures as visual aids. He devoted his whole life to evangelizing Japan.[100]

The parishioners in Nara adored him. His death mask (Plate 17) is kept at the Nara Catholic Church, where they preserve photos of Fr. Villion and talk about him with deep affection (Fig. 10). Among the Nara parishioners, Yoneda Yuki was particularly close to Villion. She attended his daily Mass and respected him deeply. The morning Mass on 1 April was the last one Villion celebrated. After the Mass, he fell ill and asked Yoneda to call a rickshaw to take him to Osaka. Before leaving, he realized that he would not return again, and asked Yoneda to dispose of his belongings. In the evening he passed away. All of the books and daily items left by Villion were carefully kept by Yoneda. Her son Shōji and his wife Yasuko have continued to preserve them until the present day (Plates 18, 19).

From the late nineteenth to the mid-twentieth centuries, the intellectual who had the strongest impact on Japanese views of history was Tokutomi Sohō. An admirer of Villion's books, Tokutomi wrote in an essay that Villion "made me feel that he is a second Xavier who came here after 370 years…Fr. Villion's modesty and love touch our hearts… He was surrounded by a peaceful aura mixed with a sense of humor, which relaxed people naturally." After reading Kariya's description of

Fig. 10, Villion with Ishihara Akira (first from the left), Chief of the Society of Youths. Photograph courtesy of Ishihara Tsutomu.

---

100 "Eimin shita Biriyon ō shinpu" 永眠したビリヨン翁・神父, *Ōsaka Asahi shinbun*, 1932. 4. 3.

Villion's parting from his beloved horse, a long-term companion, Tokutomi wrote, "this parting is more touching than the famous partings from horses of the Edo merchant Shiobara Tasuke and the Tang poet Bai Letian."[101] Tokutomi's writings, it is worth noting, later influenced Shiba Ryōtarō.[102]

Villion's love of Japan was based on his understanding of the Japanese people, through his direct communication with them. In order to learn about the Japanese people, he decided to study Buddhism before he went to Japan. After living in Japan, he again realized that knowledge of Buddhism was essential for answering the serious questions posed by Buddhist believers.[103] Among all the Catholic missionaries of his day, Villion has been regarded as the "only one who developed a friendly relationship with Buddhists."[104] Villion left a large quantity of notes from his study of Buddhism, but unfortunately they were never published. Some of them were provided to other missionaries who were interested in Buddhism, but much of what he recorded remains unknown to us.

In the last half century, for Christian missionaries in Japan to conduct serious studies of Buddhism has ceased to be a rare phenomenon. For instance, Heinrich Dumoulin (1905–1995), a Jesuit missionary from Germany, wrote a book on the mutual influence of Buddhism and Christianity (*Bukkyō to Kirisutokyō no kaikō*, 1975). Ruben Habito, a former Jesuit missionary from the Philippines, studied esoteric Buddhism and the Jōdo Shin sect, and published several books.[105] Peter Baekelmans from Belgium, a member of Congregatio Immaculati Cordis Mariae, wrote a book titled *Iesu to Kūkai* (2012) on the universality of the teachings of Jesus and the Japanese monk Kūkai (774–835). In the "Acknowledgements" section of his book, Baekelmans wrote, "My happiness as a Catholic missionary lies in the twenty years of communication and dialogue with the esoteric Shingon

---

101 Tokutomi, *Jinbutsu keikan*, 318–23.

102 Isoda, "*Shiba Ryōtarō*" de manabu Nihonshi, 16.

103 Verwilghen, "The Buddhist Studies of Father A. Villion," 252; Villion, *Cinquante ans d'apostolat au Japon*," 205.

104 Tehelle, "Buddhism and Christianity in Japan: From Conflict to Dialogue, 1854–1899," 73–75.

105 Habito, *Mikkyō ni okeru Hōshinkan no haikei* (1987); *Shinran to Kirisutokyō no deai kara: Nihonteki kaihō no reisei* (1989); *Seisho to Shinran no yomikata: Kaihō no shingaku to undō no Kyōgaku* (1990); *Shūkyō to sekai no itami: Bukkyō, Kirisutokyō no shinzui o motomete* (1991).

Buddhist sect centered on Mt. Kōya, and in my research and understanding of the religion. This book, resulting from that happiness, is intended to convey the mystery and faith of Esoteric Buddhism."[106]

Fr. Villion loved the Japanese people because he understood them well. In comparison with Xavier's stay of two years and three months, Villion spent sixty-four years in Japan. Xavier's method of propagation through understanding the Japanese language and the culture was further developed by Villion, who published books in Japanese and thereby contributed to the shaping of Japanese modern culture. By informing people about the history of Kirishitan persecution, he helped the Japanese understand their past objectively, and made them realize that Christianity provided a new view of the world and a new system of values to Japan during the premodern period.

On 7 August 2019, I visited the burial ground of Fr. Villion at Hattori Cemetery, guided by Professor Yasukawa Shunsuke of Seizan College who used to play in the graveyard when he was a small boy. Under the scorching sun, we washed the tombstone (Plate 20) together and thanked Fr. Villion for his dedication to Japan.

Chronology of A. Villion's Life[107]

Year	Age	Activities
1843	(0)	Born in Belley, Ain Province, France.
1855	(12)	Graduated from an elementary school in Lyon and entered St. John Minor Seminary in Lyon.
1861	(18)	Graduated from the Minor Seminary, and entered the Seminary of the Rue du Bac in Paris established by M. E. P.
1866	(23)	Graduated from the Seminary. 26 March, ordained. 14 June, departed from Marseille. Arrived in Hong Kong, waiting for an opportunity to go to Japan.
1868	(25)	21 October, participated in Petitjean's ordination of a bishop in Hong Kong. October, landed in Nagasaki and began work at Ōura Church.
1870	(27)	January, was saddened about the deportation of Kirishitan of Urakami to other regions.
1871	(28)	24 November, became the second pastor of Kobe Catholic Church, succeeding Fr. Pierre Mounicou (1825–71); guided foreigners and Kirishitan in exile.

---

106 Baekelmans, *Iesu to Kūkai: Fuji no sekai*, 442.

107 According to "Birion shinpu ryaku nenpu" in Ikeda, *Birion shinpu: Gendai Nihon Katorikku no chūseki, Keiō, Meiji, Taishō, Shōwa shi o haikei ni.*

1873	(30)	From 21 April until 13 May, devoted to bringing the Urakami Kirishitan back to their home via Kobe. August, established a preaching house at Onohama Shinden, Kobe.
1875	(32)	Looked after orphans from the Kansai region.
1877	(34)	July, welcomed the sisters of L'instruction Charitable du Saint Enfant Jésus to Kobe.
1878	(35)	Tirelessly took care of cholera patients.
1879	(36)	8 September, went to Kyoto as a French language teacher.
1880	(37)	Toured with preacher Nishita Yoshimatsu to Tsu and Matsuzaka to proselytize.
1881	(38)	Established a temporary church at Toiyamachi, Kyoto, and visited Chion'in to study Buddhism.
1882	(39)	During the summer holiday season, proselytized in the Ise region.
1883	(40)	Evangelization in Kyoto gained more and more followers.
1884	(41)	Toured Ōtsu, Fushimi, Wakasa, Obama, Maizuru, Miyatsu, and Tango to propagate Christian teachings.
1887	(44)	Published *Yamato hijiri chishio no kakioki (Testament in Blood)* co-authored with Kako Giichi.
1888	(45)	Purchased a piece of a former daimyō property at the intersection of Kawaramachi and Sanjō, Kyoto, and began fundraising to build a church.
1889	(46)	Transferred to Yamaguchi. Hospitalized in Bethany Hospital in Hong Kong for several months. July, returned to Japan. In autumn, went to Hagi to preach. Built a temporary chapel at Komeyachō, Yamaguchi city. Published *Baramonkyō ron*, co-authored with Kako Giichi.
1890	(47)	1 May, attended the consecration of St. Xavier Church in Kyoto. June, went to Tsuwano to proselytize. In Yamaguchi, constructed a monument to St. Francis Xavier.
1891	(48)	Went to Miyaichi, Hōfu, Tokuyama, and Shimonoseki of Yamaguchi prefecture to preach. In Yamaguchi city, utilized a slide projector and illustrated book to teach.
1892	(49)	Had monuments for martyrs built at Hagi and Tsuwano.
1893	(50)	Discovered the site of Daidōji where Xavier stayed and preached.
1895	(52)	Transferred to Hagi.
1897	(54)	Published *Yamaguchi Kōkyō shi* with Kako Giichi.
1898	(55)	Met Itō Hirobumi at Hagi, and resolved the problem of providing a cemetery for Christians. Toured Hagi, Tsuwano, and Jifuku with his beloved horse.
1904	(61)	Visited Mt. Kōya in Wakayama prefecture to study the Shingon sect of Buddhism.
1907	(64)	Visited Mt. Minobu of Yamanashi prefecture to study the Nichiren sect of Buddhism.
1912	(69)	Befriended British aristocrat Lady E. A. Gordon, and gained financial support to purchase the land incorporating the site of Daidōji.
1913	(70)	Went to Mt. Kōya again to give a lecture to Buddhist monks.
1914	(71)	Attended the consecration of Urakami Church, Nagasaki.
1919	(73)	26 May, the fiftieth anniversary of his ordination.
1918	(75)	Published *Nagato Kōkyō shi*, authored with Kako Giichi.
1925	(82)	Transferred to Azemamechō of Nara to be its pastor.

1926	(83)	16 October, attended the unveiling ceremony of the monument to Xavier at Yamaguchi, and published *Yamaguchi Daidōji no hakken to saikyojō ni tsuite*.
1928	(85)	Attended a ceremony to commemorate his sixty years in Japan at Nara Kōkaidō.
1929	(86)	Published *Kirishitan daimyō shi*, his Japanese translation of a book by Michael Steichen.
1930	(87)	Fundraising for constructing a Catholic church and student hall in Nara.
1932	(89)	1 April, died at Osaka Kawaguchi Tenshudō.

CHAPTER
4
Sauveur Candau's Enchantment with the Japanese People

1. Admiration for Xavier

Because of the similarities between Japanese and his mother tongue Basque, as noted in Chapter 1, Fr. Candau found that Japanese was easy to learn. This information helped us to determine Xavier's Japanese proficiency, as he too was a native speaker of the Basque language. Now let us examine further how Candau himself utilized Japanese.

Sauveur Antoine Candau was born on 29 May 1897 at Saint-Jean-Pied-de-Port in the Basque country in southern France, close to the border with Spain. He was the seventh of eleven children in a pious Catholic family. His father was a fabric merchant and his mother a housewife.

When he was a small boy, he saw a painting of Mt. Fuji and learned of the country Japan for the first time. After graduating from elementary school at age eleven, he attended a Minor Seminary at Larressore for six years. From 1914 he studied at the Major Seminary at Bayonne. After graduation he went to war as an army infantry lieutenant, and in 1916 he fought in the Battle of Verdun. To him, the battlefield was "the most inhumane world," and "only beastly nature and animal instinct" could enable one to survive.[1]

In recognition of his distinguished service, he was promoted to first lieu-

---

1 Ikeda, *Shōwa Nihon no onjin: S. Kandō-shi*, 27.

tenant. After the war, he left the army and decided to become a missionary. His father was happy that he would serve as a priest, but opposed his plan of going overseas. Around the same time, a document containing information about several episodes in Candau family history was found. Sauveur and his contemporaries learned that a relative of Francis Xavier had once stayed at the Candau home, and Xavier himself had spent a summer vacation there. Candau's father was moved and told him, "Well, it seems Xavier's germs were brought into this house. It cannot be helped." He agreed to let his son go to evangelize in Japan.[2]

In his book *Nanban no michi*, Shiba Ryōtarō describes his journey to the Basque country in search of the traces of Xavier and Candau. Shiba found out that not only had Xavier stayed at the Candau house, but the house of Xavier's grandfather was located next to Candau's. This discovery surprised Shiba and made him wonder why Candau never mentioned this in his writings. "He probably did not want to show off this extremely important connection with St. Francis Xavier," Shiba conjectured, concluding, "This silence reveals his humble nature."[3]

Candau joined the Paris Foreign Missions Society in 1919 and went to Rome to study at the Pontifical Gregorian University (originally named the Roman College), which had been established by the Society of Jesus in 1551. During the five years he spent there, Candau studied philosophy, theology, the Hebrew and Greek languages, and earned doctorates in both theology and philosophy. He was ordained a priest in 1923. Two years later, in January 1925, he landed in Yokohama and took the first steps toward realizing his long-held dream of evangelizing Japan.

His first stay in Japan was fourteen years (1925–1939) and his second stay, seven years (1948–1955), twenty-one years in total. After visiting the Basque region, the NHK reporters who were making a documentary about Shiba Ryōtarō's research methods wrote: "If Xavier, Candau, and many other missionaries born in the Basque region had not come to Japan, our country might have taken a very different path."[4]

Based on his frequent contacts with Candau, comparative literature

---

2 Ibid., 38.

3 Shiba, *Shiba Ryōtarō zenshū 59: Kaidō o yuku 8, Nanban no michi*, 127–28.

4 NHK Kaidō o Yuku Purojekuto, *Shiba Ryōtarō no fūkei 3: Kita no mahoroba, Nanban no michi*, 208–209.

scholar Hirakawa Sukehiro came to believe that "although it is hard to know Xavier's Japanese language skills, it is certain that the missionaries of the sixteenth century understood the Japanese people precisely through their affection for Japan. Fr. Candau was taking Xavier as his role model as they both had the character of Basque warriors."[5]

Fig. 11, Portrait of S. Candau, frontispiece of *Kandō zenshū*, vol. 1, edited by Ikeda Toshio, Chūō Shuppansha, 1970.

Candau had a great admiration for Xavier, but did not join the Society of Jesus. He once considered joining after he had chosen the renowned Jesuit scholar of theology and ethics, Arthur Vermeersch (1858–1936), to be his spiritual mentor, but realized that the obedience strictly required by the Society was not suitable for him.[6] Candau's "weak point," it came to be said, was his tendency to act "freely." He framed his opinion on this in these terms: "Freedom is the most precious gift given to humans by God," and "the privilege of being a teacher is getting a summer vacation of two to three months without asking for anyone's permission."[7] He particularly enjoyed travelling.

Yamanashi Atsushi was correct, I believe, when he argued that Candau's activities in Japan deserve to be more highly evaluated so as to give due credit to "his excellent mastery of the Japanese language and affection for Japanese culture." Yamanashi emphasized that "his extensive knowledge of the world and his charming personality enlightened the Japanese people, along with his introduction of criticisms of both modern society and contemporary European thought to Japan."[8] Kevin Doak has observed that Candau is remembered better in Japan than in his native France or the Anglophone world. Doak points a key internet-era indicator of a person's reputation: there is an entry on Candau in the Japanese Wikipedia, but none in either the French or English Wikipedia.[9]

---

5 Hirakawa, *Higashi no tachibana, Nishi no orenji*, 43.

6 Dumoulin, "'Sei Igunachio no yūbe' no Kandō-shi," 112.

7 Anouilh, "Daishingakkōchō to shite no Sōvuru Kandō," 107.

8 Yamanashi, "Sōvuru Kandō shinpu to kindai Nihon no chishikijin," 140.

9 Doak, "Kandō shinpu no Nihon bunka e no kōken," 227.

2. Exceptional Skills in Japanese

After his long trip from Marseille, Candau arrived at Yokohama on 21 January 1925. Everything he saw was new and unique, but the Japanese language sounded familiar to him—similar to Basque. Just like Xavier, Candau wanted to communicate with the Japanese directly in their distinctive tongue, and to understand them thoroughly.

Fortunately Japanese proved easy for him to master. During his second stay in Japan, Candau wrote in his diary (21 January 1947), "When we can understand the feelings of a different people by their language and by direct contacts with them, we are able to avoid the exaggerations and empty quests by 'experts.' We can feel how they feel, and can stay away from pretentious interpretations of them."[10] Here we can see why he devoted so much attention to communicating in the Japanese language, just as Xavier had declared was necessary four centuries earlier.

Early in his mission, Candau was an assistant to Lucien Delahaye (1884–1957) at the Shizuoka Catholic Church at Ōtemachi, Shizuoka city. While there he studied Japanese with Murakoshi Kinzō, a scholar of Chinese classics and head teacher of the Fuji Girls' High School (present-day Shizuoka Futaba Gakuen). According to Murakoshi's daughter, Candau had such an amazing memory that he could remember whatever he heard only once, and he was very good at applying immediately what he had just learned.[11] Candau also absorbed knowledge of Japanese customs, folklore, and cultural traditions from Murakoshi. The two of them often went together to the theatre to enjoy *rakugo* (comical storytelling) performances.

In 1926 Candau moved to Tokyo to head the Sekiguchi Seminary, and for five years after that, Murakoshi sent him letters in cursive script twice a week. The teacher's purpose was to improve Candau's facility in reading different forms of Japanese writing.[12] Candau later recalled, "Letters from Murakoshi were first written in printed style, and then gradually cursively. So I was able to understand all the styles. I also learned from him how to read aloud the Chinese classics."[13] However, not everything Candau learned from Murakoshi was utilized. Later Candau complained, "At the

---

10 Ikeda, *Shōwa Nihon no onjin: S. Kandō-shi*, 47.

11 Ibid., 48.

12 Candau, "Shisō no eizokusei: Watashi no kangaku shugyō jidai," 2.

13 Gakuen, "Gakusha junpōki 7: Shosai ni okeru Kandō shinpu," 2.

beginning, I memorized five to six thousand kanji. But now I have completely forgotten the difficult ones, as there is no opportunity to use them in daily life. I felt my effort was in vain."[14]

Candau described his method of learning Japanese as "repeat like a parrot" and "swallow like a cormorant," because there is no need to poke one's nose into why the language is as it is. "Just gulp it down humbly!"[15] After only ten months in Japan, Candau gave his first public speech in Tokyo. The occasion was a commemoration of the 700th death anniversary of St. Francis of Assisi, and he spoke for one hour. "He memorized the entire speech and astonished the audience by his fluent Japanese."[16] On the program with him were prominent Christian scholars giving lectures, such as Iwashita Sōichi, Totsuka Bunkei, and Tanaka Kōtarō. The result of his Japanese learning in less than a year can only inspire the awe of all other students of the Japanese language.

Candau once said, "After having lived in Japan for about one and half years, I managed to read all the books written by Nishida Kitarō. If I memorize 120 sets of idiomatic expressions in kanji, I can understand his philosophy."[17] It is not clear whether he liked Nishida's philosophy or not, as he himself was an expert on philosophy. But what is obvious is that his Japanese had reached

Fig. 12, Candau with the Murakoshi family, 1925, frontispiece of *Kandō zenshū,* supplementary vol. 1, Chūō Shuppansha, 1970.

Fig. 13, Candau lecturing, *Kandō zenshū,* supplementary vol. 1, Chūō Shuppansha, 1970.

14 Candau, "Furansugo to Nihongo," 125.

15 Ikeda, *Shōwa Nihon no onjin: S. Kandō-shi,* 51.

16 Miyamoto, "Nihon to sekaiteki yūjō no shito," 275.

17 Ozawa, "Kandō-shi o itamu," 15.

a level to enable him to understand abstract writings. Three years later, Candau gave a lecture entitled "Valuable Things" at a meeting to establish the Society of Catholic Research at Urawa Senior High School. The audience was amazed by his clear and eloquent manner of speaking.[18]

Candau did not depend on vocabulary cards, but diligently utilized Japanese dictionaries and memorized expressions. When he wrote articles in Japanese, at first he usually imitated the sentences of Japanese authors, then worked at conveying his own ideas by using their words, and finally incorporated their particular expressions or fine passages in crafting his own sentences and literary style.[19]

Candau was impressed by the Japanese language proficiency of some earlier missionaries. He admired, for example, the witty puns used by Jean-Pierre Rey (1858–1930), the Archbishop of Tokyo.

> Among those foreigners who completely mastered Japanese is the former Archbishop Rey, who died more than ten years ago. His Japanese was said to be a masterful art. One cold day, the archbishop was riding a rickshaw. His regular puller was complaining about many things—his miserable life, everything was so expensive, all he received could not buy him a cup of alcohol after working from morning till night, etc. Fr. Rey started to cough. "Have you got a cold?" the puller asked, and turned his head around. Fr. Rey rubbed his gray beard and replied, "That's right. As long as we live in this world, we've got to "have" (*hiku*) a rickshaw or a cold.[20]

> 日本語を自在に操る外人の中でも、名人芸に達していたのは十数年まえに亡くなった前東京大司教レイ師だった。ある冬の寒い日、大司教閣下は人力車で外出した。なじみの車屋は車をひきながら、いろいろぐち話を聞かせる。こんな暮しはまったく情けない。諸式は高くなるばかり。朝から晩まで車をひいても手に残るものは酒代にもならぬ、などとこぼすうちに、うしろの司教さまはゴホンゴホンと咳をはじめた。「おや、だんな、風邪をひきなすったね」と心配そうにふりかえるのに、レイ師はやおら白ひげを撫でながら、「そうじゃよ。ま、こうしたもんじゃ。なあ、お

18 Miyashita, "Urawa Kōtōgakkō Katorikku Kenkyūkai sōritsu," 42.

19 Ikeda, *Shōwa Nihon no onjin: S. Kandō-shi,* 52.

20 Candau, "Kuruma to kaze to jibiki to," 16.

互いこの浮世に生まれた上は、車か風邪か何かひかにゃならんもんじゃ」
と答えた。

The same Japanese verb *hiku* is used for "pulling" a rickshaw and "catching" a cold. Rey was famous for making Japanese puns, and Candau also was very good at this. He often composed *kyōka* (comical *tanka* poems of thirty-one syllables) with his teacher Murakoshi. One day after a drive to the Mishima peninsula in Kanagawa prefecture, Candau wrote a *kyōka* on a postcard to Murakoshi. "Hashinakumo Mishima no hashi de hashi o kai, Atami no hashi de Shina soba o kuu," using different meanings of the homophone "hashi." Murakoshi questioned the meaning of "hashinakumo," prompting Candau to reply, "That shall mean 'by chance'." Murakoshi was amazed by Candau's wit and remarked, "He was severely injured in the war [World War II], but his brain is intact!"[21] This poem can be translated into English as: "Unexpectedly (*hashinakumo*), at the tip (*hashi*) of Mishima, we bought chopsticks (*hashi*), and had Chinese noodles on the bridge (*hashi*) of Atami."

Novelist Kanbayashi Akatsuki (1902–1980) once listened to Candau's lecture "Criticism of Modern Thought" at the University of the Sacred Heart, Tokyo. In his essay "Listening to a Sermon," Kanbayashi observed that Candau's Japanese "has the grace of ancient Japanese poetry, and is surprisingly fluent...His sermon was about civilization, art, and humanity, and it was like a literary narrative, full of artistic flavor. There was not a whiff of religious doctrine, and he did not mention Christianity at all. This suits unbelievers like me very well." At the end of the lecture, Candau quoted "A Beautiful Poem" written by the anti-clerical philosopher François-Marie Voltaire (1694–1778). Candau first translated this French poem into Japanese, then he explained, "This means that 'If such a being as God exists, then God, please bring me happiness!'" He urged his listeners, "When you cannot fall asleep at night, please recite this poem to yourself." The audience was so enchanted by the lecture that they remained in their seats for quite a while after he finished.[22] Kanbayashi also read Candau's essay collection *Shisō no tabi* (A Journey of Thought) and wrote, "His eloquent discussion of civilization is like art. There is no trace of preaching. I

---

21 Ikeda, *Shōwa Nihon no onjin: S. Kandō-shi*, 55.
22 Kanbayashi, "Sekkyō chōmon," 246–52.

was immediately attracted, and I have been reading everything of his that I can find in newspapers and magazines."[23]

Tanaka Kōrarō (1890–1974), a jurist who became the Chief Justice of the Supreme Court of Japan, was a close friend of Candau. Tanaka wrote, "Among all missionaries born in the Basque country, we do not know anyone else who has a better command of Japanese than Fr. Candau…He mastered the language rapidly because of his affection for Japanese culture and Japan in general."[24] This tradition was started by Xavier and has been carried on by Villion, Candau, and other missionaries—that is, the more they know about Japanese things, positive or negative, the deeper their fondness for Japan becomes. And the deeper their affection is, the more they want to know about Japan. Getting familiar with the Japanese language and culture is a precondition for their mission work in Japan. In other words, they do not preach just from their point of view, but rather keep learning from the Japanese. It is a two-way street, without any sense of superiority involved.

Shimatani Toshizō, a scholar of Zen Buddhism, often met with Candau and received letters from him written in Japanese (but typed in rōmaji). Candau said, "Recently young people do not know kanji well, and if I asked them to write down what I say orally, I will discover a lot of mistakes in kanji, which would take more time to correct." Therefore he rather liked to type his Japanese writing in romaji when responding to other people. His letters, according to Shimatani, are "much more polite than we Japanese could have written." Shimatani quoted one of Candau's postcards as below.

> Thank you very much for your postcard followed by the gift with all your kindness. I drank the tea and have never before enjoyed one so fine and tasty. It is very different from the freshly picked tea I buy at shops. It has an indescribable flavor. For the first time I know what pure, refined taste is. You said that it functions like medicine. That is even better. I will treasure it. Thank you indeed.

Shimatani also mentioned Candau's careful attitude toward writing. Once Candau said, "People of a hundred years ago only published their mature

---

23 Kanbayashi, "Byōchū dokusho," 53–54.
24 Tanaka Kōtarō, *Gendai seikatsu no ronri*, 291.

thoughts. They knew what they wanted to say, then carefully considered how to present it, imagining their readers' reaction, and finally started to write slowly in a relaxed manner."[25] This attitude should be a model for today's writers as well.

The speeches made by Candau set a good example for other missionaries. For instance, Joseph Roggendorf (1908–1982), a member of the Society of Jesus, organized many public lectures by intellectuals and writers at Sophia University. He recalled, "Among all the speakers, Fr. Candau was one of the most excellent. If I ever learned something about speaking in Japanese, it is from Fr. Candau. Sadly, I have no talent like his. He could thrill his audience, enlighten them, and entertain them with a sense of humor, all at the same time." Roggendorf also provided us with an account of how Candau prepared his lectures. First he drafted the manuscript, then memorized it, and finally practiced it, sometimes in front of a mirror.[26] It also seems that Candau prepared with his understanding of the audience's psychology firmly in mind.

Many people have evaluated Candau's Japanese as "better than that of the Japanese people." Novelist Inukai Michiko wrote, "His Japanese is so excellent that it outshines ours. He is the first foreigner who wrote by himself and contributed to *Asahi shinbun*'s column 'Yesterday, Today' (Kinō, Kyō) for about a year." In radio programs, he "embarrassed Japanese presenters by his eloquent speaking in the Edo style, often using proverbs. His beautiful essay collections are best-selling books," she enthused.[27]

Novelist Shishi Bunroku (1893–1969) admired Candau's Japanese, and even learned some Shizuoka dialect expressions from him.[28] When Candau was charged with editing other manuscripts submitted by Japanese authors, he was sensitive to kanji usage and often corrected errors made by native speakers.[29] Kanō Michiko, a scholar of Basque studies, once saw a letter written by Candau to a friend. The handwriting was "as beautiful as that of those who grew up in Japan," she said.[30] Here we can see a photocopy

---

25 Shimatani, *Rōbaiju*, 16–17.

26 Roggendorf, *Ibunka no hazama made*, 143.

27 Inukai, *Seiō no kao o motomete*, 247.

28 Candau and Shishi, "Nihon are kore 'Shishi Bunroku-shi to no taidan," 146–47.

29 Imamichi, "Tōku kara no inori," 2.

30 Kanō, *Basuku monogatari: Chizu ni nai kuni no hitobito*, 181.

of handwritten draft of an essay by Candau (Fig. 14), which was provided to me by Prof. Araki Shin'ichirō of Nagasaki Junshin Catholic University.

Novelist Yoshiya Nobuko (1896–1973) met Candau for the first time when she was visiting another writer, Masugi Shizue (1901–1955). "The ruddy-faced Fr. Candau spoke in overly skillful Japanese about the benefit of moxa cautery for muscle pain."[31] The expression "overly skillful Japanese" reveals that his extraordinary mastery of the language made this Japanese writer a bit uncomfortable.

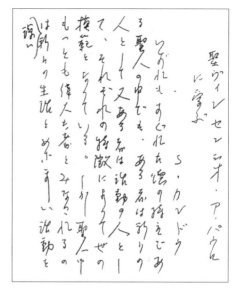

Fig. 14, A page from Candau's handwritten draft of an essay, courtesy of Araki Shin'ichirō.

Tanaka Kōtarō evaluated his writing in Japanese as equal to that of the country's most accomplished intellectuals. "His style is plain, but not mediocre; witty, but not shallow; humorous, but not tawdry. His writings are thoroughly refined with attention to all details. They have the dignity of a missionary as well. His postwar publications were enthusiastically received by the press because they suited the style and taste of well-educated people." His knowledge of Japanese culture clearly surpassed that of average Japanese.[32]

Candau introduced Western philosophy and thought to postwar Japanese readers while teaching French at the Institut franco-japonais de Tokyo and Athénée Français. Hirakawa Sukehiro attended his class frequently and was amazed, declaring, "Fr. Candau studied the Chinese classics in Shizuoka and started to learn Japanese before we were born. His Japanese was elegant, simply brilliant."[33] However, Hirakawa thought that Candau's written Japanese could not compare to his fascinating lectures. He heard from

---

31 Yoshiya, "Kozakana no kokoro," 393–95.

32 Tanaka, *Gendai seikatsu no ronri*, 291–96.

33 Hirakawa, *Higashi no tachibana, Nishi no orenji*, 47.

Candau that he wrote his World War II battlefield diary in Japanese so as not to forget the language. Hirakawa said, "I have never seen another scholar of Japanese studies who can use Japanese as skillfully as Fr. Candau did."[34]

Scholar of French literature Tatsuno Yutaka said, "It is very rare to see someone like Fr. Candau who is able to speak, read, and write perfectly… Whenever I read his essays, I am awed. His style is equivalent to that of the finest writers."[35] Tatsuno posed a direct question to Candau about his way of composition. "He does not write in kana and kanji from the beginning, as it would take too much time. He usually writes in rōmaji first, and then transcribes the letters into kana and kanji. Sometimes he asks his students to do so."[36] In other words, he gave ample time to polishing and refining the contents before putting it into kanji and kana.

Candau is famous for his slow, methodical writing. Even his short articles required much effort to create.[37] He repeatedly polished, shortened, and refined his articles for "Yesterday, Today," according to *Asahi shinbun* editor Miyamoto Toshiyuki.[38]

There were, however, a few things in Japanese that were problematic for Candau. Linguist Kindaichi Haruhiko (1913–2004) once asked Candau about any difficulties he experienced. Candau replied that neither kanji nor honorifics were difficult, but idioms using *ki* (気) were confusing to him.[39]

3. Insightful Understanding of Japan

During the twenty-one years he lived in Japan, Candau was simultaneously a missionary, an educator, a social worker, a public speaker, and a writer. It is well known that he only slept four hours a day.[40] By using his outstanding Japanese, he was able to communicate with Japanese society widely and to observe the country from different perspectives. Let us look at some excerpts from his writings that reflect his observations.

---

34 Hirakawa, *Shomotsu no koe, rekishi no koe*, 69–70.

35 Tatsuno, *Bongu shunjū*, 35–36.

36 Ibid., 141–42.

37 Okada, "Kandō-shi no kanshikigan," 137.

38 Miyamoto, "Kandō shinpu-sama no koto," 53.

39 Kindaichi, "Giongo, gitaigo," 55; *Nihongo no tokushitsu*, 158.

40 Nakata, "Kandō kōchō no omoide," 48.

Candau was particularly touched by Japanese people's "natural goodness" (*shizentoku*). One day he bought a copy of a newspaper for two *sen* at a platform from a train window. He gave five *sen* to the newspaper boy. He forgot to take the change, and was absorbed in reading until reaching the next station. Upon arrival he was given three *sen* by the station conductor who told him about what happened at the previous station. "What honest people! This was done by people who know nothing about Christianity." Like Xavier, Candau was amazed by the kindness of the people.[41] Not only Candau, but many other missionaries also wrote favorably about the Japanese, commenting that they have Christian morality without believing in Christ.

This "natural goodness" was mentioned by Xavier in one of his letters too. Xavier wrote that among the people encountered by the Europeans so far, "there can be none that has more natural goodness than the Japanese. They are of a kindly disposition, not at all given to cheating, wonderfully desirous of honour and rank."[42]

Toward the end of World War II, Candau suffered a serious injury, and for a while he stayed in Rome recovering. There he wrote in his diary on 17 July 1945, one month before Japan officially surrendered,

> Japan's current misfortune is not a result of its spiritual development, but rather of deliberate compromise that enabled the military to control the government. It is the military that derailed Japan's advancement. After overcoming the "suffering" caused by the nation's arrogance, Japan will become an attractive and fascinating country, and will continue its development, which may astonish the whole world, because Japan has much fewer corrupted people, and much more 'natural goodness' and spiritual power than other nations.[43]

Looking back seven decades later, we can see that Candau's prognosis was correct. From its defeat in war to the present day, Japan has achieved marvelous economic prosperity and cultural advancement, and has substantially contributed to world peace and improvements. Candau had confidence in Japanese people's "natural goodness" and "spiritual power." His view of

---

41 Ikeda, *Shōwa Nihon no onjin: S. Kandō-shi*, 53.

42 Coleridge, *The Life and Letters of St. Francis Xavier*, vol. 2, 237.

43 Candau, *Kandō zenshū*, vol. 4, 259.

Japan confirmed Xavier's praise of the people of four centuries ago, and it was founded on deeper observation of Japan than had been possible for Xavier during his short stay.

Candau wrote, "It is the abundance of beautiful souls that has kept me in Japan for all my life. They are the people who, in their final moments, thanked God, expressed their happiness, and left this world with composure...I am confident to say that I cannot help but love this country where I have discovered so many graceful souls."[44] As a result of Candau's evangelization in Japan, many Japanese people converted to Christianity.

As we have remarked, Candau often mentioned the similarity between Japanese and Basque. "In terms of syntax, Basque can attach different endings to sentences to express intimacy and respect at different levels, very much like the Japanese language." He also noted that Basque poetry is similar to Japanese *waka* and haiku. "In Basque poems as in Japanese *sōmonka* (mainly composed by lovers for one another), when conveying love, the first line is usually a description of a natural scene which seems to be unrelated, and the second line would express the poet's emotion. The style is brief and symbolic, containing multiple meanings, as is also the case with *waka* and haiku."[45]

His essay *Take tsukushi* (All Things Bamboo) shows us Candau's careful observation of Japanese daily life, in which bamboo is utilized for many things.

> When I tried to count with fingers, I am startled again. Outside the house there are hedges (*kakine*), fences (*saku*), drainpipes (*toi*), water pipes (*kakei*), benches (*endai*), and foldable stools (*shōgi*). Inside the bathroom and kitchen, there are duckboards (*sunoko*), ladles (*hishaku*), toothpicks (*yōji*), draining baskets (*zaru*), baskets (*kago*), bamboo blowpipes (*hifukidake*), fish skewers (*uogushi*), chopsticks (*hashi*), brooms (*hōki*), duster sticks (*hataki no e*), bamboo leaf wrappers (*take no kawa tsutsumi*), bamboo leaf sandals (*takegawa zōri*), rakes (*kumade*), bamboo poles (*takezao*), and barrel hoops (*oke no taga*).
>
> In terms of small items, there are lanterns (*chōchin*), umbrellas (*kasa*), and fan sticks (*ōgi no hone*). When you open a bamboo door

---

44 Candau, "Shingan ni eijitaru Nihon," 28–30.
45 Candau, "Banshū bōkyō," 66–71.

(*takedo*) and enter the living room (*zashiki*), you will see the outdoor bamboo deck (*take no nure'en*), bamboo curtain (*take sudare*), flower vases (*hanaike*), picture frames (*gakubuchi*), pen stands (*fudetate*), writing brushes (*fude*), bamboo flutes (*shakuhachi*), flutes (*fue*), bird cages (*torikago*), ash holders (*haifuki*), and tobacco pipes (*rau*). The inventory is endless.

An amateur like me can easily come up with this list, let alone experts or men of leisure who may produce a thick catalogue…

In the East, bamboo is a precious gift of Heaven. And bamboo products have unique characters and purposes. Look at the elasticity of bamboo baskets, the delicacy of tea whisks, how can they be made by anything else, if not bamboo? Bamboo products are our daily companions. If one day they are replaced by metal, we cannot help but feel cold.[46]

試みに指を折って数えてみて、いまさら驚いた。まず家の回りでは、垣根、柵、樋、かけい、縁台に床几、湯殿から台所では、すのこに柄杓、よう枝、ざる、籠、火吹竹、魚串、箸、ほうきにハタキの柄、竹の皮包みに竹皮草履、熊手、竹竿、桶のたが、こまかいところでは提灯、傘、扇の骨、竹戸をあけて座敷にくれば、竹の濡れ縁に竹すだれ、花いけ、額ぶち、筆立に筆、尺八、笛、鳥籠、灰吹にキセルに羅宇……ときりがない。しろうとがざっとこれだけ思いつくのだから、専門家や閑人に頼んだらたいへんな目録になるであろう。……

たしかに竹は東洋での貴重な天与の賜物である。しかも竹製品は独特の長所と趣を有する。竹籠の多種多様の自在さ、茶せんのあの繊細さは、他の何で造り出せるか。日常生活の伴侶であるこれらの竹製品がみな金属に代わる日を想像すると、寒気を感ぜずにはいられない。

These paragraphs display Candau's minute observations, rhythmic descriptions, sense of humor, and imagination of "cold" when referring to "metal." This essay exemplifies his power to captivate the hearts of readers.

Candau had a flexible attitude toward people of different denominations and religions. He showed his admiration for Protestants and Buddhists whose great personalities, honest writing, and outstanding achievements impressed him.[47] He mastered not only the Japanese language, but also

---

46 Candau, "Takezukushi," 42–43.
47 Seki, "Onshi no ningenmi," 69.

Japanese culture, which enabled him to "have a good understanding of Confucianism and Buddhism, and to utilize their inherent truths to explain Christianity." Tanaka Kōtarō observed that Candau often emphasized the universality of moral principles, or "natural law," that exist in moralities of different religions.[48]

In the 1935 general meeting of the Society of Morning Stars (Ake no Hoshi no Kai), a group of Catholic women in Tokyo established under his guidance, Candau spoke on how to "show broad-mindedness toward positive things in the society," how to "respect people's valuable thoughts different from Catholic ideals," and how to "use people's natural emotion to guide them to the real religion."[49] In other words, Candau wanted to respect other religious feelings, even as he was propagating Christianity to non-believers. The fact that he did not criticize other religions was comforting to many ordinary Japanese who were attracted to his work.

Candau's motive in studying Asian religions was to "find the most suitable way to touch the hearts of the people in the East." One Buddhist believer listened to Candau's explanation of Heaven, and concluded, "your Heaven is so open!"[50] When a woman told Candau that she was too busy with washing, cleaning, and sewing to go to church on Sundays, he replied, "You are always smiling. If there is Heaven, you are the one who should be there."[51] She was greatly comforted by his words. In Candau's living room, there was a hanging scroll of a Chinese poem. In front of it, chrysanthemums were arranged in a vase. This décor well represented his taste for Asian arts.[52]

Candau was the chairman of the board of directors of Shinsei Kaikan (its prewar name was "St. Filippo Dormitory"). This Catholic organization brings young people interested in Catholicism together and provides them with the opportunity to communicate with each other. Candau told the students that it is important to "turn the direction of Japanese culture and atmosphere to the Christian God." He asked them not to hide Catholicism in their minds, but rather to make it acceptable to the Japanese ways

---

48 Tanaka, *Gendai seikatsu no ronri*, 294.
49 Hiramatsu, "Mikan to egao," 76.
50 Dumoulin, "'Sei Igunachio no yūbe' no Kandō-shi," 113.
51 Maruta, "Kandō shinpu-sama no mitama ni," 49–50.
52 Shimatani, "Kandō shinpu to Minhō Yuian rōshi," 14.

of thinking and disposition.[53] Candau was looking for an effective way to proselytize by finding common ground between Japanese culture and Catholicism.

During Sunday School sessions, Candau often mentioned the importance of being kind and patient when guiding unrestricted spirits in the better direction of improvement, because "Japanese children's hearts are very pure and fine, and it is vital to prepare their hearts for sowing the seeds of Gospels. But we shall never monopolize their hearts."[54]

Novelist Nagata Mikihiko (1887–1964) used Candau as the model for Fr. Rosario in his novel *Ryokui no seibo* (Holy Mother in Green, 1931). That fictional priest says, "the Japanese people know the existence of God, although they are not aware of this. I have been in Japan for a long period, and I know the Japanese character very well."[55] This pronouncement mirrors the actual Candau's observations of Japan.

Called back into the French army during World War II, Candau was grievously injured in the Battle of Ardennes. His hips were crushed. After surgery in 1942, he stayed in Rome for five years to recuperate, during which time he worked for the Embassy of Japan to the Holy See (Vatican). He was told by the doctor in charge of his treatment that he had only two years to live, owing to his stomach and blood diseases. He decided to return to Japan, stating, "I want to spend the final two years in Japan." When he heard the news that Japan's defeat was imminent, he wrote in his diary on 13 August 1945,

> I devoted a greater part of my life to this country. I love its people from the bottom of my heart. I want to share their sorrow with them. When I think about the anxiety of those I know very well, the possible changes that will occur, and the difficulties Japan must face, I feel even greater attachment to the Japanese because of their defeat. They will not lose their great merits. The trial they are undergoing shall purify their demerits.[56]

---

53 Kobayashi, "Kirisuto no yoki heishi," 104.

54 Nakata, "Kandō kōchō no omoide," 47.

55 Nagata, *Ryokui no seibo*, 485–93.

56 Candau, *Kandō zenshū*, vol. 4, 260–61.

Thus Candau's affection for Japan was based on his comprehension of both the merits and demerits of the people, not a "blind love".

In the opinion of novelist Takami Jun (1907–1965), "Fr. Candau wrote about good points of Japan and the Japanese people. It was not mere flattery. He pointed out virtues of which we Japanese ourselves are unaware. He recognized good points we are at risk of losing, and he excavated merits we have lost. His sharp critique of current Japan is rooted in the deep love he feels for Japan and the Japanese people. I am touched, especially touched by his fondness for ordinary Japanese people."[57]

One day Takami visited the novelist Masugi Shizue in her hospital room, where another woman was saying to her, "Please be happy that you are approaching the day to be called by God." Takami felt the words were "too thoughtless and merciless." "Never," he believed, "would Fr. Candau have said anything like that."[58]

Regarding postwar intellectual circles in Japan, Candau wrote, "The most appropriate method of evaluating this intellectual chaos is to observe it from a religious standpoint. That is because religion gives answers to the origins of human races, issues of race and space, people's destiny in this world and after death, the relation between humans and God, obligations between humans, and human duties to all creatures. In short, it is no exaggeration to say that religion sums up all these matters."[59]

Candau also mentioned the tendency of Japanese intellectuals to learn Western things superficially. "No matter how much you study the French language and literature, if you do not pay attention to the spiritual aspects which are the foundation of French culture, you are only learning technically, and cannot at all really digest it."[60] Obviously Candau was being critical of Japanese scholars' lack of interest in Christianity, which has underpinned French culture for centuries.

Candau was often invited to participate in roundtable discussions, but was never satisfied. He named them "empty talk" (*kūdankai*), judging that there was no meaningful substance to the discussions. Noting that these events usually ended up with a banquet, he made a pun and suggested that

---

57 Takami, "Daiyonsha no shutsugen: Gendai bunshi ron danpen," 595.
58 Takami, "Kinō kyō," 47.
59 Candau, "Shingan ni eijitaru Nihon," 16–20.
60 Iwase, "Kandō-shi no ikun," 135.

they could be called "eating talk"—one Chinese character pronounced *kuu* means "empty," but a homophone written with a different character means "to eat".[61] In his writings we can often see this kind of ironic humor. Tanaka Kōtarō pointed out that one characteristic of Candau's works is criticism of contemporary culture. "Fr. Candau offered Japanese students an invaluable warning against highly specialized and exclusive knowledge which resulted in the obliteration of unified perceptions of each other. This is a disease of today's culture."[62] Candau's affection for Japan also enabled him to criticize Japan's problems of thought without hesitation.

4. Contribution to Japan

From 1929, when Candau became the principal of the Sekiguchi Seminary, until 1939 when he was drafted for military service for the second time, he devoted himself to educating future priests. During this decade he also compiled a Latin-Japanese dictionary—*Rawa jiten (Lexicon Latino-Japonicum)*. According to the preface, "I came to Japan in January 1925. From autumn of the same year, before I had enough time to concentrate on the Japanese langauge, I was asked to teach theology and philosophy. I realized there was an urgent need to compile a Latin dictionary in Japanese. Since then, everyday from 8:00 in the morning to 5:00 in the afternoon, I had only ten to fifteen minutes of each class break available to write the dictionary." He disclosed that he had a collaborator, Kokura Gujin, in working on the dictionary.[63]

According to a commentary by Seya Yukio, this dictionary "is highly useful and practical, and has historical value as the first Latin-Japanese dictionary in Japan." It not only has ancient Latin vocabulary, but also medieval Latin words, especially many Catholic terms, with "rare value." A Latin-Japanese dictionary currently in print, *Rawa jiten* published by Kenkyūsha includes many entries from Candau's dictionary as supplements.[64] Candau's dictionary has played a role in introducing European classics to modern Japan.

---

61 Candau, "Tōzai no zadankai," 73.
62 Tanaka, *Gendai seikatsu no ronri*, 295.
63 Candau, *Lexicon Latino-Japonicum*, "Jo."
64 Seya, "Fukkokuban ni tsuite," 10–12.

Candau actively engaged in public speaking and writing for a wide-ranging audience in order to introduce Christian knowledge and culture. In the four years after the speech he gave in his tenth month in Japan, he delivered nearly two hundred more speeches.[65] He also wrote numerous essays, many of which were compiled and published under seven titles (in eleven volumes) as follows:

1) *Shisō no tabi* (思想の旅, A Journey of Thoughts), Sanseidō, 1952.
2) *Sekai no ura omote* (世界のうらおもて, The Two Sides of the World), Asahi Shinbunsha, 1955.
3) *Eien no kessaku* (永遠の傑作, Eternal Masterpieces), Tōhō Shobō, 1955.
4) *Basuku no hoshi* (バスクの星, The Stars of Basque), Tōhō Shobō, 1956.
5) *S. Kandō ikkan senshū* (S・カンドウ一巻選集, One Volume of Selected Works by S. Candau), Shunjūsha, 1969.
6) *Kandō zenshū* (カンドウ全集, Complete Works by Candau), 7 volumes, Chūō Shuppan, 1970.
7) *Shisaku no yorokobi: Kandō shinpu no eien no kotoba* (思索のよろこび：カンドウ神父の永遠のことば Delight in Contemplation: Fr. Candau's Eternal Words), Shunjūsha, 1971.

From 1949 to 1953, he also published Japanese translations of four French books.

1) *Ai no tetsugaku: Kami no awase tamaishi mono* (愛の哲学：神の合せ給ひしもの), co-translated with Kanayama Masahide, Kawade Shobō, 1949; the original was Gustave Thibon, *Ce que Dieu a Uni* (1947).
2) *Kirisuto to sono jidai* (キリストとその時代), 3 volumes, co-translated with Kanayama Masahide, Sanseidō, 1949–50; the original was Henri Daniel-Rops, *Jésus et son temps* (1945).
3) *Kaimiroa* (カイミロア), Hōsei Daigaku Shuppankyoku, 1953 ; the original was Éric de Bisschop, *Kaimiloa: D'Honolulu à Cannes par l'Australie et Le Cap, à bord d'une double pirogue polynésienne* (1935).

---

65 Candau, "Shingan ni eijitaru Nihon," 15.

4) *Seijin jigoku e iku* (聖人地獄へ行く), Hōsei Daigaku Shuppankyoku, 1953 ; the original was Gilbert Cesbron, *Les Saints vont en enfer* (1952).

Candau co-authored a book in French with Paul Martin, *Le sport et l'homme*, which was translated into Japanese by Kanayama Masahide as *Supōtsu ningen gaku* スポーツ人間学 and published by Shin Taiikusha in 1952. This book on the psychology and techniques of people engaging in sports was reprinted by Terateia in 2012 because of its relevance to sports education today. Candau also partially translated Kamo no Chōmei's *Hōjōki* (An Account of a Ten-Foot-Square Hut) into French. This was published by the Institut franco-japonais de Tokyo in 1957, two years after his death.

Keen to familiarize Japanese with European thought after the war, Candau was probably the first person to introduce the names of intellectuals such as Simone Weil (1909–1943), the French philosopher and activist, and Max Picard (1888–1963), the Swiss writer and thinker.[66] According to Tanaka Kōtarō, Candau's greatest achievement was the product of his endeavor to introduce and critique thinkers and writers from the French philosophical and literary worlds with whose work he was intimately familiar. He was critical of the Japanese reception of novelist André Gide (1869–1951) and philosopher Jean-Paul Sartre (1905–1980), who were viewed as if they were representative of France. In reaction Candau introduced French philosopher Gustave Thibon (1903–2001) and Catholic writer Henri Daniel-Rops (1901–1965) to Japan.[67]

During his twenty-one years of residence in Japan, Candau energetically promoted Catholicism in public lectures and writings. He emphasized the importance of publications, quoting what Pope Pius XI said to newspaper reporters in 1930: "If St. Paul were to come again in the twentieth century, he would definitely be a newspaper reporter." "Until now," he declared, "most Catholic missionary work in Japan had been done by foreigners like us. However, there is no one among us who can completely understand Japan and its language, therefore we cannot communicate our deep thoughts as well as we wish. With the assistance of certain Japanese

---

66 Yamanashi, "Sōvūru Kandō to kindai Nihon no chishikijin," 108; Candau, "Gendai Furansu no shisōkai," 291.

67 Tanaka, *Gendai seikatsu no ronri*, 293.

believers who are knowledgeable about Christianity, we have managed to convey our ideas as missionaries, but this has been inadequate." He called the time of his mission a "transitional period," and looked forward to the day when leadership in evangelization would be taken over by Japanese priests and philosophers like Iwashita Sōishi (1889–1940) and Totsuka Bunkei (1892–1939).[68]

Candau spoke many languages and advocated cultural exchanges. "Advancement is based on exchange," he maintained. "Only by exchanging technology, arts, and ideas between countries, can human society make progress, share common wealth, and improve intelligence."[69] His introduction of European thought to Japan was intended to enrich Japanese culture.

Some of Candau's essays were selected for inclusion in Japanese language textbooks used in junior high schools. For instance, in the section on criticism in *Kokugo 3* (National Language 3, published by Chikuma Shobō from 1957 to 1961), Candau's essay "Gimu to rieki" (Responsibility and Profits) was included along with pieces by renowned Japanese writers such as "'Ningen rashisa' to iu koto" (On "Humanity") by Kishida Kunio, "Ningen no heian" (The Peace of Humanity) by Itō Sei, and "Aruki nagara kangaeru" (Thinking while Walking) by Ryū Shintarō.[70]

Another essay by Candau, "Chinmoku no kōyō" (The Effect of Silence), was printed in *Chūgaku Kokugo 2* (Junior High School National Language 2, published by Nihon Shoseki in 1962). These might be the first times a foreigner's essays written in Japanese were chosen for Japanese language textbooks. Anthropologist Hagio Shō thought it worth remarking that "around the early 1960s, Japanese children were actually learning 'National Language' from works written by a Basque man." He continued to say, "The reason Candau's name remains in the memory of Japanese people to the present day is his mastery of refined and elegant Japanese, [and people appreciate] his teaching and commentating endeavors in his 'second home country, Japan'…He greatly influenced Japanese intellectuals who are now of middle age and older."[71]

In *Tetsugaku yōgo no kiso chishiki* (Basic Knowledge of Philosophical

68 Candau, "Oriori no mondai," 14–16.
69 Candau, "Tōzai no zadankai," 78.
70 Chikuma Shobō, *Sōgyō 50 shūnen: Chikuma Shobō tosho sōmokuroku, 1949–1990,* 837.
71 Hagio and Yoshida, *Gendai Basuku o shiru tame no 50 shō,* 98–99.

Terms) by scholar of philosophy Takama Naomichi (1915–1996), there is an entry for "Ishi no jiyū" (freedom of will). In it the author cites Candau: "Freedom means no restriction by others. However, this does not only mean a situation without restriction. The late Fr. Candau skillfully defined this term, 'Freedom is like a train running on the rails'."[72] This shows that even a renowned specialist such as Takama benefited from reading Candau's philosophical writings.

In postwar Japan, Candau was as famous as Xavier. To illustrate this we can use the example of Wada Sei (1890–1963), who introduced European ethnicities in his book *Tōyō shijō yori mitaru kodai no Nihon* (Ancient Japan in East Asian History, 1956). He wrote, "Basque people live at the foot of the Pyrénées Mountains and at the tip of Biscay Bay...The famous Xavier is a Basque, and so is Fr. Candau."[73]

The trailblazing scholar of modern folklore studies Yanagita Kunio (1875–1962) received a copy of *Kirisuto to sono jidai* (Christ and His Time), Candau's Japanese translation of Henri Daniel-Rops' *Jésus et son temps* (1945). Yanagita underlined several passages in the sections headed "Brothers of Jesus," "The Issue of Miracles," "Mary's Virginity," and "The Process of Transmitting Oral to Written Documents." This suggests that Candau's translation was useful to Yanagita's research in Japanese folklore as well.[74]

Yamanashi Atsushi, in the article mentioned above, remarked on Candau's influence on Tanaka Kōtarō, Iwashita Sōichi, Abe Yoshishige (1883–1966), and others, noting that "because of Candau, there have been many in Japan who became sympathetic to the Catholic church."[75] He continued to say, "Because Candau talked and wrote just like a Japanese, he was able to convey his thoughts directly to readers. Most missionary writings were co-authored with Japanese assistants, while Candau's works were written by himself. This enabled him to express thoughts and emotions freely, which made his work even more appealing."[76] The direct communication between Candau and his readers fostered a favorable relationship of mutual understanding. Candau loved the Japanese people, and they loved him too.

---

72 Takama, *Tetsugaku yōgo no kiso chishiki*, 70.
73 Wada, *Tōyō shijō yori mitaru kodai no Nihon*, 5.
74 Takagi, *Yanagita Kunio to Yōroppa: Kōshō bungei no tōzai*, 95–102.
75 Yamanashi, "Sōvūru Kandō to kindai Nihon no chishikijin," 103.
76 Ibid., 115.

Okazaki Kaheita (1897–1989), Japanese entrepreneur and the second president of All Nippon Airways, was another person who quoted Candau's words. "Just as Candau said," Okazaki wrote in an essay, "the healthiest society is where an ordinary person would not like to become a 'big shot'," because the higher the position, the more self-sacrifice is required, and that is very hard to endure.[77] Here we can see how widely Candau's words have been disseminated in Japanese society. In the *Encyclopedia Nipponica* published by Shōgakukan in 1985, an entry on Candau says this about him: "His extensive knowledge and excellent Japanese fascinated intellectuals during the postwar period, and gained him many friends. He worked as the Director of the Institut franco-japonais de Tokyo, professor of the University of the Sacred Heart, and he exerted religious and cultural influence on many young people, especially at Shinsei Kaikan in Shinanomachi, Tokyo."[78] The Jesuit missionary Heinrich Dumoulin praised Candau saying, "Among all the missionaries who have ever come to Japan, no one other than Candau has influenced so many non-believers by his spoken and written words."[79]

5. Guided by Candau

Now let us look at some of the people in Japan who were particularly strongly influenced by the Catholic teaching they received from Candau. Ono Toyoaki (b. 1912), former chairman of the Department of Economics at Sophia University, was baptized by Candau after attending a summer theology seminar organized by him; participants read about St. Thomas Aquinas and Ono decided to convert to Catholicism.[80] Scholar of East Asian history and ethnology Shiratori Yoshirō (1918–1998) studied Catholicism with Candau for one year, during which he decided to become a Catholic. Stimulated by Catholic priests' research on ethnology, Shiratori became "extremely interested in their research, and wanted to professionally study ethnology."[81]

Literary critic Suzuki Hideko (b. 1932) listened to Candau's lecture "Crit-

---

77 Okazaki, *Watashi wa omou: Nihon no kadai*, 259.
78 Shōgakukan, *Nihon daihyakka zensho*, vol. 6, 250.
79 Dumoulin, "'Sei Igunachio no yūbe' no Kandō-shi," 111.
80 Ono, "Hitō shūkyōhan no katsudō," 570–71.
81 Arima, "Shiratori Yoshirō-shi," 145–47.

icism of Modern Thought" at the University of the Sacred Heart, and found Candau's philosophical knowledge and logical interpretation convincingly resolved the riddle posed in Mori Ōgai (1862–1922)'s short story "Takase-bune" (1916)—was it a crime or not when the older brother "killed" the young sibling to relieve him from suffering? "He made us see the unimaginably emotional richness and literary elegance of the story which is well known by most Japanese people, and he prompted us to think about life and its origins."[82] Suzuki felt that Candau's works suggested a way of enriching Japan's spiritual world. When she was studying Christianity and Buddhism and could not make up her mind whether to convert to Catholicism, she consulted Candau, and was asked by him, "What will you do?" Immediately she responded, "I would like to be baptized."[83]

Mori Ōgai's second daughter Annu (1909–1998) lost her father when she was thirteen years old. She met with Candau only once, when she was forty-one, but she was impressed that he was the only person who made her feel like her father. "When I saw his eyes full of mercy, I instantly felt that they were 'the eyes of my father!'"[84] She was baptized when she was fifty in November 1959.[85] Regarding the end of "Takase-bune," where Shōbei could not determine whether "euthanasia" meant murder or not, no matter how much he thought about it, he sensed that "it would be better to leave it to a higher 'authority' than myself to decide, and I shall just abide by the decision." Candau said that Ōgai was great precisely because he recognized the existence of a higher "authority." Upon hearing this, Annu understood for the first time why her father was so obedient to her grandmother. "My father," she said, "was obedient to God who gave him life through his mother!"[86]

After reading her father's short story "Goji'ingahara no kataki uchi" (Revenge at Goji'ingahara), Annu started to respect her father even more deeply, regarding him as great as Candau and Sawaki Kōdō, master of the

82 Suzuki Hideko, "'Gendai shisō hihan' no kurasu," 139.

83 Genyū and Suzuki, Bukkyō, Kirisutokyō shinikata ikikata, 153.

84 Kobori, Fugū no hito Ōgai: Nihongo no moraru to bi, 172–73.

85 Kracht/Kurahato and Kracht/Kurahato-Tateno, Ōgai no Kōtansai (Kurisumasu): Mori-ke o meguru nendaiki, 380–81.

86 Kobori, Fugū no hito Ōgai: Nihongo no moraru to bi, 317.

Sōtō sect of Buddhism.[87] It is through Candau that Annu discovered the excellence of her father's literature. As for Candau's literary style, she described it as "very concise, plain, easy to be understood by most people. Because he was a priest, he put much effort in to communicating profound thought in his writings while making them easily understandable so as to provide guidance… Fr. Candau's books are like Gospels to readers like me."[88]

Masugi Shizue got to know Candau through Tanaka Mineko, Kōtarō's wife. Terminally ill with cancer, Masugi started to read the Bible.[89] She regretted her past and wrote in her will, "If my sins can be redeemed by religion, if I still have time, I would like to pursue it." She asked Candau to baptize her before her death. Her funeral was held at the St. Ignatius Church at Yotsuya, Tokyo.[90] According to Tanaka Mineko, Masugi behaved like an infant, pressing Fr. Candau to visit her from early morning until late evening. The aging priest tried his best to satisfy her. At one point Mineko told Masugi, who was suffering severe pain, "You will go to Heaven soon." Candau reproved Mineko, saying, "My policy is to keep patients' hope as long as possible. Masugi seems to have messed up her life, as she wrote in her autobiography. She wishes to be redeemed, even if only slightly. We must let her keep her hope for redemption."[91] Masugi passed away on 29 June 1955, almost exactly three months before Candau's death on 28 September.

Let us return briefly to the time when Candau was living in Rome, recovering from his war wounds. When the news of the atomic bombs dropped on Hiroshima and Nagasaki reached him, he was furious, and through Vatican channels he registered a strong protest against the U. S. government. He exclaimed, "If the United States wanted to show off its most powerful weapon and make Japan stop the war, they could have just dropped the bombs into the mouth of Mt. Fuji. If the symbol of Japan is blown away, the military would definitely surrender unconditionally, no matter how stupid they are. Instead, the Americans dropped bombs on Hiroshima and Nagasaki, killing hundreds of thousands of innocent people. Isn't Nagasaki the sacred place where the twenty-six martyrs sacrificed themselves? What

---

87 Ibid., 325.
88 Kobori, *Jinsei butai: Kobori Annu zuihitsushū*, 221–22.
89 Yoshimi, "Masugi Shizue," 239.
90 Ōmura, *Bundan eiga monogatari*, 358.
91 Tanaka Mineko, "Chinmoku no Seibo," 116.

nonsense! The United States does not choose means appropriate for the end it seeks!" Kanayama Masahide, a Japanese diplomat posted to the Vatican, learned of Candau's letter of protest and wrote about it in his memoirs.[92]

Kanayama had become acquainted with Candau when he was studying at the First Higher School. When he heard that Candau had been injured critically and was in Rome, he decided to invite the priest to be an advisor to the Embassy of Japan to the Holy See in the Vatican. He wanted to connect Japan and the Vatican through Candau, who knew Japan well and was friendly to it. In Rome, Kanayama noticed, Candau was "constantly visited by many people, regardless of social status or political position. Candau created a warm atmosphere, and on any single occasion the topics discussed might be arts, philosophy, or the economy and social problems...There was no one who could match Candau's knowledge or verbal facility."[93]

After Italy's surrender, the victorious Allies placed staff members of the Embassy of Japan in Italy under house arrest in Salsomaggiore in northern Italy. Disregarding the pain he was suffering, Candau visited them in the capacity of "envoy of the Vatican," traveling 500 kilometers by car over a bumpy road. Over an eight-month span, he called on them three times, bringing food and cigarettes. The staff members were more interested in Candau's personality than the treats he delivered, and they were encouraged by his heart-warming talk.

Candau discussed the discourse on modern civilization in Japan that had been started by Fukuzawa Yukichi, and he talked about postwar French thought, philosophy, and literature. When requested, he also talked about "religion." Three members of the embassy decided to convert to Christianity as "their hearts respectfully absorbed Candau's words." Surprised by this, the British officer supervising the house arrest gave permission for them to be baptized at a church in the town. He even summoned a bishop from a nearby city to perform the sacrament. But the converts wanted to be baptized by Fr. Candau in Japanese, and their wish was granted.[94]

Modern Japanese literature has fictional characters patterned on Candau. For example, in his autobiographic novel *Wakai hi no deai* (Encounters in Young Days), musicologist Nomura Yoshio (1908–1994) created a

---

92 Kanayama, *Daremo kakanakatta Bachikan*, 62–63.
93 Ibid., 73–76.
94 Ibid., 79–80; Hidaka, "Itaria ni okeru Kandō shinpu no omoide," 82–84.

much-admired priest called Fr. Dubara who is obviously a fictionalized proxy for Candau, who had baptized the author in 1934.[95]

Novelist Kaga Otohiko (b. 1929) studied French with Candau and said that he would not have become a Catholic novelist without Candau's influence. Kaga first got to know Candau when he was working as a medical officer for the prison where the culprit of the "Mekka Bar Murder Case" of 1953, Shōda Akira (1929–1969), was incarcerated. Shōda also was converted to Christianity because of Candau's teaching.

In his novel *Shikeishū no kiroku* (A Record of a Death-Row Prisoner, 1980), Kaga quoted Shōda's "Appeal Statement," which contained this comment about Candau: "Father is completely different from others. He quietly smiled at me, accepted who I am. Before teaching me trust and love, he gave me trust and love first." Shōda was baptized in July 1955, two months before Candau's death.[96] Shōda said, "Fr. Candau asked me to believe in God. If it is his God, I want to believe wholeheartedly."[97]

Kaga's novel *Senkoku* (The Sentence, 1979) takes Shōda as the model for the protagnist Kusumoto Takao, and Candau for priest Fr. Shōmu. When meeting Takao for the first time, Fr. Shōmu talked about his pets.

> Priest: "At home I have a goat, a cat, a dog, a Java sparrow, and gold fish. They are getting along with each other well. They are very playful...Sometimes the cat fights with the dog. And it is always the cat who wins. That is why she walks around proudly, expanding her chest, raising her tail, as if saying, "Akanbē" (You, silly!). So her name is Bē. Well, she is a mixed breed. Who knows her background! One day she came and forcefully joined the family. The dog is a pure Maltese with white fluffy hair. But he is a coward. At night, he is chased by Bē, and will run into my bed, whimpering."
>
> Takao laughed in spite of himself. "What do you call the dog?"
>
> "That's easy. He often cries and has NO courage, so he is Nay."
>
> "Interesting!" Replied Takao.
>
> "Isn't it? I am a careless man and often cannot find things. So, I search around the house and shout "No, no, no! Hearing this, Nay is

95 Nomura, *Wakai hi no deai*, 129–33.
96 Kaga, *Shikeishū no kiroku*, 172–73, 180.
97 Dandō, "*Shikei haishi ron* o kaita Keihō Gakkai no jūchin," 85–86.

worried too, and rushes to me and starts to search too."

"Do you find it?" Asked Takao.

"Never. Nay doesn't have a good nose, and we end up having a commotion." The two laughed, and so did the guard.[98]

With regard to the relations between Candau and Shōda, former judge of the Supreme Court and legal scholar Dandō Shigemitsu (1913–2012) wrote that Fr. Candau "is a great man. I admire him deeply…Of course his exceptional personality exerted religious influence on Shōda. But it is his faith and complete dependence on God that inspired Shōda to improve."[99]

The sentence handed down at the end of Shōda's first trial includes this statement: "Now the defendant greatly regrets his past, repents his crime, and is trying to return to an honest life after being guided and baptized by Fr. Candau. The Court sympathizes with his feelings as he spends all his time in repentance and redemption."[100] Nevertheless, Shōda was executed in 1969. His repentance was recognized, but his crime was not pardoned.

6. Loved by the Japanese People

Fr. Candau devoted his affection and life to Japan. He was also loved by the Japanese people. When he first arrived in Japan at the age of twenty-eight, he attracted parishioners immediately. It is said that church attendance increased wherever he was celebrating the holy mass.[101]

Shiba Ryōtarō included a chapter titled "Fr. Candau" in his book, reporting on his visit to the priest's hometown. He wrote:

> Fr. Candau is a theologian, philosopher, and above all a "Japanese." Since he came to Japan in 1925, he received deep affection and respect from many non-believers. He loved the Japanese people and culture, and wrote essays of high quality with a great sense of humor. His Japanese is perfect. We can see his clear and pure spirit in his writings. Fortunately the *Complete Works of Candau* (*Kandō zenshū*, seven

---

98 Kaga, *Senkoku*, 205–206.

99 Dandō, "*Shikei haishi ron* o kaita Keihō Gakkai no jūchin," 85–86.

100 Horikawa, *Shikei no kijun: "Nagayama saiban" ga nokoshita mono*, 163.

101 Suzuki, "Kandō-shi no omoide," 43.

volumes, Chūō Shuppan) was published, and we can learn more about him from his writings.[102]

This passage makes it unmistakably clear that Shiba evaluated Candau's significance in Japanese culture (and not just in the field of religion or his contributions to newspapers and magazines) very highly. Philosopher and critic Tsurumi Shunsuke also, as noted earlier, lauded Candau along with Xavier as foreign men who "constructed Japanese culture with the Japanese people."[103]

Scholar of Christian literature Takeda Tomoju asserted in a 1973 book review, "In postwar Japan, the most famous Catholics are Tanaka Kōtarō and Fr. S. Candau. At least ten years ago, these two men were frequently mentioned in church and their books were widely read." Takeda contended that there were extremely few people who have been loved as much as Fr. Candau, by both believers and non-believers. "His famous essays written in lucid Japanese are admired by many readers. As the author of the *Asahi shinbun* column 'Yesterday, Today,' he has been welcomed enthusiastically because his essays are fascinating and enjoyable. He is loved by readers because of his sharp sense of observation and rich wisdom."[104]

After reading Kaga Otohiko's work, novelist Nogami Yaeko (1885–1985) wrote, "Fr. Candau has had unparalleled influence on postwar Japan's Catholic world. He is not just an ordinary missionary…There are fervent believers in my family, and because of them I had the opportunity to meet Fr. Candau directly."[105] She visited Candau as he was to officiate at the wedding for her son Soichi, a scholar of Italian literature. She recorded her impression of her first encounter with Candau in her diary entry dated 2 July 1952. "Fr. Candau really looks like a Basque man with his joyfulness. Many followers hold him in high esteem because of his warmth and kindness, full of God's grace. I too would like to have a friend like him, even though we may have different political views."[106]

On the wedding day (14 July), Nogami was again impressed by Candau.

102 Shiba, *Shiba Ryōtarō zenshū 59: Kaidō o yuku 8, Nanban no michi*, 16.

103 Tsurumi, "Basuku made kita nagai nagai michi," 394.

104 Takeda, *Shūkyō to bungaku no setten*, 297–98.

105 Nogami, "Omoi dasu koto," 308–309.

106 Nogami, *Nogami Yaeko zenshū*, vol. 11, 263–64.

She wrote: "Fr. Candau said that when people reached a certain age, they naturally reexamine themselves and search for God. He quoted a poem by Charles Baudelaire to illustrate this, and wished the couple a happy life. His speech was not a formulaic blessing such as an average priest would have given, neither was it like a Shinto priest's chanting of a *norito*, which sounds like a business deal. Although Candau's speech was a bit conceptual, his eloquence is rare. Very few Japanese people can match his level."[107]

Novelist Shishi Bunroku also described Candau's performance of a wedding—that of his daughter. In his autobiographical novel *Musume to watashi* (My Daughter and Me), Shishi tells how the priest expressed his joy and appreciation to all the guests who attended the wedding. "His words are not conventional ones, but full of warmth, as he is a loving teacher of the couple. I listened to his speech as if immersed in a gentle mist, in a tender dream."[108]

Hirakawa Sukehiro felt "happiness" when being taught by Candau. There was a morning radio program featuring Candau talking in Japanese. "His warm personality must have attracted many listeners and have encouraged them a lot. My parents and I often listened to the program attentively." Hirakawa was also "infected" by Candau's accent. When he read aloud from French books, he was told by a young French woman, "You sound like a priest preaching." Hirakawa's diary also testifies about Candau's influence on his own view of life. He often skipped classes at the University of Tokyo, but diligently attended Candau's classes at the Institut franco-japonais de Tokyo, four times a week, nine hours in total. Later, during his five years of study in France, Hirakawa did not find any teacher better than Candau. He was saddened by the fact that when he returned to Japan, "Fr. Candau was no more."[109]

Mori Eisuke (1917–1951) dedicated to Candau a poem that is included in his collection *Hi no seijo* (The Holy Woman of Fire). The poem, "Rairaiken," expresses the emotion of a person from overseas who decides to stay in Japan and open a *ramen* shop to provide noodles to people in distress. The collection was published shortly before Mori's premature death. The dedication "to S. Candau" reflects the poet's respect for the priest and also the religious education received from him. This collection was favor-

---

107 Nogami, *Nogami Yaeko zenshū*, vol. 11, 270.

108 Shishi, *Musume to watashi*, 550.

109 Hirakawa, *Higashi no tachibana, Nishi no orenji*, 43–52.

ably reviewed by Takamura Kōtarō (1883–1956), a prominent poet who praised Mori's "novel Japanese language completely different from those of other poets."[110]

Another of Candau's many Japanese admirers was the Catholic priest Ikeda Toshio. Ikeda edited *Shōwa Nihon no onjin: S. Kandō shinpu* (A Contributor to Shōwa Japan: S. Candau) which introduces Candau's activities in Japan comprehensively and includes contributions by numerous people who were personally familiar with him. Another admirer, author of children's literature Murotani Kōkichi (b. 1912), published *Kandō shinpu: Nihonjin no kokoro no tomo* (Fr. Candau: A Friend of Japanese Hearts), a book that was selected by the Japan Library Association for inclusion in its 1979 list of recommended books for educating young people. Murotani's book, which is mostly based on Ikeda's edited volume, highlights two characteristics of the Candau figure: one, that he was a good friend of young Japanese people, with an example of how he became close friends with a university student and persuaded him to give up his idea of committing suicide; and two, that Candau was a pacificist and animal lover who followed St. Francis of Assisi.[111]

A researcher who studies the local culture of Aomori prefecture, Toyabe Yōnosuke, quoted Candau in a book about the famous Lake Towada. Toyabe wrote that he feared Candau's words— "If a list of 'International Silence Parks' were to be compiled, I would recommend Lake Towada first"—could no longer be said. He doubted Candau would feel the same if he saw the current situation of the lake because of the pollution caused by tourism.[112] The fact that a scholar of local culture chose to quote Candau's words in support of his own concern about the future of a scenic spot is yet another indicator of how deep Candau's writings have permeated into Japanese culture.

In *Minzoku to iu na no shūkyō* (A Religion Called "Nation", 1992), the author and psychiatrist Nada Inada (1929–2013) imagines the following dialogue. One person asks, "How about the Basque people?" The other replies, "There are Spanish Basque people who want to be independent from Spain by all means, and there are also Basques who identify with the

---

110 Takamura, "Jo."
111 Murotani and Tomiga, *Kandō shinpu: Nihonjin no kokoro no tomo*, 128–39, 148–60.
112 Toyabe, *Shin Towada-ko monogatari: Shinpi no mizuumi ni tsukareta hitobito*, 34.

French. Candau, who came to Japan, clearly had a double identity, Basque and French."[113]

During World War II, the French military intended to employ Candau's Japanese skills in its intelligence service. Candau rejected the proposed assignment, saying, "I learned Japanese for the sake of spreading the Gospel to the Japanese people."[114] To Candau, his Japanese skill should be used to bring happiness, not destruction, to Japan.

Tazaki Yūzō, a medical doctor who was adept in physiognomy, met with Candau once and described his appearance as "perfect." This opinion was immediately seconded by others who were acquanted with Candau, such as the film director Kumagai Hisatora and actress Hara Setsuko. Tazaki and his wife were members of a group of "Candau fans" who got together with the priest to discuss various matters twice a month, usually from seven p.m. till midnight. These regular meetings continued for two to three years in the early 1950s.[115] According to Horie Shigeo, the former president of the Bank of Tokyo, the attendees included businessmen, politicians, and intellectuals, among them deputy president of the Bank of Tokyo Ijūin Toraichi and his wife, journalist and chief director of the International House of Japan Matsumoto Shigeharu, mountainer and journalist Matsukata Saburō, industrialist and politician Asō Tagakichi (whose son Tarō would become the 92nd prime minister of Japan), medical doctor Tazaki Yūzō and his wife, trading company executive Ikebuchi Shōjirō and his wife, and Mr. and Mrs. Horie.

Horie wrote, "Rather than religious teaching, Fr. Candau talked more about human life, philosophy, and literature, and participants actively expressed their own opinions... Discussion topics were quite broad, ranging from historical themes such as Pascal's philosophy to contemporary topics such as Camus' literature. Fr. Candau's talks were humorous, and we learned an enormous amount from his teaching about human beings in general and about the ways people live. Every time we had lively discussions until late at night." Most of the couples consisted of enthusiastic Catholic wives and non-believer husbands. But later most of the husbands converted to Catholicism. Horie himself "unconditionally surrended."[116]

---

113 Nada, *Minzoku to iu na no shūkyō*, 185–86.

114 Tomizawa, "Onshi no omokage," 24.

115 Tazaki, "Wasure enu hito," 89.

116 Horie, "Ikebuchi san to Kandō shinpu no tsudoi," 131–33.

Sociologist Nagashima Kan'ichi said, "Fr. Candau loved the Japanese people, and has been loved by all the Japanese regardless of their religious beliefs. He captivated everyone who came into contact with him, without exception." Nagashima's father-in-law was touched by Candau's personality and decided to convert to Catholicism, disavowing a long family tradition. Nagashima wrote that Candau made his audience realize the importance of thinking and contemplation.[117]

7. Premature Death Lamented by Millions

On Sunday, 25 September 1955, Candau suffered from severe abdominal pain and swelling, but assuming it was just another of the attacks he put up with daily, he stayed home and endured the pain. On the 27th he was diagnosed with "acute swollen abdomen" and underwent surgery at Seibo Hospital. But it was too late to treat the "gastric torsion." He left this world at fifty minutes past midnight on the 29th.[118]

The news of his death spread instantly across the country and saddened hundreds of thousands of people. In the view of journalist Miyamoto Toshiyuki of the *Asahi shinbun* office, it was probably unprecedented that all newspapers, TV channels, and radio programs mourned for a foreigner's death.[119] At the *Asahi shinbun*, from novice reporters to the editor-in-chief, all were moved by Fr. Candau's "unshakeable faith, deep wisdom, and unexplainable tolerance that transcends race and religion." Miyamoto estimated that among the 7.5 million readers of the newspaper's column "Yesterday, Today," at least 10 percent were "Candau fans." He quoted many letters which were received but never published by the newspaper. The ordinary people who sent those letters read his articles, admired him, and lamented his death.[120] Tatsuno Yutaka, who had interviewed the priest-author about his composition techniques, wrote this when Candau died:

> Again we are given an opportunity to know how precious Candau has been to Japan. Not only Catholics, but also those outside the church

---

117 Nagashima, "Kandō-shi to 'toriko'," 92–93.
118 Ikeda, *Shōwa Nihon no onjin: S. Kandō-shi*, 261.
119 Miyamoto, "Kandō shinpu-sama no koto," 53.
120 Miyamoto, "Kyoju no kage ni: Kandō shinpu o mishiranu hitobito no koe," 95–98.

are thrown into desperation and sorrow. This shows us the wide influence Candau has had on Japan. After the war, he returned to Japan and intensively undertook cultural activities for newspapers, magazines, and radio programs. Now we see that he knew his days were limited.

Tatsuno further praised the excellent thought, steadfast faith, and affection for the Japanese people that distinguished Candau's essays and radio talks, no matter how short they were. His incomparably beautiful Japanese and first-class international personality always moved his readers and audience, and his penetrating criticism of modern Japan's lack of universal and lasting values will be sorely missed.[121]

Candau's nephew Jacques Candau (1920–1990) also became a Catholic missionary and served as the priest of Kawagoe Church from 1952 till 1954. He sorted out his uncle's correspondence and diaries, and translated the writing into Japanese,[122] enabling readers in Candau's second homeland to view the whole picture of his thought.

Tanaka Kōtarō wrote one year after Candau's death, "In Japanese society, which is forgetful, only Candau's work has transcended the temporary popularity of journalism to retain its status as a best-seller."[123] Today as I write, it has been sixty-five years since Candau's death, and it seems that his image has become dim in Japanese memory.

Chronology of S. Candau's Life[124]

Year	Age	Activities
1897	0	Born at Saint-Jean-Pied-de-Port, Basque, southern France.
1908	11	Graduated from elementary school, and entered the Minor Seminary at Larressore.
1914	17	Graduated from the Minor Seminary and studied at Major Seminary at Bayonne.

---

121 Tatsuno, "Basuku no hoshi," 1–2.

122 Archives des Missions Étrangères de Paris, http://archives.mepasie.org/fr/notices/notices-biographiques/candau-1/

123 Tanaka Kōtarō, *Gendai seikatsu no ronri*, 285.

124 Ikeda, *Shōwa Nihon no onjin: S. Kandō-shi.*

1916	19	Mobilized, attended École Spéciale Militaire de Saint-Cyr, and fought in the Battle of Verdun.
1917	20	Met Fr. Mateo, the "Apostle of the Sacred Heart," and was impressed by his talk. Later, decided to become a priest.
1918	21	August, joined the Flanders Offensive and took part in victorious battles. November, World War I ended. December, received an award from the commander.
1919	22	Joined the Paris Foreign Missions Society and studied at the Pontifical Gregorian University in Rome.
1923	26	22 December, ordained a priest.
1924	27	Graduated from the University, awarded doctoral degrees in theology and philosophy. Departed from Marseille.
1925	28	21 January, arrived at Yokohama Port. Started working for Shizuoka Catholic Church at Ōtemachi; learned Japanese from Murakoshi Kinzō.
1926	29	Headed the Sekiguchi Seminary in Tokyo.
1929	32	Headed the newly established Tokyo Major Seminary (named "National Seminary" in 1932). Became the chief editor of magazines *Koe* (Voice) and *Catholic*, and helped to edit the *Catholic Newspaper*.
1934	37	Published *Lexicon Latino-Japonicum* (*Rawa jiten*).
1936	39	Helped edit the magazine *Actio Missionaria*.
1939	42	Called up as first lieutenant of French Army upon outbreak of war.
1940	43	Seriously injured in northern France. June, France surrendered to Germany unconditionally.
1945	48	Recuperating in Rome, working at the Vatican. Visited members of the Embassy of Japan in Italy, who were under house arrest in Salsomaggiore, northern Italy. 15 August, Japan surrendered unconditionally.
1946	49	January, saw Japanese diplomats and priests off to return home, at Nàpoli.
1948	51	Decided to return to Japan via the United States. 11 September, arrived in Japan.
1949	52	Travelled to Hokkaidō, Tōhoku, Nagano, etc. and recorded the trips in his diary. Published two co-translated books, *Ai no tetsugaku: Kami no awase tamaishi mono* and *Kirisuto to sono jidai*.
1950	53	Became a contributor for the magazine *Kokoro*.
1952	55	Held monthly meetings with "Banseikai" (Society of Late Bloomers). Published *Shisō no tabi* and co-authored book *Supōtsu ningen gaku*.
1953	56	Published two translated works, *Kaimiroa* and *Seijin jigoku e iku*.
1954	57	Visited death-row prisoner Shōda Akira.
1955	58	June, baptized novelist Masugi Shizue. July, baptized Shōda. 29 September, died of acute duodenal ulcer. He was buried at the Catholic Fuchū Cemetery. His essay collections *Eien no kessaku* and *Sekai no ura omote* were published.
1956		His essay collection *Basuku no hoshi* was published.

CHAPTER
5
Hermann Heuvers' Poetic Evangelization

1. Enlightenment from A. Villion

Hermann Heuvers was born on 31 August 1890 in Dreierwalde village, Westfalen, in northern Germany. He joined the Society of Jesus when he was nineteen years old, and studied philosophy and theology at the Ignatius College in Valkenburg, Holland. He was ordained as a priest in 1920 and resolved to devote himself to missionary work in Japan. Before leaving for Japan, he studied the *Manyōshū* and noh chants at the University of Hamburg with Japanologist Prof. Karl Florenz (1865–1939). He arrived at Yokohama on 25 August 1923, eight days before the Great Kantō Earthquake took place on 1 September.

Heuvers lived in Japan for the rest of his life, for fifty-four years, during which he taught at Sophia University and became its second president (serving for three years). He also concentrated on his vocation as a priest, first at the St. Theresa Church in Kōjimachi and later at the St. Ignatius Church next to the university campus in Yotsuya. He is famous for his short sermons and his writings, which influenced many Japanese people. Legal scholar Morita Akira (b. 1943) analyzed the reason why people continued to cherish Heuvers long after his death: "... because we continue to share the emotion generated by his ordinary Japanese. He responded to people's general questions about the Gospels, giving answers that were concrete and detailed, and easy to understand."[1] It seems that "ordinary Japanese" (*futsū no Nihongo*) was the most effective medium for conveying his messages.

Heuvers' life as a missionary was immersed in the Japanese language and culture. He once reckoned that he baptized about three thousand people.[2] This means that he converted four to five people to Christianity per month, on average, for half a century. When he was teaching at Sophia University (established in 1913), students often asked him why he had come to Japan. He responded by quoting the answer Luís Fróis (1532–1597) gave to Oda Nobunaga, who asked the identical question. Quickly taking out a world atlas and showing Nobunaga the long route by sea from Portugal via the southern tip of Africa, Fróis had said, "Half of the missionaries who

Fig. 15, Photo of Hermann Heuvers, from Heuvers, *Vierzig Jahre in Japan, 1923–1963*, Tokyo: Die Japanisch-Deutsche Gesellschaft, 1965.

boarded the ships would vanish in the sea. Those who arrived in Japan would face hardship and difficulties with no worldly rewards. The only reason we came here is to deliver the true happiness to people's hearts from God."

Heuvers also quoted the famous sentence written by St. Francis Xavier: "Japan is the joy of my heart…" (*Hi izuru kuni wa, waga kokoro no tanoshimi*).[3] As discussed in Chapter 2, the Latin, English, French, and the first Japanese translations of this sentence all emphasized the "joy" Xavier experienced in Japan, while the original Portuguese expression did not have that nuance. But it seems that Heuvers liked the translations more than the original, which he may have felt better conveyed Xavier's sentiments.

Later Heuvers wrote a play entitled "St. Francis Xavier's Japan Visit" for publication in the magazine *Bōrō* (July and August, 1949), which made his admiration for Xavier abundantly clear. Heuvers is another missionary who closely followed Xavier's footsteps in Japan.

In October 1923, two months after his arrival in Japan, Heuvers went to

---

1 Doi and Morita, *Hoiverusu shinpu: Shinkō to shisō*, 5.

2 Bitter, "Shinpu no hito to shōgai," 20.

3 Heuvers, *Nihon de yonjūnen*, 146.

Okayama to teach German at the Sixth Higher School, and to teach French conversation to military officers at the Army Training Camp. His missionary talents were quickly recognized by Aimé Villion. In his essay "The Father Burning with Enthusiasm for Evangelization," Heuvers described the time he spent with Villion. After a short stay in Okayama, Heuvers was called back to Tokyo to teach at Sophia University. He was disappointed by the new assignment, as he had "wanted earnestly to learn many things about propagating Christian teaching in Japan from Fr. Villion." For his part, Villion was so angry at the decision by the Society of Jesus to transfer Heuvers that the young priest likened him to an erupting volcano.

During the following spring holidays, Heuvers went with friends to visit Villion. From the city of Yamaguchi, they crossed mountains and valleys, and eventually reached Hagi at night. Villion was extremely happy to see them, and joyfully talked about his fifty years in Japan, full of hardship and difficulties. Later Heuvers saw him several times at Sophia University. "Fr. Villion came and went like the wind. I usually saw him at the university chapel (Plate 22). He never leaned on the kneeler, but always knelt on the wooden floor, bowing low like an old Japanese woman and praying intently."

From Villion, Heuvers received one of the hooves of Villion's beloved horse that he had ridden on missionary trips when he was serving as pastor in Hagi. Villion had turned the hoof into an ink container (Fig. 16), and asked an artisan to carve a Latin phrase into the hoof and inlay the words with gold: "Quadrupedante putrem sonitu quatit ungula campum" (the horses' hooves with four-fold beat shake the crumbling plain),[4] from the Latin epic poem *Aeneid* written by the ancient Roman poet Publius Vergilius Maro. This special gift shows Villion's intention to pass on to Heuvers the determination he had brought to his own missionary work. Heuvers considered himself "the last student of Villion."[5]

After coming to Japan, Heuvers

Fig. 16, Ink container made from the hoof of Villion's beloved horse. Frontispiece of Yamazaki Tadao, *Idai naru Viriyon shinpu: Viriyon shinpu ni manebite*, 1965.

---

4 Ikeda, *Birion shinpu*, 555–57.

5 Heuvers, *Vierzig Jahre in Japan, 1923–1963*, 14–16.

poured great effort into learning Japanese. It was not easy at the beginning, but he progressed and before long was able to freely conduct daily conversation. Later, he could deliver orally to his Japanese friends what he intended to write down. According to psychiatrist Doi Takeo (1920–2009), Heuver's Japanese contained occasional grammatical imperfections and his use of Japanese vocabulary was unique. Those who knew him called it "Heu-go" (Heuvers' speech). His way of speaking had a subtle flavor because of his poetic sensitivity to language. Every word coming from his mouth had a fresh meaning...He tried to use very plain Japanese to express Christian doctrine.[6] It is this highly distinctive Japanese that Heuvers used to compose literary works that included dramas, poems, and essays.

Catholic artist Murada Kayoko (b. 1944) visited Heuvers at St. Ignatius Church in Tokyo when she was a high school pupil. She wanted to learn more from him about Hosokawa Gracia, a heroine of late sixteenth-century Japan. Heuvers answered her questions slowly, carefully selecting his words and pausing between sentences, conveying to her an impression of honesty. He tended to use more written expressions than colloquial, and often put "ne" at the end of sentences, which sounded more feminine. Murata told me that she often noticed this tendency in the spoken Japanese of male missionaries.[7]

Many Japanese intellectuals had contact with Heuvers. One was the playwright and novelist Inoue Hisashi (1934–2010), who had been baptized as a child in an orphanage and who once, while studying at Sophia University, asked for Heuvers' opinion regarding "the next world." Heuvers replied: "I do not know whether such a world exists. There are three possibilities a person can imagine while dying: a happy place to go, a desolate desert with a foul-smelling wind in which to wander forever, and a void or nothingness. Of course the first one is the best. Catholics spend all their lives imagining a happy world after this life, so that they can be certain, while dying, that they will go to a beautiful and joyful place."

Upon hearing Heuvers' reply, Shiba Ryōtarō was impressed and said to Inoue, "What a great man Fr. Heuvers is! In the Kamakura era Shinran adopted a similar stance. He never clearly indicated that people will definitely go to the Pure Land. He only said, as Heuvers did, that someone may

---

6 Togawa and Doi, *Hoiverusu shinpu no kotoba*, 63.

7 Interview with Mrs. Murata Kayoko at her home in Kamakura on 17 December 2017.

go." Inoue was surprised to hear that Heuvers did not know with certainty about the next world, hinting only what one might imagine while one is still living. To Inoue, it was a revelation that there was someone who had been contemplating death so seriously all his life.[8]

Psychoanalyst Doi Takeo, famed as the author of *Amae no kōzō* (1971, English translation: *The Anatomy of Dependence*, 1973), was another of Heuvers' students. He felt he learned much from his teacher's style of evangelization, because Heuvers always attempted to understand the characteristics of Japanese culture and the Japanese, and saw deep "religiosity" in everyday Japanese life, which was no different from the essence of Christianity. Doi learned from Heuvers to live as both a Japanese person and as a follower of Christianity, a universal religion essentially separate from Western culture. He developed the theory of *"amae"* by going beyond both Japanese-style and American-style psychoanalysis. He emphasized that although the sentiment of *amae* and its expression are specific to the Japanese, the desire to depend and presume upon another's love is universal.[9]

Curiously, another person who benefited from Heuvers' preaching was medical researcher Ishii Shirō, mastermind of the infamous Imperial Army Unit 731, which conducted human expriments in China during World War II. According to Ishii's daughter Harumi, he asked Heuvers to baptize him and took the Christian name Joseph shortly before he died. "It seems to me," Harumi declared, "that my father felt relieved somehow."[10] Although Ishii's baptism has not been confirmed by documentary evidence,[11] his desire to be baptized suggests that he felt guilty about his wartime atrocities and was searching for forgiveness.[12] It is very possible that Heuvers helped him to feel remorse for his past, and encouraged him to look forward to a new life in the next world.

---

8 Inoue and Shiba, "Shūkyō to Nihonjin," 267.

9 Ando, "Doi Takeo and the Development of the 'Amae' Theory," 137–49.

10 Williams and Wallace, *Unit 731: The Japanese Army's Secret of Secrets*, 279.

11 Aoki, *731*, 374.

12 Guo, "Discovering Traces of Humanity: Taking Individual Responsibility for Medical Atrocities," 114–15.

2. Graceful Essays and Poems

Heuvers published some twenty books in Japanese: most of them were collections of essays, two were book-length plays, and one a co-translation. They are listed below chronologically.

1) *Kami e no michi* (神への道, A Road to God), Shunjūsha, 1928.

2) Co-translation, *Kirisuto no shōgai* (キリストの生涯, The Life of Christ), Shibun Shoin, 1935; the original was Franz Michel Willam's *Leben Jesu im Lande und Volke Israel* (1933).

3) *Hosokawa Garashia fujin* (細川ガラシア夫人, Madame Hosokawa Gracia), Katorikku Chūō Shoin, 1939. 【play】

4) *Uguisu to shijin* (鶯と詩人, A Bush Warbler and a Poet), Enderure Shoten, 1948.

5) *Sanjō yori no mikoe: Seisho o yomite* (山上よりの御声：聖書を読みて, A Voice from the Mountain Top: Reading the Bible), trans. Togawa Keiichi, Enderure Shoten, 1950.

6) *Toki no nagare ni* (時間の流れに, Along the Flow of Time), Chūō Shuppansha, 1953.

7) *Kobune yori no koe: Kirisuto no tatoe* (こぶねよりの御声：キリストの喩, A Voice from a Small Boat: Parables Used by Christ), Chūō Shuppansha, 1956.

8) *Kirisuto no kotoba* (キリストのことば, Christ's Teaching), Shunjūsha, 1963.

9) *Nihon de yonjūnen* (日本で四十年, Forty Years in Japan), ed. trans. Hayashi Mikio, Shunjūsha, 1964.

10) *Waga furusato* (わがふるさと, My Hometown), Chūō Shuppansha, 1968.

11) *Jinsei no aki ni: Heruman Hoiverusu zuisōshū* (人生の秋に：ヘルマン・ホイヴェルス随想集, In the Autumn of Life: Collection of Hermann Heuvers' Thoughts, Shunjūsha, 1969.

12) *Jinsei sanka: 12 no seika ni yoru kami e no michi* (人生讃歌：12の聖歌による神への道, Hymns in Praise of Life: A Road to God by Way of 12 Psalms), Shunjūsha, 1971.

13) *Gikyoku senshū* (戯曲選集, Selected Plays), Chūō Shuppansha, 1973. 【plays】

14) *Hoiverusu shinpu sekkyōshū* (ホイヴェルス神父説教集, Selection of Fr. Heuvers' Sermons), Chūō Shuppansha, 1973.

15) *Watashi no sukina kotoba: Shisōka to shijin no kotoba* (私の好きな言葉：思想家と詩人の言葉, My Favorite Words by Thinkers and Poets), trans. Doi Takeo, Enderure Shoten, 1974.

16) *Shi to sono deshi: Timoteo sho kaisetsu* (師とその弟子：ティモテオ書解説, The Teacher and His Disciples: Interpretation of the Epistles to Timothy), Chūō Shuppansha, 1975.

17) *Toki no magarikado* (時の曲り角, A Turning Point of the Times), trans. Doi Takeo, Chūō Shuppansha, 1976.

18) *Hoiverusu shinpu no kotoba: Kirisutokyō to Nihon no hitotsu no deai* (ホイヴェルス神父のことば：キリスト教と日本の一つの出会い, Fr. Heuvers' Teaching: An Encounter between Christianity and Japan), Kōbundō, 1986.

18) *Hoiverusu shinpu: Nihonjin e no okurimono* (ホイヴェルス神父：日本人への贈り物, Fr. Heuvers' Gifts to the Japanese People), Shunjūsha, 1996.

19) *Hoiverusu shinpu: Shinkō to shisō* (ホイヴェルス神父：信仰と思想, Fr. Heuvers' Faith and Thought), ed. Doi Takeo and Morita Akira, Nagasaki: Seibo no Kishi Sha, 2003.

20) *Kokoro dake wa eien: Heruman Hoiverusu shinpu no kotoba* (心だけは永遠：ヘルマン・ホイヴェルス神父の言葉, Only the Heart Is Eternal: Fr. Hermann Heuvers' Words), ed. Doi Takeo and Morita Akira, Don Bosuko Sha, 2009)

Among the above, four books were penned in German by Heuvers and translated into Japanese by his students. They are (using the English translation of their titles): *A Voice from the Mountain Top*, *Forty Years in Japan*, *My Favorite Words of Thinkers and Poets*, and *A Turning Point of the Times*.

Heuvers wrote many fine essays. One of them, "Musashino no hibari" (The Larks of Musashino), is particularly interesting. To convey a sense of the high quality of this short piece, let me quote several paragraphs.

Each March I like to go to Musashino, strolling through the fields of tall wheat stalks. I do this to listen to the singing of the larks. Fortunately, the larks of Musashino and those of my hometown sing the same melody. They fly high from the wheat fields and sing beautifully and restlessly, "tirilirili, tirilirili…" as they fly upward infinitely. They become small dots and then disappear from the blue sky. But their song is like dew, dropping down to me... In ancient Latin, there are these lines describing larks.

Laudat alauda Deum, dum sese tollit in altum,
dum cadit in terram, laudat alauda Deum.
(The lark praises God while flying high; when descending to the earth, it still praises God.)[13]

毎年三月はじめごろ、わたしは武蔵野に出かけ、伸び育つ麦畑のあいだを通って歩きます。それは、ひばりの声を聞くためです。うれしいことに、武蔵野のひばりも、わたしの故郷のひばりそっくりな歌をうたいます。麦畑のなかから舞い上がり、tirilirili と玉を転がすように歌っています。絶え間なく、休みなく、どこまでも高く昇りながら。そして、その姿は青空のなかの一点となって、やがて見えなくなってしまいますが、さえずり声だけは、露の玉のように空から下のほうへなおも垂れてきます。……
　　古いラテン語の格言は、ひばりに関するすべてを簡潔に表しています。
Laudat alauda Deum, dum sese tollit in altum,
dum cadit in terram, laudat alauda Deum.
（ひばりは神をほめたたえる、高く高くのぼりながら、地面に向けて低く低くおちながらも、ひばりは神をほめたたえる。）

Heuvers observed larks closely and discovered a religious meaning in their flying and chirping. He was also interested in how larks were described in Japanese literature, and was touched by a *waka* poem written by the Meiji Emperor, Mutsuhito (1852–1912): *Tsugitsugi ni / noboru o mireba / kumo no ue ni / irishi hibari ya / tomo o yoburamu* つぎつぎにのぼるを見れば雲の上に入りし雲雀や友を呼ぶらむ Watching the larks enter the clouds, one after another, as if inviting their friends. Heuvers interpreted this poem to mean "Humans all have to go through the clouds of death. There is something frightening about death, but it should not be feared. In the sky above us, there is nothing but bright light. Everyone must be prepared to reach the beautiful and transparent world, which is well symbolized by the Emperor's *waka*."[14] He quoted the Latin poem and the Japanese *waka* to show that

---

13 Heuvers, *Jinsei no aki ni: Heruman Hoiverusu zuisōshū*, 33–35.

14 *Koe*, "Meiji tennō no gyosei o kinyaku suru Hoiverusu Jōchi Daigaku gakuchō," back cover.

people in both West and East long for a beautiful world after death.

Heuvers' essay collection *Jinsei no aki ni: Heruman Hoiverusu zuisōshū* (In the Autumn of Life: Collection of Hermann Heuvers' Thoughts) has become famous recently because a poem "Saijō no waza" (The Greatest Task) that appears in this collection was frequently quoted in the 2012 film *Tsunagu* (To Connect). An adaptation of the novel with the same title by Tsujimura Mitsuki (b. 1980), winner of the 32nd Yoshikawa Eiji Literary New Writers Prize in 2011, the movie recounts several episodes of how a medium brings a dead person to life for just one night to meet his/her family member or friend to talk about the matters that concern them most after death. The lines of the poem are spoken by the grandmother, played by actress Kiki Kirin (1943–2018).

Tsujimura's novel does not have anything Christian about it, except the idea of reviving the dead for one night. However, the film is different. The poem "The Greatest Task" is repeatedly recited by the main characters, especially the grandmother, who intends to humbly pass her role of "tsunagu" to her grandson, played by Matsuzaka Tōri (b. 1988), and to retire quietly.

This poem was originally written in German. It was given to Heuvers by a friend in southern Germany when he returned home on a furlough. He translated it into Japanese and included it in his essay "Toshi o toru sube" (The Way of Aging). Below is Heuvers' Japanese version, along with an English translation by his nephew Konrad Heuvers (Konrad translated it from the German, not the Japanese), titled "Life's Greatest Task."

What is this life's most important task?
To grow old with a cheerful heart,
To be still even when I would like to be active,
To be silent when I would like to talk,
To have hope in times of frustration,
To carry my cross in humility and serenity of heart,

To put aside envy even when I see younger people walking God's path full of health and energy,
To humbly accept help from others when I would rather work for the sake of others,

So when I can no longer be useful for others because of frailty, I need
   to gently and humbly accept the heavy burden of old age as a gift
   from God.
I have an aged heart that has been in use a long time and now God is
   giving it a final polishing so that I can return to my true home all
   shining.
To gradually release myself from the chains that bind me to this world
   is indeed a wonderful work.
When I cannot do things let me humbly accept these circumstances in
   humility.

However, for my closing years God has kept for me the most important work of all, and that is: prayer.
Even if I can no longer do anything else with my hands, right to the
   very end I can join those hands in prayer.
I can pray, asking for God's blessings upon all those I love.

And when I come towards my end, approaching death may I hear
   God's voice when He says to me;
"Come! You are my friend! I will never desert you." [15]

最上のわざ

この世の最上のわざは何？
楽しい心で年をとり、
働きたいけれども休み、
しゃべりたいけれども黙り、
失望しそうなときに希望し、
従順に、平静に、おのれの十字架をになう。

若者が元気いっぱいで神の道を歩むのを見ても、ねたまず、
人のために働くよりも、
謙虚に人の世話になり、
弱って、もはや人のために役だたずとも、

---

15 Barillas, "A Prayer for the Autumn Years of Life," 2011. 7. 3, *https://www.speroforum.com/a/56477/A-Prayer-for-the-Autumn-Years-of-Life*

親切で柔和であること。

老いの重荷は神の賜物、
古びた心に、これで最後のみがきをかける。
まことのふるさとへ行くために。
おのれをこの世につなぐくさりを少しずつはずしていくのは、
真にえらい仕事。
こうして何もできなくなれば、
それを謙遜に承諾するのだ。

神は最後にいちばんよい仕事を残してくださる。
それは祈りだ。
手は何もできない。
けれども最後まで合掌できる。
愛するすべての人のうえに、神の恵みを求めるために。

すべてをなし終えたら、
臨終の床に神の声をきくだろう。
「来よ、わが友よ、われなんじを見捨てじ」と。[16]

The poem's linguistic symbolism and poetic meaning have been discussed by Taniguchi Sachiyo in her article on Heuvers' writing.[17] This verse shows a state of mind that accepts aging and death calmly before heading quietly to God's arms. This is probably a state all people would like to reach, no matter whether they possess Christian faith or not. Ōhira Ken, a neurologist at St. Luke's International Hospital in Tokyo, placed a copy of this poem under the sheet of glass on his office desk after reading it. "I am not a Catholic," he said, "but I felt so comforted by the final moment described by Fr. Heuvers."[18] By introducing this German poem into Japanese, Heuvers brought the universality of Christianity into Japanese culture, and his verses echo among people whose anxiety about death is soothed.

Kiki Kirin was extremely fond of this poem, and often quoted it in her

---

16 Heuvers, *Jinsei no aki ni: Heruman Hoiverusu zuisōshū*, 308–309.

17 Taniguchi, "Nihongo no kakite to shite no Hoiverusu: 'Saijō no waza' o chūshin ni," 239–52.

18 Ōhira, "'Saijō no waza' ni tsuite," i–iii.

public talks. A collection of her essays published posthumously in September 2019 takes its title from one of its lines ("Oi no omoni wa kami no tamamono" 老いの重荷は神の賜物, The Heavy Burden of Old Age is a Gift from God), and the entire poem was placed at the beginning of the book. Since her death in 2018, all of Kiki's books have become bestsellers. A common feature of her writing is her longing for a "modest" attitude toward aging and a "calm" welcome of the end, as expressed in the poem. Thanks in no small measure to Kiki's popularity, Heuvers has once again become widely known in Japan.

Before his own death, Heuvers prayed, "Jesus, Jesus, please come to me."[19] He quipped to visitors, "I am just practicing for death."[20] His good humor was a product of his composure in the face of mortality.

3. Veneration of Hosokawa Gracia

Heuvers was deeply interested in the life of Hosokawa Tama Gracia (1563–1600), wife of Hosokawa Tadaoki, a daimyō of the Warring States period, and wrote a script about her life. As Shinmura Izuru pointed out, no other Kirishitan women has won as much praise from the missionaries as Madame Hosokawa. Shinmura thought that her conversion to Christianity was prompted by missionaries' respect for "women's status and feelings."[21]

Missionary writings about her courage and beauty are introduced in Chapter 3 of this book. A thorough discussion of Tama Gracia's life, based on primary sources of the Jesuits' correspondence and reports, can be found in Haruko Nawata Ward's *Women Religious Leaders in Japan's Christian Century, 1549–1650*, published in 2009.[22]

Tama was born in 1563 as the third daughter of Akechi Mitsuhide (?–1582), who was one of the most trusted generals in Oda Nobunaga's military force. When she was fifteen years old, Nobunaga arranged for her to marry Hosokawa Tadaoki (1563–1645), the son of Hosokawa Fujitaka (*also* Yūsai, 1534–1610), famous for his military role and expertise in

---

19 Togawa and Doi, *Hoiverusu shinpu no kotoba*, 21.

20 Doi and Morita, *Hoiverusu shinpu: Shinkō to shisō*, 217.

21 Shinmura, "Kirishitan josei no hanashi," 323; Gössmann, "Garasha Hosokawa Tama no jitsuzō to kyozō," 132.

22 Ward, *Women Religious Leaders in Japan's Christian Century, 1549–1650*, 199–292.

waka poetry. Their marriage took place in 1578. Four years later, in 1582, Tama's father Mitsuhide revolted. His troops surrounded his lord Nobunaga while he was sleeping at Honnōji temple in Kyoto. Taken by surprise, Nobunaga fought hard, but eventually committed *seppuku* knowing there was no chance to win the battle. Mitsuhide asserted governing power, but his rule only lasted eleven days before he was killed by an alliance of Nobunaga loyalists led by Toyotomi Hideyoshi.

Hideyoshi ordered that the Akechi family be eradicated, but spared Tama's life, as her husband Tadaoki had not taken part in Mitsuhide's rebellion, but rather sided with Hideyoshi. Tama was taken to Midono, deep in the Tango mountains, about 100 kilometers north of Kyoto, and confined there for two years. Later, she was pardoned by Hideyoshi and returned to Osaka to be reunited with her husband.

Tama learned about Christianity through Takayama Ukon (1552–1615), a Kirishitan daimyō. As her husband banned her from going outside of their residence, she visited a nearby Catholic church only once in her life in 1587, at a time when Tadaoki was away fighting the Satsuma domain in Kyushu. Several months later, when she was twenty-four years old, she was baptized by her Kirishitan lady-in-waiting Kiyohara Ito Maria. Her Christian name became Gracia.

Gracia attracted much attention from the missionaries. Luís Fróis wrote that she "had extraodinary sensitive talents and knowledge." She "had many concerns and endless questions," and her soul "fell into deep doubt and darkness," even after studying Zen Buddhism with great effort. When she visited the church, she listened to Brother Takai Cosme's teaching and argued about the immortality of the soul, drawing on her knowledge of Zen. Cosme professed, "During the last eighteen years, I have never met a Japanese woman of such a clear mind and strong determination." She joined her hands to ask for Christian baptism. However, because of her "beautiful dress and elegant appearance," Fr. Gregorio de Céspedes and Cosme suspected her of being one of Hideyoshi's mistresses and did not baptize her.

Gracia borrowed catechism books from the church and studied at home. She sent questions about Christian doctrine to the church and received answers through her ladies-in-waiting, seventeen of whom were baptized. She also sent gifts to young students and priests of the seminary in Osaka, and gave rice to poor people in her neighborhood. After hearing of Hideyoshi's proscription policy, she said that if Hideyoshi intended to kill the priests, "I would like to be a martyr first, with other Kirishitan women." After she was baptized, Gracia's personality changed dramatically, and she became a happy, patient, humble, and gentle person.[23]

In his letter dated 3 March 1588 from Shōdoshima where he was in exile, Gnecchi-Soldo Organtino (1533–1609) wrote about her "extraordinary enthusiasm," her suffering from Tadaoki's violence, and her help to her lady-in-waiting Luisa to avoid Tadaoki's lust. He also mentioned that "everyone is ready to die for Christ's love" in the Goki region (part of present-day Kyoto, Nara, Osaka, and Hyōgo prefectures), where there was strong opposition to Hideyoshi's prohibition of Christianity.[24] In a letter of 6 May, Organtino also reported that he persuaded Gracia to give up her intention to divorce her violent husband.[25]

In 1600, thirteen years after her baptism, the famous Battle of Sekigahara took place between the Eastern army, led by Tokugawa Ieyasu (1542–1616), and the Western army, led by Ishida Mitsunari (1560–1600) who was loyal to Hideyoshi's heir. Hosokawa Tadaoki sided with Ieyasu. Before he left home to join the Tokugawa forces, Takaoki ordered his retainer Ogasawara Shōsai to kill Gracia in the event that Ishida's forces threatened to take her hostage. Therefore when Ishida's soldiers arrived, she was killed, as Tadaoki ordered. Ishida was eventually defeated and Tokugawa established governance over the entire country. Gracia's final moments were witnessed by her lady-in-waiting Shimo, who informed Fr. Organtino who then reported her death to Europe.

Gracia's life stimulated much interest and imagination in Europe. She was featured in a Jesuit musical drama *Mulier fortis: Gracia* (A Strong Lady: Gracia), performed in Vienna in 1698 for the purpose of educating girls of the House of Habsburg. In the drama, unlike the historical facts, as punishment for her baptism Gracia was tortured to death by her husband, who later regretted what he had done, felt guilty, and eventually became

---

23 Fróis and Matsuda, *Nihonshi 5 Gokinai hen III*, 219–41.

24 Fróis and Matsuda, *Nihonshi 2 Toyotomi Hideyoshi hen II*, 18–22.

25 Fróis and Matsuda, *Nihonshi 5 Gokinai hen III*, 246–48.

Fig. 17, Gracia's image in Theophilus Nelk's book *Gratia, Reine de Tango* (Paris: Chez Gaume Frères, Libraires, 4th edition, 1836; courtesy of the Twenty-Six Martyrs Museum in Nagasaki, Japan)

a messenger of the Christian faith.[26] Later, this German drama inspired a French moral story by Theophilus Nelk of the Franciscans (OFM), *Gratia, Reine de Tango*, first published in 1834 (Fig. 17).

Three centuries later, this drama was performed in 2013 to celebrate the 100th anniversary of the establishment of Sophia University. It was staged again in 2014 in the city of Nagaokakyō, Kyoto prefecture, where Tama and Tadaoki were married in 1578; their wedding was held in Shōryūji Castle, which belonged to Tadaoki's father Hosokawa Yūsai. Since 1992, Nagaokakyō has been organizing an annual "Gracia Festival" that features a reenactment of Tama's wedding palanquin scene in a parade.

In the story of Gracia's abandonment of belief in Buddhist transmigration and transience and her discovery of the meaning of life in Christianity, Heuvers probably saw possibilities for evangelizing Japan. To him, Gracia was "strictly guided by the divine Providence, and was able to break through

---

26 The play script was translated into English by Ann Louise Cole, "Becoming All Things to All Men: The Role of Jesuit Missions in Early Modern Globalization" (PhD dissertation, University of Arkansas, 2015), and into Japanese by Niiyama Karitsuki, *Kijō na kifujin: Hosokawa Garasha*. Also see Yoneda, "Hosokawa Garasha to Iezusukai no Ongakugeki," 91–98; An, *Hosokawa Garasha: Kirishitan shiryō kara mita shōgai*, 190–94; Niiyama Karitsuki, "Yōroppa ni okeru Nihon junkyōsha geki: Hosokawa Garasha ni tsuite no Ongakugeki Uīn Iezusukai dorama," 284–94; Takao, " 'In what storms of blood from Christ's flock is Japan swimming?': Gracia Hosokawa and the Performative Representation of Japanese Martyrdom in *Mulier fortis* (1698)," 87–120.

the balance of the silent cosmos with the fire of the Holy Spirit, and eventually managed to reach the harmony created by God's sacred heart."[27] The so-called "silent cosmos" (or a peaceful state of mind) means, according to Zen Buddhism, a world which denies the existence of life, death, virtue, and evil. There is no creator, nor human spirit, but only "nothingness."[28]

Based on Villion's book *Yamato hijiri chishio no kakioki* (Japanese Martyrs' Testament in Blood), Heuvers wrote the screenplay for the film *Junkyō ketsushi Nihon nijūroku seijin* (A History of Martyrs: Japan's Twenty-six Martyrs, 1931). Gracia appeared twice in the movie.[29] In 1936, Heuvers wrote a play titled *Hosokawa Garashia fujin*, and it was performed that same year in Tokyo and Berlin. His script was published in a book format in 1939.[30] An opera based on the play was composed by Italian missionary Vincenzo Cimatti (1879–1965) of the Salesians of Don Bosco (SDB, or Salesian Society) in 1940, and re-composed in 1960.[31] The opera was performed numerous times in 1940, 1942, 1960, 1965, 1966, 1967, 1989, 2004, and 2016 in Tokyo, Osaka, Sendai, and Kumamoto.[32]

Regarding his motivation for writing, Heuvers said that he wanted to inform the world of this Japanese woman who embodied "the great virtue of bushidō," a spirit of self-sacrifice, courage, and earnestness. He also highlighted her enthusiasm for learning, her acquiring of the Latin and Portuguese languages, her aid to the poor, the sick, and children, and her "pure, deep, and kind heart toward others."[33] When the opera was performed in 1940, Heuvers hoped it would be "the first step for Gracia to appear in world literature."[34]

This hope was materialized in 1952, when a Japanese film based on his play was produced. Entitled *Ransei no yuri* (A Lily amid Turbulence), the film was intended mainly for an overseas audience. Mitarai Hikoroku wrote the screenplay, Ōiwa Daisuke directed, and Maria Mitarai acted the part

---

27 Heuvers, *Nihon de yonjūnen*, 42.
28 Fróis/Furoisu, *Historia de Japam*, II. Chp. 106; *Nihonshi 5*, 219.
29 Ibid., 43; Kurata and Rin, *Kindai Nihon geinō nenpyō*, vol. 1, 401.
30 Heuvers, *Hosokawa Garashia fujin*.
31 Bitter/Bittā, "Shinpu no hito to shōgai," 13.
32 Sekine, *Nihon opera shi*, 267, 570–73; Compri, "Opera 'Hosokawa Garashia' konshū jōen." A DVD format of the 2016 performance was produced in 2017 (Fig. 42).
33 Heuvers, *Hosokawa Garashia fujin*, 14.
34 Heuvers, *Nihon de yonjūnen*, 185.

of Gracia. The film immediately received purchase orders from European countries.[35] The same movie was released in the domestic market in 1955 under a new title, *Sengoku hibun* (A Hidden Story of the Civil War Era).

In January 1965, a kabuki drama based on Heuvers' script was performed with Kon Hidemi as its director and Nakamura Utaemon IV playing the role of Gracia (Fig. 18 and Fig. 19).[36] Fourteen years later, in June 1979, Nakamura performed it again as "the last kabuki drama at the Enbujō theatre," which was to be demolished soon after.[37] In fact, when the play was first staged in 1936, Heuvers already hoped that it would one day be performed as a kabuki drama, because "I wanted to inform the world of the hearts and characteristics of the Japanese people." He is recorded as saying that by transforming it into a kabuki drama, "I hope to add fresh color to kabuki."[38] These words are testimony to his cultivated interest in kabuki and more generally to his commitment to contributing to Japan's performing arts.

According to Heuvers, the primary objective of his play is to show the totality of Gracia's life, not only her "brave death." He thought that focusing on her death would give rise to a fixed unidimensional image of Gracia, which would be a "wrong interpretation."[39] His play portrayed Gracia as "a fine Japanese woman, a figure to be proud of in the history of world literature," because she "eventually received happiness and grace from God, after having faced death several times during eighteen years of intense civil conflict, from the age of twenty." By becoming a Kirishitan, she found "the meaning of her life" for the first time.[40] The real meaning of her life is that

---

35 "Garasha fujin no shōgai, Ho shinpu no gensaku, rokugatsu kansei, Rōma Hōō e" ガラシャ夫人の生涯、ホ神父の原作、六月完成、ローマ法王へ, *Yomiuri shinbun*, 1952.2.12, morning issue; "Shijitsu no shōryaku ni muri 'Ransei no yuri'" 史実の省略に無理『乱世の百合』, *Yomiuri shinbun*, 1952.11. 5, evening issue.

36 "Enmoku no sentei ni nan ga 'Hosokawa Garasha fujin' mo shūkyō emaki ni owaru" 演目の選定に難が『細川ガラシャ夫人』も宗教絵巻に終わる, *Yomiuri shinbun*, 1965.11.16, evening issue.

37 "Kōkoku, nagori kōen, rokugatsu meisaku kabuki" 広告・名残り公演、六月名作歌舞伎, *Yomiuri shinbun*, 1979.5.22, evening issue.

38 "Gekisakukai ibun Doitsujin no kakioroshi, gikyoku 'Garasha Hosokawa'" 劇作界異聞　独逸人の書卸し、戯曲ガラシャ細川, *Asahi shinbun*, 1935.12.20, morning issue; Leiter, *Kabuki at the Crossroads: Years of Crisis 1952–1965*, 709–10.

39 Heuvers, *Nihon de yonjūnen*, 185.

40 Heuvers, *Jinsei no aki ni: Heruman Hoiverusu zuisōshū*, 100–101.

Fig. 18, Gracia performed by Naka-mura Utaemon VI, from Heuvers, *Vierzig Jahre in Japan, 1923–1963* (Tokyo: Die Japanisch-Deutsche Gesellschaft, 1965).

Fig. 19, Nakamura Utaemon VI and Heuvers backstage at the theatre in Tokyo, from Heuvers, *Vierzig Jahre in Japan, 1923–1963.*

she overcame the sufferings of this world and an unreasonable death in her quest for eternal life, the ultimate goal in Christianity.

In order to understand the heroine's existence during her confinement in the deep mountainous area, Heuvers followed the description by novelist Morita Sōhei (1881–1949)[41] and paid a visit to "Midono" (Noma village, Yosano county, Kyoto prefecture). There, at the bottom of a valley between two mountains, Heuvers sensed the enormous desperation Tama must have felt.[42]

Heuvers also probed historical documents, including them as appendices in his book *Hosokawa Garashia fujin*. Among them are excerpts of the historical record of the Hosokawa family, *Menkōshūroku 9 and 12* (compiled in 1778), a memoir by Shimo who witnessed Gracia's death ("Shimojo oboegaki," dated 1648), and letters written over fourteen years by Jesuit missionaries Antonio Prenestino (1587), Luís Fróis (1588, 1592, 1595, 1596, 1597), Gnecchi-Soldo Organtino (1589, 1595), Valentim Carvalho (1601), and Francisco Pasio (1601), as well as the Jesuit Annual Report on Japan, edited in Nagasaki and sent to Rome in 1600 and 1601.

41 Morita Sōhei 森田草平, "Omoi tsuku mama ni (3) Tango no Miyazu" 思いつくまゝに（3）丹後の宮津, *Yomiuri shinbun*, 1935.5.23.

42 Heuvers, *Hosokawa Garashia fujin*, 2–14.

These letters provided Heuvers with important knowledge about Gracia. For instance, Prenestino emphasized her psychological transformation because of her new faith. Her previous "depressed mood" became "a cheerful atmosphere," her "anger" became "patience," and her "stubborn and bitter temper" became "gentle and calm."[43]

In his letter dated 20 February 1588, Fróis quoted the letter Gracia wrote to the priest Céspedes whom she met during her only visit to the church: "Dear Father, as you know, I wanted to become a Kirishitan, not because of other people's persuasion, but because the almighty God's grace made me seek baptism. Even if the sky falls to the ground, trees and grasses all die out, my faith in God will never change."[44] These records made it possible for Heuvers to focus on the process of Gracia's spiritual development.

4. Interpretations of Gracia's Death

In 1873 the Japanese government finally revoked its prohibition of Christianity, and historical facts about Kirishitan were gradually made public. Jean Crasset's book on the history of the church in Japan, *Histoire de l'eglise du Japon* (1689), was translated into Japanese in 1880 by a Japanese government agency. It introduced Gracia's visit to the church, her longing for baptism, and her correspondence with the Jesuit missionaries via her ladies-in-waiting.[45]

Gracia's death inspired different interpretations: manslaughter, suicide, or martyrdom. Léon Pagés' book on Japan's Christian history, *Histoire de la religion chrétienne au Japon depuis 1598 jusqu'à 1651* (published in 1869), was translated into Japanese in 1938–1940. Pagés took her death as manslaughter perpetrated in accordance with samurai ideology, which was simply wrong. He narrated how she evacuated her children and ladies-in-waiting and then "knelt down and positioned her neck in front of the sword. Then the retainers went to the next room, set fire to the castle, and

---

43 Heuvers, Appendix to *Hosokawa Garashia fujin*, 6–14.

44 Ibid., 14–26. This letter was included in the Jesuit Annual Report on Japan in 1587, a Portuguese translation of Gracia's original letter. Heuvers translated the Portuguese back to Japanese for the Appendix. The English translation is from Charles R. Boxer, "Hosokawa Tadaoki and the Jesuits, 1587–1646," 89.

45 Crasset and Daijōkan Honyaku Kakari, *Nihon Seikyō shi*, 1104–16.

committed *seppuku*. All turned to ashes in the fire."[46] A similar story was recounted in *Kirishitan daimyō shi* (1929), Villion's Japanese translation of Michael Steichen's *The Christian Daimyos* (1903).[47] Heuvers also said, "The truth is that she was killed by the chief retainer Ogasawara who carried out her husband's order."[48]

For most of the twentieth century, Tokutomi Sohō (I'ichirō)'s (1863–1957) *Kinsei Nihon kokumin shi* (A History of the Japanese People in the Early Modern Period; 100 volumes, published from 1918 to 1962) had a strong influence on Japanese people's understanding of their history. After examining many documents written by missionaries, Tokutomi concluded that Gracia's death was not suicide, and there was no reason for her to kill her children.[49]

This opinion went counter to the widespread story about her suicide. Popular literature published in the Meiji period (1868–1912) portrayed Gracia as a pious and brave follower of Confucian ethics. She was believed to have committed suicide after killing her two children in order to comply with her husband's request, thereby contributing to the eventual victory of his side at the Battle of Sekigahara. This theory was presented in books like *Nihon retsujo den* (Biographies of Japanese Brave Women, 1878),[50] *Daitō retsujo den* (Biographies of Brave Women in the Greater East, 1884),[51] *Fujo kagami* (Models for Women, 1887),[52] *Chūgaku kanbun* (Chinese Classics for Middle Schools, 1894),[53] *Shūshin no maki* (On Moral Teaching, 1905),[54] and *Sekai Nihon shin otogi jusshu* (Ten New Tales of the World and Japan, 1909).[55]

Gracia's death was beautified as a factor that brought victory to her hus-

---

46 Pagés and Yoshida, *Nihon Kirishitan shūmonshi*, vol. 1, 46.

47 Steichen and Villion, *Kirishitan daimyō shi*, 229–30.

48 "Doitsujin shinpu ga kabukigeki 'Hosokawa Garasha fujin' rikisaku, chikaku butai ni" ドイツ人神父がカブキ劇『細川ガラシャ夫人』力作、近く舞台に, *Asahi shinbun*, 1965.10.26, evening issue.

49 Tokutomi, *Kinsei Nihon kokuminshi, Toyotomi-shi jidai Hei hen*, 439–44; *Kinsei Nihon kokuminshi, Ieyasu jidai Jōkan Sekigahara no eki*, 236–37.

50 Kojima, *Nihon retsujo den*, 26–28.

51 Hayashi, *Daitō retsujo den*, 20–21.

52 Nishimura, *Fujo kagami*, 7–8.

53 Iida, "Hosokawa Tadaoki fujin," pp. 20–21.

54 Yūbunkan Henshūbu, *Shūshin no maki*, 33–35.

55 Kōtō Otogi Kai, *Sekai Nihon shin otogi jusshu*, 122–28.

band's faction. Essays written by Christian pastor Ii Matsuzō relate that her death saved other daimyō family members from being taken hostage, thus providing an advantage to the Tokugawa forces.[56] Tatsui Matsunosuke, a scholar of Japanese cultural history, praised Gracia's refusal to be taken captive by Ishida Mitsunari as an act that affected the outcome of the Battle of Sekigahara.[57]

The "suicide" interpretation of Gracia's story was adopted in famous scripts and performances as well, such as Kawatake Mokuami's kabuki drama "Hosokawa Tadaoki no tsuma" (Hoskawa Tadaoki's Wife, 1903)[58] and Fujisawa Kosetsu's script "Garashia, Shigeki" (Gracia: A Historical Drama, 1907).[59] Tsuchiya Motosaku's noh play "Garashiya" (1931) also focused on the suicide aspect.[60]

Shinmura Izuru thought that Gracia died for the sake of two ideals, "the family tradition and the Christian faith."[61] Her psychological struggle as whether to follow Christian faith (which condemns suicide) or to die as a samurai wife was portrayed in several dramas, among them Fujii Hakumin's play *Hosokawa Garashia*,[62] performed in June 1922 at the Yūrakuza Theatre,[63] and Okamoto Kidō's *Hosokawa Tadaoki no tsuma* (The Wife of Hosokawa Tadaoki) performed at the Empire Theatre in 1926.[64] The textbook *Kokushi kyōju ni hitsuyō naru Nihon joseishi* (History of Japanese Women for Teaching National History, 1931) also discussed whether her death should be viewed as suicide or as manslaughter.[65]

Martyrdom is another category of interpretation for Gracia's death. In Luis de Guzman's book on Jesuit missions in India, China, and Japan, *Historia de las missiones que han hecho los religiosos de la Compañia de*

---

56 Ii, "Garashiya fujin o omou," 13.

57 Tatsui, *Nihon meifu den*, 293–307.

58 Nadehara, "The Emergence of a New Woman: The History of the Transformation of Gracia," 107–19.

59 Fujisawa, *Garashia: Shigeki*.

60 Tsuchiya, "Garashiya," 788–91.

61 Shinmura, "Kirishitan josei no hanashi," 323.

62 Fujii, *Hosokawa Garashiya*.

63 Osanai, "'Hosokawa Garashiya' o mite," 62–63; Okada, "Yūrakuza no 'Hosokawa Garashiya'," 64–65.

64 Okamoto, "Hosokawa Tadaoki no tsuma," 361–98.

65 Isogo Jinjō Kōtō Shōgakkō, *Kokushi kyōju ni hitsuyō naru Nihon joseishi*, 63–65.

Iesus (1601), Gracia was depicted as opposing Hideyoshi's policy of prohibiting Christianity and was said to have "prepared clothes for crucifixion at any time." She said that if a notice came in the middle of the night, she would be the first to rush out barefoot. "I am ready to die for my holy faith. But I might be frightened like an ordinary woman when seeing a sword pulled out. So, if the time comes, please take me to the executors and ask them to kill me along with other believers."[66]

Tabata Yasuko's biography *Hosokawa Garasha* (2010) claims that Gracia avoided suicide by making the retainer thrust a spear into her chest, so that she could fulfill her obligation to the Hosokawa family on the one hand and become a martyr on the other.[67] In her research monograph *Hosokawa Garasha* (2014), An Jon'on regards Gracia's death as martyrdom because she was ready to die several years earlier with persecuted priests.[68] This opinion is similar to Villion's in *Yamato hijiri chishio no kakioki* (Japanese Martyrs' Testament in Blood). Haruko Nawata Ward concludes that Gracia's death was "liberation not only from the bondage of the mortal body and from the political siege but also from the long years of marriage under siege by her husband who imprisoned her in exile in Mitono [sic] and her own residence in Osaka."[69]

A parody of the above-mentioned memoir "Shimojo oboegaki" was published by Akutagawa Ryūnosuke. His short story *Itojo oboegaki* (A Memoir of Itojo, 1924) satirically described the bad temper of Gracia from the view of Itojo, a fictional maid. When Gracia extended her neck to a young samurai and blushed, Itojo for the first time felt a bit positive toward her. One critic characterized this story as "transcending" the contradiction between bushidō and Christianity, and between Japan and the West that Gracia has been thought to exemplify, arguing that it freed her from the popular image of a loyal and brave Confucian woman.[70]

There are also works that focus on Gracia's Christian faith. For instance,

---

66 Guzman, *Historia de las missiones que han hecho los religiosos de la Compañia de Iesus: Para predicar el sancto Evangelio en la India oriental, y en los reynos de la China y Iapon*, vol. 2. 568; Guzman and Arai, *Tōhō dendōshi*, 691.

67 Tabata, *Hosokawa Garasha: Chirinu beki toki shirite koso*, 213.

68 An, *Hosokawa Garasha: Kirishitan shiryō kara mita shōgai*, 176–77.

69 Ward, *Women Religious Leaders in Japan's Christian Century, 1549–1650*, 270.

70 Okuno, " 'Itojo oboegaki': Retsujo o koete," 328.

Wakaba Sei's *Hosokawa Tadaoki fujin* (1907–1908),[71] Fukuda Kingetsu's short story "Hosokawa Garasha,"[72] and Washio Ukō's short story "Hideyoshi to Hosokawa"[73] all describe her conversion to Christianity by putting emphasis on her misfortune caused by her father's revolt, her conflicts with her husband, her dissatisfaction with Buddhist views on life, and her deep interest in the Christian religion. Ōi Sōgo's *Hosokawa Tadaoki fujin*[74] and Mitsue Iwao's *Hosokawa Garasha fujin*[75] also give accounts of her final "martyrdom."

Consciously or unconsciously, almost everyone who is exposed to stories about Hosokawa Gracia—whether as a reader of biography or fiction or as a member of the audience of a play, film, or musical work based on her life—comes to feel that Christianity was the only ray of light in the darkness of her life, which was full of suspicion, mistrust, betrayal, and conspiracy.

5. The Characteristics of Heuvers' Play

Heuvers' script *Hosokawa Garashia fujin*, published in 1939, treats the seventeen years from 1583 to 1600. The major characters are Hosokawa Tadaoki, Madame Hosokawa [Gracia], chief retainer Ogasawara Shōsai, and lady-in-waiting Kyōbara. Below is a synopsis of the play.

Scene 1, Act 1, Midono, in 1583: Shōsai, who has heard that Toyotomi Hideyoshi's retainers will arrive soon, attempts to persuade Madame Hosokawa to commit suicide.

Scene 2, Act 1: Madame Hosokawa laments that she has in a single night gone from being the most fortunate woman in the realm to the most unfortunate person. She gazes at the lotus flowers and asks, "How can Nothingness create such a beautiful thing, and then destroy it with such malevolence?" She wonders if a creator of everything in the world exists, and she seeks to find the meaning of life and death.

Scene 1, Act 2, Spring of 1587, new residence of Hosokawa family in Osaka: Before her husband Tadaoki goes to Satsuma, she says to him,

---

71 Wakaba, "Hosokawa Tadaoki fujin."
72 Fukuda, "Hosokawa Garasha," 86–90.
73 Washio, "Hideyoshi to Hosokawa," 85–97.
74 Ōi, *Hosokawa Tadaoki fujin.*
75 Mitsue, *Hosokawa Garasha fujin.*

"Now cherry blossoms are winking at me. They surprise me too. They look like a person from a faraway corner of this world winking at me." Tadaoki responds by telling her about the faith of the Kirishitan daimyō Takayama Ukon who used to say, "I believe in the almighty God who created the heaven and the earth. His name is Deus."

Scene 2, Act 2: Madame Hosokawa summons Kyōbara and seeking to know the eternal truth, they secretly go to the church, disobeying Tadaoki's command that they not leave the residence.

Scene 3, Act 2: Japanese Brother Vincentio, while taking a walk in cherry-blossom viewing season, encounters some drunken picnickers. He asks them, "Don't you wonder who on the earth made the flowers blossom?" They reply, "Obviously, must be the springtime sun. Anyway let's have another drink." Meanwhile, Madame and Kyōbara ask the Spanish priest Céspedes, "We want to know more about this world. Why do the flowers blossom and wither? Why do people feel happy and sad? Why are we born and have to die?"

Scene 4, Act 2: After learning Christian doctrine at the church, Madame holds her six-year-old son and joyfully says, "You are so lucky! I knew nothing until this spring when I am twenty-four. I did not know who created the heaven and the earth and everything in the world, and endowed them with colors...But you are just six, and you know all of this now."

Scene 1, Act 3, Summer of 1587: After learning that Tadaoki will return from war and Takayama Ukon has been exiled, Madame decides to be baptized by Kyōbara, who has already become a Kirishitan. Here is their dialogue.

Kyōbara: Madame, your new name is Gracia.

Madame: Gracia! That is a smile to me from the Lord.

Kyōbara: Bathed by this smile, the first flower of your heart will sprout.

Madame: Gracia! That is the everlasting love to me from the Lord.

Kyōbara: Breathed upon by this love, the spring of happiness will gush out.

Madame: Gracia! That is the forgiving kiss to me from the Lord.

Kyōbara: Touched by this kiss, you are God's child, and my sister.

Madame: Gracia! That is the heavenly dew dropping on the barren land.

Kyōbara: Quenched by the dew, the garden of your heart will bear many fruits.

Scene 1, Act 4, street of Osaka, 1600: Italian priest Organtino talks with Japanese Brother Vincentio, and praises Gracia. "She is such a wonderful person. I do not think you can find anyone like her in this country...She learned Portuguese only by reading books. She writes letters more skillfully than you do, excuse me! She also studied Latin. Above all, she made her husband, an angry man like a lion, be friendly to us."

Scene 2, Act 3: Before going to join forces with Tokugawa Ieyasu's army, Tadaoki meets Shōsai, and asks him to "assist" Gracia's death if Ishida Mitsunari's army tries to take her away, because she will not commit suicide by herself.

Scene 3, Act 3: Ishida's army arrives to take Gracia as hostage. She evacuates her children and ladies-in-waiting, and then composes a *waka* poem before her death. Gracia prays before her death.

今こそ命すつべき時	Now is the time when I have to desert my life.
光輝くデウスの御国の、 尊きひかり、我を召させ給ふ。	The holy lights from the heaven of Deus are beckoning me.
紫のけぶり、紅のほむらに、	With the purple smoke and red flames,
五体は空に帰するとも、	Even my body will be nothing,
我が魂の故郷へ我は召されて帰る。	I am called to return to the home of my soul.
救ひ給へや、我が主よ。	Save me, my Lord.
愛の御手、さしのべ給へ。	Give me your loving hands,
最後の御めぐみ、たれ給へ。	Give me your final blessing.
花は咲き競ふ、その中に	Among the proudly blooming flowers,
天に帰する喜びは鳴り響く、	There is resonating joy of returning to Heaven,
五彩の雲に、天使の微笑み、	There are smiles of angels above colorful clouds,
妙なる楽の音は讃歌をかなで、	A beautiful melody accompanies the Psalms,
高らかに歌声は、四方にひゞく、	Their voices resound widely,
お召しの声、我を招く、	The Lord's call is summoning me,
遥かなる天より	From the faraway Heaven,
遥かなるこの地上へ	To this earth.
尊きみこゑす	Holy voice,
天主の御こゑ	My Lord's voice,
我が父の……	My Father's…

In this play we can see that the Christian name "Gracia" has evoked lasting resonance between the two, and for Gracia, brings divine happiness. "Smile," "everlasting love," "forgiving kiss," "sisterhood," and "heavenly dew" all represent exact opposites of the atrocities of the era of civil strife in which they lived. These are the most important things to Gracia's life, as she has suffered so much from the uncertainty of her fate.

Fig. 20, Gracia's final poem with melody composed by Vincenzo Cimatti, in Heuvers' *Vierzig Jahre in Japan, 1923–1963*.

Her final poem "Chirinu beki toki shirite koso yo no naka no hana wa hana nare hito wa hito nare" (散りぬべき 時知りてこそ 世の中の 花は花なれ 人は人なれ) has been translated into English by Ogawa as, "Blossoms shall be blossoms/ people people/only when they come to know/the right time to fall).[76] Another translation by Makoto Harris Takao reads, "A flower is most beautiful when it knows the time to fall. People are like flowers, I will die without hesitation,"[77] and one by Haruko Nawata Ward, "One must know the time to leave this world. As the flowers perish, so do human lives."[78]

Heuvers wanted to create a character who first sees "the world, the universe, and human life all in a meaningless chaos, quickly changing and swirling, with no purpose." She struggles to find a way out of this chaos.[79] After converting to Christianity, Gracia escapes the chaos. Therefore, in the context of this play, we can interpret her final poem as meaning, "It is the time to depart, I shall leave this world gracefully like the flowers." Heuvers also loved this poem. Vincenzo Cimatti set the text to music, and Heuvers included a photograph of the score in his essay collection written in Ger-

---

76 Ogawa and Ogawa, "A Short Study of *Jisei* (Swan Songs): Death, Cosmos and Its Transmigration," 325.

77 Takao, "'In what storms of blood from Christ's flock is Japan swimming?': Gracia Hosokawa and the Performative Representation of Japanese Martyrdom in *Mulier fortis* (1698)," 94.

78 Ward, *Women Religious Leaders in Japan's Christian Century, 1549–1650*, 262.

79 Heuvers, *Hosokawa Garashia fujin*, 7–8.

man, *Forty Years in Japan* (Fig. 20). In Heuvers' play, Gracia happily walks toward Heaven by her own will.

6. God's Wrapping Cloth with Flower Patterns

Heuvers made clear that he wished to make a place for Gracia in world literature. Now let us consider the meaning of this term "world literature." Commonly thought to have been proposed first by Johann Wolfgang von Goethe (1749–1832) in 1827, this term (*Weltliteratur* in German) was in fact already in use about half a century earlier, as Wolfgang Schamoni, a scholar of Japanese literature, has shown.[80]

Schamoni argues that it was August Ludwig von Schlözer (1735–1809), a German Enlightenment historian, who introduced the word *Weltliteratur* in his writing on Icelandic literature and history in 1773. Comparing Icelandic literature to other literatures, Schlözer maintained that Icelandic literature is "as important to the whole world literature" as Anglo-Saxon, Irish, Russian, Byzantine, Hebrew, Arabic, and Chinese literatures. When he asserted this, Schlözer was teaching at the University of Göttingen, an institution with an international character that was rather rare at the time. He was conducting research on histories of Phoenicia, Scandinavia, Poland, and Russia. He had a good command of Swedish and Russian, as well as German, and was presenting papers in Latin. It seems that "his interest in and curiosity about the world spread to literary research as well." However, as Schamoni points out, Schlözer's "world literature" is simply an accumulation of each nation's literature; it is unlike Goethe's concept of "world literature," which means the "current and future process of global exchange of writers and their literary works".

Heuvers respected Goethe highly and often quoted his words.[81] He probably understood well the meaning of Goethe's "world literature." However, because Goethe did not provide a precise definition of this term, its meaning is still being debated today.

We can find several instances where Goethe mentions "world literature" in 1827. The earliest one is in his letter to Johann Friedrich Cotta on 26

---

80 Schamoni, " 'Sekai Bungaku': Gēte yori hanseiki mo mae ni shoshutsu shite ita go," 173–82.

81 Tamura, *Waga Heruman Hoiverusu shinpu*, 58–64.

January 1827, declaring that "a world literature is forming, that all nations are inclined towards it and therefore take favorable steps." A few days later, in his conversation with Eckermann on 31 January, he stressed, "National literature does not count for much now; it is time for the epoch of world literature and everyone must help to advance this epoch." Soon thereafter he wrote in an article for the journal *Über Kunst und Altertum* (vol. 6, no. 1, 1827), "I am convinced of the formation of a general world literature, in which an honorable role is reserved for us Germans. All nations look round for us, they praise, censure, adopt and dismiss, imitate and disfigure, understand or misunderstand us, open or close their hearts." In his draft for an address at the Society of Natural Philosophers in Berlin, he remarked that "world literature" meant "the living and striving literators come to know each other and feel moved, by inclination and a sense of community, to work together."[82]

We can assume what Goethe proposed is the spirit of "world literature," rather than "world literature" itself. The spirit may have four salient features: (1) literatures shall be created based on insightful observation and representation of the essence of things; (2) writers shall have a broad perspective and be familiar with other languages and literatures; (3) literary effects shall distinguish universality from particularity, and eternity from momentariness; (4) literary endeavors shall nurture refined taste for reading and improve the intelligence of the human race.[83]

It is in this spirit that Heuvers wished to represent Gracia. In his play, Gracia searches for the truth of world creation, social changes, and the meaning of human life and death. She studies the Portuguese and Latin languages in order to communicate with missionaries and familiarize herself with Christian thought. She overcomes the sufferings of this life and the horror of death by finding a sublime spiritual world. Heuvers' intention of establishing Gracia in "world literature" was not only to make her known overseas through drama, opera, kabuki, noh or other performing arts, but also make her a person who embodies the spirit of "world literature."

---

82 Hoesel-Uhlig, "Changing Field: The Directions of Goethe's *Weltliteratur*," 34–40; also in Kogishi Akira's translation "Sekai Bungaku ron" (On World Literature) in *Gēte zenshū* [Complete Works by Goethe] (Shio Shuppansha, 1980; revised version, 2003), vol. 13, 91–102.

83 Guo/Kaku, *Shiga Naoya de "Sekai Bungaku" o yomitoku*, 210.

One more thing we need to pay attention to is the fact that Heuvers wrote the script in Japanese. And interestingly, he did not clearly remember which language he used when writing. When the kabuki play was performed in 1965, he said, "I wrote the script thirty years ago. I have already forgotten whether I used Japanese or German."[84] To him, which language he used was not important. Using Japanese instead of German or English would in itself contribute toward making the play "world literature." This spirit is a common feature in missionary writings in the Japanese language.

Heuvers absorbed much nourishment from the Japanese language and culture. He studied Japanese classical literature for a long period, and using the Japanese classic style gave him considerable satisfaction. He said, "I followed St. Augustine's teaching to conserve and preserve each race's good tradition, by utilizing Japan's excellent classical arts to preserve the old and good Japanese minds in the light of Christian spirit."[85]

Heuvers' books have shed new light on "the Christian virtues the Japanese people were born with," as Togawa Keiichi has remarked. By connecting Christianity to Japanese customs and traditions, Heuvers tried to inspire the Japanese to accept Christian values naturally.[86] One example of how Heuvers articulated this rhetoric was expressed in a roundtable talk. He employed a comparison with the gift-giving custom in Japan. When preparing a gift, he noted, the Japanese will first choose an item the receiver will like, then put it into a nice box, wrap it with a *furoshiki* cloth, and finally take it to the receiver. God followed the Japanese custom by choosing his only son Jesus, putting him into a treasure box, which is Mother Mary, then wrapping it with "the cosmos" and presenting it to the world.[87]

Among the many writings by missionaries, Heuvers' works are unquestionably the most poetic. His literature, it might be said, adds flower patterns to God's wrapping cloth.

---

84 "Man'in no kankyaku kara hakushu, Kageki 'Hosokawa Garashia'" 満員の観客から拍手、歌劇『細川ガラシア』, *Yomiuri shinbun*, 1965.1.24, morning issue.

85 Heuvers, *Nihon de yonjūnen*, 191.

86 Togawa and Doi, *Hoiverusu shinpu no kotoba*, 31–32.

87 Ibid., 172.

Chronology of H. Heuvers' Life[88]

Years	(Age)	Activities
1890	(0)	31 August, born at Dreierwalde village of the state of Westfalen.
1909	(19)	19 April, joined the Society of Jesus in Holland; studied philosophy and theology at Ignatius College in Valkenburg, Holland.
1913	(23)	Studied philosophy at Stonyhurst College in England.
1914–16	(24–26)	Taught the Latin language and earth science at St. Stanislaus School in Mumbai, India.
1920	(30)	Ordained a priest at Ignatius College in Valkenburg. Decided to devote himself to missionary work in Japan.
1922	(32)	Studied Japanese language and literature at the University of Hamburg.
1923	(33)	25 August, arrived in Japan; taught German at the Sixth Higher School, Okayama city.
1928	(38)	Published *Kami e no michi* (A Road to God).
1935	(45)	Co-translated *Kirisuto no shōgai* (The Life of Christ).
1937	(47)	Installed as the second president of Sophia University.
1939	(49)	Published *Hosokawa Garashia fujin* (Madame Hosokawa Gracia).
1941	(51)	Resigned from post as university president; became an assistant priest of St. Theresa Church in Kōjimachi, Tokyo.
1946–59	(56–69)	Taught at the First Higher School, the Imperial Univeristy of Tokyo.
1947	(57)	Became the priest-in-charge of St. Ignatius Church (formally St. Theresa Church).
1948	(58)	Became the director of the Japanese Catholic Students Association and published *Uguisu to shijin* (A Bush Warbler and a Poet).
1953	(63)	Published *Toki no nagare ni* (Along the Flow of Time).
1956	(66)	Published *Kobune yori no koe: Kirisuto no tatoe* (A Voice from the Little Boat: Fables used by Christ).
1964	(74)	Published *Nihon de yonjūnen* (Forty Years in Japan).
1968	(78)	Published *Waga furusato* (My Hometown).
1969	(79)	Received Order of the Sacred Treasure from the Japanese Government. Published *Jinsei no aki ni: Heruman Hoiverusu zuisōshū* (In the Autumn of Life: Collection of Hermann Heuvers' Thoughts).
1971	(81)	Published *Jinsei sanka: 12 no seika ni yoru kami e no michi* (Songs in Praise of Life: A Road to God by Way of 12 Psalms).
1973	(83)	Published *Gikyoku senshū* (Selected Plays) and *Hoiverusu shinpu sekkyōshū* (Selection of Fr. Heuvers' Sermons), for the 50th anniversary of his life in Japan.
1975	(85)	Published *Shi to sono deshi: Timoteo sho kaisetsu* (The Teacher and His Disciples: Interpretation of the Epistles to Timothy).
1977	(87)	9 June, died while celebrating Mass.

---

88 Based largely on the chronology in Tamura's *Waga Heruman Hoiverusu shinpu.*

CHAPTER
6

Georges Neyrand's Unconventional Preaching

Finally let us look at the life and work of Georges Neyrand, another extraordinary missionary from France. After arriving in Japan, Neyrand attentively read Candau's writings, probably because he was particularly interested in the Basque priest's method of evangelization. In the summer of 1955, he noticed that Candau "wrote only about death recently." Several months later, Candau passed away. Neyrand went on to develop his own style of missionary work with Candau in mind as his model. He earned a reputation for being "highly knowledgeable" and "well representing the French Catholic spirit of modern worker-priests."[1]

Neyrand became famous for his unconventional approach to missionary work. When he was young, his ambition was to become an actor in order to "perform the subtleties of human nature." He especially desired to play the role of a clown. After coming to Japan, he saw how money seemed to take precedence over all else, and how likely it was that a missionary following Jesus Christ would be taken as a fool. Nevertheless, in Japan he was happy to be able to realize his childhood dream.[2] Sometimes his actions even surprised novelist Endō Shūsaku who was renowned for astonishing others

---

1 Nomura, "Wareware no oyaji," 127.
2 Seibo no Kishisha, "Kono hito 2000: Neran shinpu," unpaginated.

with his mischievousness.

Neyrand loved Georges Rouault (1871–1958)'s paintings because "all the images he painted, whether a king or a beggar, resemble Christ. Even a clown painted by him has the dignity of Christ."[3] Neyrand decided to develop a new style of preaching to suit the Japanese people's psychology, by performing like a clown.

1. Praise for Japanese Aesthetic Sensibility

Georges Neyrand was born in Lyon on 2 February 1920 as the second son of a bourgeois family. Living on the interest of an inheritance from his grandfather, his family "kept their lifestyle barely at the middle-class level." His parents were enthusiastic Catholics, who raised him with a deep faith.

After graduating from high school, Neyrand entered the École Spéciale Militaire de Saint-Cyr, from which Candau also had graduated, in September 1939. The reason he attended this school is that he sensed the approach of war, and in addition the entrance examination had been made easier. After training for just six months, he graduated. The school's program was curtailed because of the outbreak of war. Neyrand was dispatched to fight at Narbonne in the south of France. Three months later, in June 1940, France surrendered to Germany, and his military career ended.[4]

At that point he was undecided about his future occupation. He was interested in land surveying, but did not feel it was his true vocation. When contemplating the meaning of life, he heard a voice from deep in his heart repeating "Become a priest!" Neyrand did not like church rituals, nor was he attracted to priests with their black soutanes. However, one day when he was riding a train, a priest was sitting in front of him, reading a prayer book. Neyrand could not help but feel that the man possessed "a marvelous dignity and charm." He thought it would be wonderful if he could become a priest too, and devote himself to the absolute value of Christianity rather than relative worth of the state.[5]

From September 1943, he studied at the Grand Séminaire de Lyon for six years, and on 29 June 1950 he was ordained a priest. He was deeply

---

3 Neyrand, *Sakariba shisai no mōgoroku*, 126.

4 Neyrand, *Obaka-san no jijoden hanbun: Seisho katate ni Nippon 36 nenkan*, 42–51.

5 Ibid., 19–21, 49.

moved and described the occasion rhetorically: "Christ came to me like a thief. He suddenly intruded into my home at night. He snatched away within one second all the knowledge and experience I had accumulated over the years. He quietly filled up my empty shell with His energy." That same day, he submitted his application for missionary work in Japan, "a country of respectable culture in Asia." His interest in Japan had been aroused by a newspaper article about a Japanese person who stopped a passing missionary and entreated him, "Please teach me Christianity!" He was also amazed by the "rich sense of beauty of Japanese paintings and ceramics" that he viewed at exhibitions in Paris.[6]

Ten days after his ordination, Neyrand welcomed three Japanese students who had just arrived at the Marseilles: future novelist Endō Shūsaku, future scholar of ethics Mikumo Natsuo, and Mikumo's brother Subaru, future scholar of nuclear science. Neyrand took them to Lyon and looked after them there. Meanwhile, he was getting ready for his Japan mission. In September 1951, he joined the Société des Auxiliaires des Missions in Belgium. One year later, on 9 December 1952, he landed in Yokohama.

Neyrand studied elementary Japanese at a language school in Tokyo for six months before starting to work for the Nagasaki diocese. He continued to study Japanese in Nagasaki, progressing to an advanced level. He tried to read the daily column "Tensei jingo" (Vox Populi, Vox Dei) of the *Asahi shinbun* newspaper because of its conciseness and good literary style.[7] In Nagasaki, he also studied the *Analects* of Confucius (551?–479 BC), saying that he "understood its excellence for the first time" because he had been unable to appreciate this work when he read it in French translation. Neyrand stayed in Nagasaki for three years, during which time he felt unsatisfied because there was little opportunity to discuss theology and the Bible with other priests, and the parishioners he was looking after were already Christians. He was eager to deliver Christianity to non-believers, and he was not getting a chance to do so.[8]

He tried every possible means to leave Nagasaki, and was eventually allowed to move to Tokyo in 1956. He took a position at the Shinsei Kaikan (formerly known as the St. Filippo Dormitory; the former chief director was

---

6 Ibid., 57–61.
7 Ibid., 64–66.
8 Ibid., 22–23.

Candau) to provide Christian education to young students. In the five years he worked there, he baptized eight students.

2. Seeing from a Japanese Point of View

In January 1958, Neyrand was invited by the Archbishop of Tokyo to edit a Japanese-language journal of theology. The journal was intended for the education of future priests, and Neyrand was selected because of his knowledge of theology as well as his good command of Japanese. He considered the level of theology in Japan at that time to be low, in part owing to the fact that there were very few books and journals on theology available in Japanese. Wanting to utilize the theological knowledge he had acquired in the seminary and in self study, he immediately accepted the invitation. Instead of publishing regular journal issues, however, he decided to publish a series of books.

In the process of editing the series, Neyrand realized that simply translating theological articles written by foreigners would not be satisfactory, because these articles were written originally for overseas readers. Japanese translations would not make them easy for Japanese readers to understand. He chose a new method—he would personally draft articles in French, based on foreign sources but written with a Japanese readership in mind, and then ask other people to translate his articles into Japanese. To his disappointment, the translations seldom met his demand for "authentic Japanese." Eventually he had to do the translation, proofreading, and revision by himself.[9]

What this illustrates is that Neyrand wrote for Japanese readers from their point of view. He thoughtfully devised a strategy of what to write, for whom to write, and how to write when editing the series. All of the successful writings in Japanese by missionaries have followed the same carefully conceived strategy.

From 1959 until 1964, thirteen volumes of *Rogosu: Kirisutokyō kenkyū sōsho* (Logos: Research Series on Christianity) were published, with Neyrand as both editor and publisher, Katō Bunmeisha as printing house, and Kinokuniya Shoten as distributor. Each volume had a particular theme.

Vol. 1, *Fukkatsu* 復活 (The Resurrection, December 1959)

Vol. 2, *Kirisuto no karada* キリストの体 (The Body of Christ, March 1960)

---

9 Ibid., 76–79.

Vol. 3, *Eremia* エレミア (Jeremiah, June 1960)

Vol. 4, *Kekkon, dokushin* 結婚・独身 (Marriage and Single Life, October 1960)

Vol. 5, *Inori* 祈り (Prayer, February 1961)

Vol. 6, *Seisho no yomikata* 聖書の読み方 (How to Read the Bible, May 1961)

Vol. 7, *Kami no kiseki* 神の軌跡 (The Locus of God, September 1961)

Vol. 8, *Keizai shakai to ningen* 経済社会と人間 (Economical Society and Human Beings, February 1962)

Vol. 9, *Hito to natta kami* 人となった神 (God Who Became a Man, June 1962)

Vol. 10, *Kami no kuni* 神の国 (The Kingdom of God, October 1962)

Vol. 11, *Saishi to shisai* 祭祀と司祭 (Rites and Priests, March 1963)

Vol. 12, *Senrei shiki* 洗礼式 (Baptism, July 1963)

Vol. 13, *Senkyōron* 宣教論 (On Evangelization, February, 1964)

Neyrand wrote an "Introduction" and "Postscript" in Japanese for each volume. His other articles were first written in French, and later translated into Japanese by Japanese persons and himself.

Even before he took responsibility for this series, he was publishing in Japanese. For example, he was invited to contribute articles to the magazine *Tabi* (Travel) by Okada Kishū, one of its editors. Okada later reminisced, "I asked him to write for the magazine three or four times. . . I was surprised to see his articles written in neat kanji and hiragana, not long after he came to Japan." Okada liked Neyrand's "unique personality" and changed his view of Christianity after having met him. According to Okada, Neyrand loved Mishima Yukio's novel *Kinkakuji* (The Temple of the Golden Pavilion, 1956), which he read three times, and had an extraordinarily good understanding of Japanese literature.[10]

In fact, whenever he wrote in Japanese Neyrand focused on Japanese people's perspectives. For instance, his book *Kirisuto no fukkatsu* (The Resurrection of Christ, 1997) states, "There are very few books written in Japanese about Christ's resurrection. There are only some Japanese translations of books written in European languages, and those reflect Western points

---

10 Okada, *Tabi no ki no mi*, 88–89.

of view. They do not necessarily satisfy Japanese people's curiosity." Therefore he believed his book, written in their language, would be helpful to Japanese readers. He stated explicitly, "This book is not a Japanese translation. I wrote it in Japanese. I received a lot of advice regarding my Japanese expressions from Professor Endō Orie of the Department of Literature at Bunkyō University."[11] He often consulted Japanese linguists such as Endō and Nakamura Akira about Japanese usage.[12]

The theological level of Neyrand's *Kirisuto ron* (On Christ) was highly praised by Endō Shūsaku, who repeatedly referred to this book. Another reviewer wrote, "This book is concrete and detailed. The author is very good at the Japanese language and his literary style is straightforward and plain, which reminds us of his engaging personality. Its theme is believed by the reviewer to be beneficial to the Japanese."[13]

Neyrand often imitated the rhetoric of the New Testament. After quoting French philosopher Paul Ricoeur's words —"expressions of faith are metaphorical"—Neyrand wrote, "Jesus did not use many abstract concepts but only metaphor. Neither the Gospel According to Mark nor that According to Mathew ever used the word 'salvation.' Instead we see only metaphors of seeds, bread, wine, salt, and pearl, etc. After reading 'foxes have holes, and birds of the air have nests,' the image of 'the reeds are swaying in the winds' can lead us to imagine vividly 'the Son of Man hath not where to lay his head.' Jesus is a real poet, because he used metaphor so well." Neyrand continued to say that metaphor is not only a rhetorical device, but also a way to show invisible reality by means of visible signs. He himself endeavored to use metaphorical expressions to advantage. He noted that Ricoeur rarely cited the thinking of theologians, but frequently quoted passages from the poetry of Dante and the philosophical writing of Pascal. In Neyrand's judgment, Ricoeur showed the direction in which interpreting and understanding Christ's teaching should be pointed,[14] and metaphor is a suitable tool for evangelization.

Neyrand's wide knowledge of the language surprised a scholar of French literature, Tobari Tomoo, who often asked for his help in editing a Japa-

---

11 Neyrand, *Kirisuto no fukkatsu*, 201–203.

12 Neyrand, *Obaka-san no jijoden hanbun: Seisho katate ni Nippon 36 nenkan*, 230.

13 Takahashi, "Shohyō G. Neran cho 'Kirisuto ron' Sōbunsha, 1979," 32.

14 Neyrand, "Gendai ni okeru Kirisuto ron to wa," 4–5.

nese-French dictionary.[15] Neyrand was very familiar with both Japanese literature and Japanese cinema. This is clear from his selection of material for translation classes he taught at universities. Among the works he used are Mishima Yukio (1925–1970)'s *Rokumeikan* (1956), Ozu Yasu-jirō (1903–1963)'s film *An Autumn Afternoon* (1962), Fukunaga Takehiko (1918–1979)'s *Kaishi* (Mirage, 1968), Atōda Takashi (b. 1935)'s short stories, Ogawa Kunio (1927–2008)'s *Eriko e kudaru michi* (The Road to Jericho, 1957), and Terada Torahiko (1878–1935)'s *Hana monogatari* (Stories of Flowers, 1908).[16]

Neyrand called himself a "translator" because his mission was to convey Christian messages written in Greek, Latin, French, English, and German languages into Japanese.[17] By introducing Christian culture, he made Christianity easier for the Japanese to understand and to accept. Neyrand was keenly aware of the relationship in his mind between Japanese and his mother tongue French. "For daily conversation, I often think in Japanese," he said. "But when I face difficult matters, I cannot do that. When thinking deeply, most people will use their mother tongue. The process is: first thinking in the mother tongue and then translating the idea into a foreign language." Meanwhile, he noticed that native speakers often get away with imprecision. "When using one's mother tongue, vague expressions are tolerated. But when one translates a thought into a foreign language, the vagueness must be eliminated. As a result, writing in a foreign language usually brings clearer words and expressions."[18] Neyrand's own experience gave him invaluable insight into the approach of writers in languages other than their native tongues. In general, I have found that writing in Japanese by non-native speakers tends to be more logical in content, and clearer or simpler in expression, than their speech in their first language.

3. Meticulous Attention to Japanese Life

In his fifth year in Japan, Neyrand contributed articles describing his trip to Kyushu to the above-mentioned magazine *Tabi* (Travel). They display

---

15 Tobari, "Kabukichō no kaisō Neran shinpu," 399.
16 Neyrand, *Obaka-san no jijoden hanbun: Seisho katate ni Nippon 36 nenkan*, 91–92.
17 Ibid., 124–25.
18 Ibid., 88.

his precise observations about the world around him. One of them, "From Yabakei valley to Higo-Oguni" (June 1957), opened with a portrayal of his delight at seeing the beauty of the Yabakei valley, often depicted in ink paintings, with his own eyes. Then he focused on village architecture. He wrote, "Farmers' houses with thatched roofs look noble and majestic. The *chigi* [forked finials] at the ends of the roof ridges are elegant ... The simple splendor of the houses reminds us of the acute sensitivity of the ancient Japanese people. Seeing Oguni's scenery, I am amazed by their refined sense of beauty, even though I may not understand the mythology of Prince Ninigi no Mikoto's descent from the sky to Mt. Takachiho-no-mine in Kyushu."[19]

Neyrand was always quick to notice Japanese aesthetic sensibilities, and his descriptions of them are impressive. The following paragraph shows how he appreciated the details of Japanese rooms.

> A Japanese-style room of six straw-mat *tatami* is full of indescribable charm. The room size is in perfect proportion to the whole structure of the house. Moreover, each of its four corners has a visible pillar, which makes the structure obvious and provides an extremely stable atmosphere. Not only the corners, but also the horizontal beams under the ceiling, the pillars that frame the *tokonoma* alcove space, and the decorative *nageshi* timbers surrounding the walls are all geometrical, and naturally construct vertical and horizontal lines which add a sense of repose. In short, the room is an assembly of naked walls fitted into a square frame. The walls of rooms are partitioned by the pillars, beams, and baseboards. The sliding door *fusuma* and the lightweight sliding door *shōji* have more visible geometrical features. The *tatami* mats have borders, and the ceiling beams are exposed. The surfaces within these frames are of a single hue. But the space is not lifeless, although it may lack decorative patterns. The wood grains of the ceiling board, the texture of the walls, the woven straw appearance of *tatami*, and the latticed *shōji* paper are all living, like the monochromatic sea...It is this extraordinary sense of beauty that produced such a harmony. It is both a heritage of tradition and a sense of modern times...A Japanese room has no shining metals and glittering glory, but quietly whispers

---

19 Neyrand, "Yabakei kara Higi Oguni e: Nebukuro motte shinwa no Kyūshū o tabi suru," 71.

to our hearts with its soft light and shade. The harmonious colors of trees, grasses, and earth play a pastoral melody.[20]

(六畳の日本間は、描き難い魅力に溢れている。それは、日本式家屋の構造から言っても最も手頃な空間に切り取られているからだけではない。四隅には柱が見えて、つまり建築の構造があらわであるために、極めて落ち着いた空気が漲る。そして、それは、角に限らず、天井の梁、床柱、長押などが、幾何学的で、かつ自然な鉛直線や水平線を描いて、更に安心感を添えている。日本間は、要するに、四角な輪郭の中にはめ込まれた裸の面の組み立てである、と言っていい。壁面は、柱と長押や幅木で仕切られる。襖や障子なら、なおさら明らかである。また、畳には縁があり、天井には梁がある。四角な枠にはめられた面はくすんだ単色である。しかし、その面は、模様がないにもかかわらず、決して死んではいない。天井板の木理、壁の肌、畳の編み目、障子の和紙の目も、海の単色の面のごとく、絶えず生きているのだ。……こういう調和を齎もたらす奥には不思議な美の感覚が光っている。伝統の遺産ともいえるし、現代的なセンスもうかがわれる。……輝く金属や目映ゆい栄光を退けた和室の柔かい濃淡は、我々の心に静かに語りかける。色の調和といえば、木の色、草の色、土の色が牧歌調の旋律を奏でる。)

This meticulous description shows Neyrand's fresh eyes coming from a foreign culture and his excellent command of the Japanese language. His depictions of Japanese scenery are rich in literary and visual effects. They function simultaneously as panorama and close-up, as in the following passage: "The contrast between the horizontal lines of the rice paddies and the sloping lines of the mountains make the landscape stand out in relief. The rooftiles of the houses within this scene make wave patterns that are pleasing to the eye. The color of the tiles becomes part of the surroundings, and their delicate curves display endless ripples."[21]

Neyrand toured Japan extensively, showing particular interest in temples and Buddhist images. Every year he went to the Nara region to search out the beauty of traditional Japan. He discovered that Shinto shrines were usually situated in the most beautiful locations, and their presence in turn made the surrounding area even more attractive. He recommended, "If you go to

---

20 Neyrand, *Sakariba shisai no mōgoroku*, 12–13.
21 Neyrand, *Obaka-san no jijoden hanbun: Seisho katate ni Nippon 36 nenkan*, 210.

an unknown place and want to see good scenery, you should head directly to a Shinto shrine. There you will not only find beautiful views, but also graceful architecture and delightful rituals." He concluded, "After all, Shinto is a religion that worships beauty."[22] Neyrand reminds us of many things in Japan we may overlook if we are not sensitive to their aesthetic qualities.

It was not just visual images that fascinated Neyrand; Japanese psychology was also a focus of his attention. Once he said satirically, "The strength of the Japanese people comes from their forgetfulness and concentration on the future."[23] This kind of paradoxical expression is another distinctive feature of his writings.

4. Appearances in Endō Shūsaku's Literature

Neyrand used money from his inheritance to support Japanese students' stays in France. Instead of naming his fund the "Neyrand Foundation," he called it "Scholarship for Overseas Catholic Students." His aim was to recruit students from Japan, and among those who were accepted were Endō Shūsaku and the Mikumo brothers. According to Endō's wife Junko, Endō would not have had the opportunity to study in France if it had not been for Neyrand's scholarship.[24] Endō did not know that the funding had come from Neyrand and assumed that it represented donations from French Catholics. When he met Neyrand, he complained that the amount was almost too small for him to survive. Later, learning that it was Neyrand's money, he was embarrassed, and after returning to Japan, he wanted to thank his benefactor personally. Neyrand rejected this idea and became upset with Endō for thinking that it was necessary to offer gifts of gratitude.

Endō returned from France just as Neyrand was moving to Tokyo from Nagasaki, and he hosted the French priest at his home for one month. The novelist observed Neyrand's interesting way of relating with Japanese people at a time when his Japanese language skills were not yet very good. Endō, who believed Jesus would be called a fool if he lived in today's world, wanted to write a novel portraying a contemporary man who mirrored the image of Jesus Christ, and he thought that Neyrand would serve as a good

22 Ibid, 211–12.

23 Asahi Shinbunsha, *Kaigai hōdō ni miru Shōwa tennō*, 89.

24 Endō and Suzuki, *Otto Endō Shūsaku o kataru*, 115–16.

model. The product of Endō's aspiration was *Obaka-san* (Wonderful Fool), the first of his novels to be serialized in a newspaper, published in the *Asahi shinbun* in 1959.[25] He himself admitted that he inserted several Neyrand episodes into this novel.[26]

Neyrand and Endō were very close, though they often argued while drinking together. After publishing his novel *Chinmoku* (*Silence*, 1966), Endō phoned his friend and asked his opinion. Neyrand replied, "It is a popular novel...[but] The style is boring." Endō was offended and cried out, "I don't ever want to see you again." Neyrand responded, "That's fine with me." But the two quickly reconciled, as always.[27]

According to Endō, Neyrand "is a person who has the all-too-human qualities of any man. He loves alcohol and good food. He travels all around Japan enjoying hot springs." At the same time, Endō regarded Neyrand's Christian faith as "living" and saw it manifested in his opening of the bar "Epoppe" in the red-light district of Shinjuku, Tokyo. There Neyrand could preach to people—his customers—who otherwise would not have had access to Christianity. Once when he was tipsy, Neyrand murmured to Endō, "Someday you should write about Christ living in the crowds of Shinjuku." Inspired by these words, Endō would portray a Christ living at the bottom of society, in "the narrow streets of Shinjuku, a filthy place contaminated by human desires,"[28] in his novels *Kanashimi no uta* (Song of Sadness, 1977) and *Sukyandaru* (*Scandal*, 1986).

Neyrand was the model for the character Gaston in three of Endō's novels: *Wonderful Fool* (1959), *Song of Sadness* (1977), and his final masterpiece *Fukai kawa* (*Deep River*, 1993). Gaston is a clumsy but passionate man who will help others at any time by sacrificing himself. His clumsiness is the source of humor in these novels.

In *Wonderful Fool*, Gaston has an unintelligent manner of speaking and a horse-like face. He is not skillful in Japanese, but is able to communicate with people despite his many mistakes. Endō provided a concise profile of the man: He is "laughed at and taken as a fool, and he failed at many things

---

25 Tsuge and Kojima, "Intabyū, Endō Junko fujin ni kiku: Hanseiki no kioku, Shōsetsu wa dono yō ni kakareta ka," 5.

26 Endō Shūsaku, *Kawaru mono to kawaranu mono*, 91–93.

27 Yamauchi, "Neran-san wa Nihonjin ni nani o katatta ka," 61.

28 Endō, "Waga shōsetsu no moderu ni tsuite," 1–3.

he tried. But he left the seeds of love in the hearts of the Japanese, and disappeared in the blue sky far away." What the author wanted to convey is the "strong faith and love" shared by Gaston and Neyrand. In a later essay he wrote, "Gaston sacrifices his life for his Japanese friends, and Fr. Neyrand devoted his life to his Japanese friends."[29]

Scholar of Christian literature Yamane Michihiro interpreted *Wonderful Fool* as the prototype of the images of Jesus in *Silence*, *Shikai no hotori* (Beside the Dead Sea, 1973), and *Deep River*. That is, a Jesus who is weak and unable to change reality, but accompanies those who are suffering and gives them his love.[30]

Neyrand saw the main theme of Endō's literature as "the frailty of human beings," because Endō aimed to reflect Christ's tolerance for and kindness to weak and sinful people. He stated that "Only when people are fully aware of their weakness will they entrust themselves completely to God... Endō's literature shows how God magically transforms their weakness to strength." In *Wonderful Fool*, Gaston's naivité, stray-dog-like pitifulness and sweetness enable the heroine Tomoe to "discover the profundity of his understanding of human existence." He "has no talents, no job, no status, and even no aims. The only thing he has is love for Japan." He embodies the ideal of "having nothing, yet possessing everything" that is remarked on in the New Testament (2 Corinthians 6:10).[31]

Jesuit priest and scholar of Japanese literature Francis Mathy pointed out that Gaston "loves people so much that he forgets about his own fear." Even after he has been mistreated by a professional hit man named Endō whom he is trying to save, Gaston continues to follow that man to prevent him from committing a crime. "This is 'strength.' This is 'love.' This unconditional 'love' becomes his power."[32]

Eighteen years later, Gaston appeared in another novel written by Endō Shūsaku, *Song of Sadness*. This time, Gaston tries to help a terminally ill old man who lives on a back street in Shinjuku. He takes part-time jobs, one of which is wrestling. His weak body cannot withstand the wrestling, but he endures the torment anyway. His weakness is both applauded and ridiculed

---

29 Endō, "Waga shōsetsu no moderu ni tsuite," 1–3.
30 Yamane, "Kaidai," 338–39.
31 Neyrand, "Kaisetsu," 383–91.
32 Mathy, "Ippiki no daken ga tsukuru dorama: Kaisetsu," 327.

by the spectators. Endō probably knew that there actually was a priest in Mexico who became a professional wrestler in order to earn money for the construction of an orphanage. Although he was getting older and weaker, the priest planned to continue wrestling until he reached the age of sixty, as he needed more funds to educate the children.[33]

In Endō's final novel *Deep River*, Gaston appears again. He volunteers to push wheelchairs, deliver meals, and use his "poor Japanese" to chat with the patients at a hospital after the working hours of his regular job at the Berlitz Foreign Language School in Shibuya. This charming but clumsy foreigner provides "temporary comfort" to the suffering patients. He holds one person's hand and talks to him, kneeling beside his bed like a "bent nail," sharing his sufferings.

Endō may have been influenced by a French novel by Georges Bernanos (1888–1948) that interested him greatly—*Journal d'un curé de campagne* (1936; English translation *The Diary of a Country Priest*, 1937). In France, Endō watched a 1951 film adaptation by Robert Bresson. The protagonist, a priest who suffers from a stomach illness, comes to a small village for parish work. The villagers avoid contact with the priest, ridiculing and mocking him. He can relieve his stomach pain only by drinking alcohol, but he continues to devote himself to serving the villagers. Everything he does fails and appears to be meaningless. Yet when he dies, his last words are "All is God's grace." Endō was deeply touched by this ending.[34] The Gastons in the three novels by Endō are like this country priest.

5. Evangelization at a Bar

Neyrand liked to teach at universities while he was supervising students at the Shinsei Kaikan, because having a teacher's "authority" was useful for his communication with them. He taught translation at the Institut franco-japonais de Tokyo and French at the College of Arts and Sciences at the University of Tokyo for seventeen years. He also lectured at Keiō University and Rikkyō University.[35] He told his students that a *cultured* person is not necessarily an *erudite* person, but must have the ability and sensitivity to

---

33 Inoue and Shiba, "Shūkyō to Nihonjin," 270.
34 Endō, "Shinpu tachi (sono 2)," 213–14.
35 Neyrand, *Obaka-san no jijoden hanbun: Seisho katate ni Nippon 36 nenkan*, 80–81.

understand other people's opinions and to appreciate works of art.[36] In fact, for a missionary, understanding of Japanese culture largely depends on this ability and sensitivity.

Neyrand's unique personality caused some people to doubt that he really was a Catholic priest. On first meeting he seemed short-tempered and arbitrary, but at the same time he was instructing people around him, fostering an approach that he called "think in an essential manner about what is essential."[37] An article titled "What Neyrand Said to the Japanese" by journalist Yamauchi Keisuke, who in his youth spent a lot of time with Neyrand, depicts Neyrand's personality more clearly. According to Yamauchi, Neyrand decided intuitively how best to fulfill his mission. In rapid succession, Neyrand initiated a student newspaper called *Shio* (Salt), and established a private-tutoring school called Neran Juku (Yamauchi suggested the name; Neyrand had wanted to call it Ryōzanpaku, after a place in Shandong made famous in the great Chinese novel *Shuihu zhuan* [Water Margin]).[38] During the four and half years of Neran Juku's operation, Neyrand baptized dozens of students.[39] In fact, one of the school's graduates would look after him during his final days.

Yamauchi became one of the editors of *Shio* and learned from the other student editors. He felt that the example of Neyrand's missionary work and faith "opened his eyes" to the world. Throughout his service as supervising priest at Catholic Research Centers at the University of Tokyo, Tokyo University of Education, and Chūō University, and also as a teacher of French at the University of Tokyo, Neyrand adhered strictly to his belief in the existence of the risen Christ.[40]

Neyrand once said that the Japanese would not reveal their true feelings unless they were drunk. Thus a good place to to propagate Christianity, he decided, would be a bar. In such an establishment he could pour alcohol and Christian doctrine simultaneously for his customers. He found a location in the Kabukichō neighborhood of Shinjuku, an area densely populated with bars and clubs, and in June 1980 named the bar エポペ (Épopée). He

---

36 Ibid., 35–37.
37 Yamauchi, "Futoccho na oyaji no koto," 8–9.
38 Yamauchi, "Neran-san wa Nihonjin ni nani o katatta ka," 62.
39 Neyrand, *Obaka-san no jijoden hanbun: Seisho katate ni Nippon 36 nenkan*, 97.
40 Yamauchi, "Neran-san wa Nihonjin ni nani o katatta ka," 49–53.

said that he chose this name because it is easy for Japanese to pronounce.[41] He registered Épopée Corporation as a "Food service for Christian propagation." Advertising the bar's opening in an "Invitation Letter," he wrote, "We have no cosmetics or karaoke, but this is a small, quiet, and relaxing place to drink. The name of the bartender is Neyrand." The name of the place, he explained, means "a beautiful adventure" in French.

The idea of opening an evangelization bar sounds eccentric, but Neyrand justified it by saying that there are many priests who have side jobs like writing books, working at offices, managing business companies, becoming legislators, and teaching at schools, as well as worker-priests who have blue-collar jobs. He also made reference to a deep relationship between Christianity and alcohol. For instance, the Old Testament (Genesis 9) says that the first person who made wine from grapes was Noah. Psalm 104 praises God for bringing humans food, "wine that gladdens human hearts, oil to make their faces shine, and bread that sustains their hearts." In the New Testament, the Gospel According to John tells of Jesus' first miracle, the changing of water to wine at the wedding party at Cana of Galilee. Neyrand took wine as a symbol for paradise. He intended his bar to trace back to the origin of Christianity and to spread the aroma of the wine served at the wedding feast at Cana. He believed that it was the most suitable place to propagate Christianity to office workers who are too busy to visit a Christian church. He often quoted a Latin proverb popular in France, "in vino veritas" (in wine lies truth).[42]

Endō Shūsaku was surprised by Neyrand's strong determination and believed that he was the only priest in the world whose side job was bartending.[43] Two months after the bar opened, a *Yomiuri shinbun* journalist visited Neyrand there. He reported that "There is nothing about religion in the shop. The friendly priest was extremely popular…He chatted with customers in fluent Japanese…Touched by his enthusiasm, about ninety people invested 20 million yen in Épopée, including the archbishop of Tokyo and four other priests who became its stockholders."[44]

Every year, Neyrand invited customers to a Christmas party that included

---

41 Tobari, "Kabukichō no kaisō Neran shinpu," 396.

42 Neyrand, *Obaka-san no jijoden hanbun: Seisho katate ni Nippon 36 nenkan*, 134–43.

43 Endō, *Kawaru mono to kawaranu mono*, 91–93.

44 "Furansu shinpu Sunakku fukyō" フランス神父 スナック布教, *Yomiuri shinbun*, 1980. 8. 31.

a Mass and baptism. For many, this was the first Mass or baptism they had ever seen. When Neyrand asked a new believer, "Do you believe in Christ?" The answer "Yes, I do" made an "extremely strong impression" on dozens of others.[45] About seventy people from Épopée were baptized by Neyrand. Endō visited the bar and noticed that the patrons included young people, office workers, and female company employees, discussing religion and marriage while enjoying alcohol.[46]

Sociologist Nakano Osamu introduced Épopée in his book *Kī shinboru* (Key Symbols). "The priest talks to people of different occupations, issues several newsletters a year, and goes on overnight trips with his customers. The priest is a philosopher and evangelist who observes modern Japan very well. If you ask him about religion, he will give you an answer. In the toilet of the bar, there is a poster on the wall with the words 'Je crois parce que J'ai cru' (I believe because I believed)."[47]

Wada Makoto, the designer of the book jacket for Neyrand's *Obaka-san no jijoden hanbun* (Half-Autobiography of a Wonderful Fool), wrote that since the author was a priest in the daytime and a bartender at night, he drew a caricature of Neyrand shaking a cocktail shaker for the front cover and holding the Bible in his hand on the back. This illustration was used for the bar's promotional materials too.[48] The cover of the pocket-size edition of the book combined the two illustrations (Plate 25).

At Épopée, Neyrand asked customers not to call him "Neran shinpu" or "Neran sensei," but just "Neran san" in order to foster a sense of intimacy. He wanted to invite Pope John Paul II to Épopée when he was visiting Japan in 1981, but predictably his attempt to get on the Pope's schedule did not succeed.[49] Nor was the bar immediately successful as a vehicle for converting non-believers. During the first three years of Épopée, only seven customers were baptized. A frustrated Neyrand took this as "resistance" against Christianity, and attributed it to "the unique way of thinking of the Japanese people."[50]

---

45 Neyrand, *Obaka-san no jijoden hanbun: Seisho katate ni Nippon 36 nenkan*, 149–50.

46 Endō, *Watashi no rirekisho*, 255.

47 Nakano, *Kī shinboru: Kotoba no shakai tanken*, 54–55.

48 Wada, *Sōtei monogatari*, 256–56.

49 Yamauchi, "Neran-san wa Nihonjin ni nani o katatta ka," 58.

50 "Zainichi 30 nen, ima 'Sunakku dendō' chū no Furansujin shinpu Joruju Neran" 在日30年、いま"スナック伝道"中のフランス人神父ジョルジュ・ネラン, *Asahi shinbun*, 1983.2.5, morning issue.

Eight years after its opening, an *Asahi shinbun* correspondent visited Épopée and found it comfortable and warm. To him, it called to mind the warmth of Jesus.[51] Neyrand provided a peaceful place to drink alcohol along with Jesus' words. In later years, he baptized more than ten customers per year.[52] The barkeeper-priest opened the hearts of the Japanese by serving them alcohol, and he poured in words of the Gospels as well. In 1993, a young man by the name of Hirayama Tatsuya became the bartender, and started Épopée Net, a network to attract customers' attention to undeveloped regions in the world.[53] At the age of eighty, Neyrand stopped working regularly, cutting his visits to the bar to three times a week. The new manager, Shindō Shigemitsu, started an NGO with support from three hundred customers. They sent donations to the UNICEF, visited Vietnam, and provided financial support for building schools, constructing wells, and other social welfare programs there.[54]

During the period of the Pope's visit to Japan (Feburary 1981), Épopée was featured on several French TV programs. Neyrand was referred to as "a priest resembling Michel Galabru,"[55] who is a famous French comedian. Neyrand must have been happy about this comparison, since he had once wanted to become an entertainer and to play the role of a clown.

Eighty percent of Épopée's customers were fans of Endō Shūsaku. After the author's death in 1996, they rushed to Neyrand's Kabukichō bar to get a glimpse of the model for *Wonderful Fool*.[56]

Neyrand died in March 2011, and seven months later Épopée was closed, ending its history of thirty-one years. It seems the evangelization bar could not be sustained without a "missionary bartender" like Neyrand.

---

51 "Kirishitan bāten" 切支丹バーテン, *Asahi shinbun*, 1988.2.18, evening issue.

52 Yamauchi, "Neran-san wa Nihonjin ni nani o katatta ka," 59.

53 " 'Suramu ni kanshin motte' okyaku to kataru bāten"『スラムに関心持って』お客と語るバーテン, *Mainichi shinbun*, 1993.6.27.

54 "Shēkā furu shinpu" シェーカー振る神父, *Asahi shinbun*, 2000.3.27, morning issue.

55 Tobari, "Kabukichō no kaisō Neran shinpu," 398.

56 "Korian fuan ga tsudou mise: 'Obaka-san' no moderu Neran shinpu ga keieisha" 狐狸庵ファンが集う店：「おバカさん」のモデル　ネラン神父が経営者, *Mainichi shinbun*, 1996. 10.7, evening issue.

6. Tolerance towards Local Beliefs

Neyrand tried to teach the Catholic Catechism to Endō's mother-in-law, who was a pious Buddhist. But no matter how hard the priest endeavored, she could not understand it at all. Neyrand assured Endō's wife, "Your mother does not need to learn the Catechism. She will go to heaven without this knowledge."[57] Endō was impressed by Neyrand's broad-mindedness, and his wife too was touched and said, "He did not want to disturb my mother's mind. She had already reached a state of peace. I am grateful for his understanding."[58] A while later, shortly before her death, Endō's mother-in-law voiced her concern about his advancing cancer and told her daughter, "I will take Shūsaku's illness away with me."[59] This expression is very similar to Jesus' words "I will carry your sufferings," to which Endō repeatedly referred in his novels. Neyrand did not see any necessity to teach this old woman, as she was already equipped with a sense of morality similar to that of Christianity.

For many Japanese, the similarity between Buddhist morality and Christian morality makes it hard to distinguish them from each other. An old woman in Kyushu referred to Pope John Paul II as "a person like the Buddha" and prayed to him during his visit.[60] This comment exemplifies the mixing of Buddhism and Christianity in ordinary people's minds.

In Xavier's letters, the obstacles to his Japan mission were often called "demons." For instance, he wrote that he would "pray that our Lord Jesus Christ will give us victory over the two demons Xaca [Shakyamuni] and Amida." As Xavier saw it, the goal of Japanese Buddhist temples was to take away believers' posessions by promising them that "all the money they give to the bonzes [monks] in the names of Xaca and Amida will be returned to them with large interest after their death." Several monks, disappointed by the lack of "salvation" in Buddhism, decided to convert to Christianity after learning its teaching from Xavier.[61]

Xavier wanted to lead the Japanese to salvation—a salvation that was unrelated to monetary compensation. Some Japanese were saddened to hear

---

57 Endō and Suzuki, *Otto Endō Shūsaku o kataru*, 77.

58 Endō Junko, *Saikai: Otto no shukudai sorekara*, 143.

59 Endō and Suzuki, *Otto Endō Shūsaku o kataru*, 77.

60 Tobari, "Kabukichō no kaisō Neran shinpu," 399.

61 Xavier's letter written on 29 January 1552 from Cochin to the Society of Jesus in Europe, in Coleridge, *The Life and Letters of St. Francis Xavier*, vol. 2, 341–46.

that their family members who died without Christian baptism might go to Hell. Xavier was sympathetic to their sorrow, but told them that giving money or just praying would not save their family members, which saddened them even more. He wrote, "I can hardly restrain my tears sometimes at seeing men so dear to my heart suffer such intense pain about a thing which is already done with and can never be undone."[62]

In the twentieth century, Neyrand told Endō's mother-in-law that she could go to Heaven without learning Christianity. What he said seems heretical. But he probably judged that she was "Christian" enough. This reminds us of how Xavier reponded to Kagoshima people who complained about why God did not appear to them earlier. Xavier told them "the reason itself teaches us to avoid evil and to do good, and that this is so deeply implanted in the hearts of men, that all have the knowledge of the divine law from nature and from God the Author of nature before they receive any external instruction on the subject."[63] In other words, the good nature of a person, regardless of whether he or she knows Christianity or not, is already a sign of God's work.

Neyrand frankly wrote, "After coming to Japan, I have met many people who know nothing about Christ. They all live a good human life and have no moral deficiency. After World War II, Japan attained affluence with astonishing speed, and yet still has maintained a high level of social morality. Many Japanese are engaged in humanitarian activities or are devoting themselves to improving social welfare. Among them there are almost no Christians. When the society does not require Christian faith, I question the raison d'être of myself being a Christian and a missionary." Nevertheless, Neyrand wanted to convert the Japanese. It is a deficiency in the philosophical understanding of Japanese people, he stated in an essay, that they believe only in what they see with their own eyes—what is invisible cannot exist. He speculated that this was the primary reason Christianity had stagnated in Japan. In sharp contrast with such thinking, Plato had argued that things invisible do indeed exist, and his theory had acted to stimulate the development of Western culture. But in Japan, no one took this proposition seriously. Neyrand wrote, "What Japan needs is not an excellent theologian, but rather a Japanese Plato."[64]

---

62 Ibid., 347.
63 Ibid., 339.
64 Neyrand, "Iesu wa ikite iru," 64–70.

Neyrand wanted to convey to Japan the teaching about the immanent Christ, the Christ who is living in the world today. "His disciples testified to his resurrection. Moreover they risked their lives to bear witness. From two thousand years ago to the present, there have been countless people who died for this testimony. Can you still say that they only saw an illusion?," questioned Neyrand.[65]

He taught that the difference between the words *shūkyō* in Japanese and "religion" in the West could be expressed as follows. The former prizes faith itself above all else, while the latter emphasizes the object of faith most. In the case of belief in Amida, the emphasis is placed on complete reliance on Amida rather than on pursuit of the existence or the essence of Amida. In contrast, Christianity places importance on Christ's life. Therefore, passionate Buddhists deepen their faith, and pious Christians their understanding of Christ himself. To Neyrand, Buddhism and Christianity were not contradictory. A person can be both a Buddhist and a Christian, just as a person can be a pianist and an artist simultaneously.[66]

7. Relations with Japanese Intellectuals

Neyrand's close relationship with Endō Shūsaku is widely known, but he also had contacts with other writers. Novelist Miura Shumon (1926–2017) studied the Bible with him when he was thirty-three, and was baptized by him four years later in 1963.[67] He took Endō as his godfather. Writer Suga Atsuko (1929–1998) also knew Neyrand. In her diary written during her stay in Italy, she mentioned him numorous times—when expecting him to find a job for her in Japan (2 and 6 Feburary 1971), upon being inspired by his opinion (17 February), and upon replying to a letter from him (19 March), for example.[68]

Novelist Yasuoka Shōtarō (1920–2014) seemed to have gone to Épopée frequently. When writing about the grand reconstruction of Paris carried out by Napoleon III, he mentioned Neyrand. "An eccentric priest who is managing a bar in Shinjuku called Napoleon 'the Tanaka Kakuei of

---

65 Neyrand, *Obaka-san no jijoden hanbun: Seisho katate ni Nippon 36 nenkan*, 160–61.
66 Ibid., 168–71.
67 Miura, "Miura Shumon nenpu," 407.
68 Suga, *Suga Atsuko zenshū*, vol. 7, 440–515.

France.'"[69] Former prime minister Tanaka is famous for his plan of reconstructing Japan in the 1970s.

Neyrand's frankness was impressive. According to Yamauchi Keisuke, he once said that Miura Shumon's Christian faith was insufficient, and claimed that he had seen the baptism record of Shōda Michiko (b. 1934), the Empress Emerita, by looking at the baptism register of Azabu Catholic Church, Tokyo, when he was an assistant priest there. He also criticized Cardinal Taguchi Yoshigorō (1902–1978) and Cardinal Satowaki Asajirō (1904–1996) for not acknowledging their responsibility for misleading the church during World War II.[70]

Endō Shūsaku thought that Neyrand's contribution to the Catholic Church in Japan had not been properly recognized, and decided to organize a ceremony to commemorate the thirtieth anniversary of his service in Japan and to express gratitude. Without letting his friend know, Endō invited Neyrand's older brother and his wife from Strasburg, France to this event. When all the attendees had arrived, Endō began the ceremony by surprising Neyrand with the appearance of his brother. The two embraced each other tightly.[71] Neyrand later recalled this moment saying, "In an instant I thought it was a dream. What an unexpected gift!"[72] The ceremony was held at Shinsei Kaikan and was attended by more than 230 people, including Mushanokōji Kinhide (b. 1929; a scholar of international political studies), Arai Sasagu (b. 1930; a scholar of theology), and Shirayanagi Seiichi (1928–2009; Archbishop of Tokyo and later cardinal).[73]

Endō spoke at another ceremony honoring Neyrand, an event held to publicize the publication of *Obaka-san no jijoden hanbun* (Half-Autobiography of the Wonderful Fool). On that occasion, Endō declared that "Neyrand married Japan." In response, Neyrand announced, "Missionaries are clowns, and I will continue to perform as a clown."[74]

As the years went by, Neyrand was happy to see more and more young

69 Yasuoka, "Daiseikimatsu sākasu," 68.

70 Yamauchi, "Neran-san wa Nihonjin ni nani o katatta ka," 61–62.

71 Ibid., 61.

72 Neyrand, *Obaka-san no jijoden hanbun: Seisho katate ni Nippon 36 nenkan*, 153.

73 Kirisutokyō Nenkan Henshūbu, *Kirisutokyō nenkan*, vol. 27, 59.

74 "Nippon to kekkon?! 36 shūnen" ニッポンと結婚?!　36周年, *Yomiuri shinbun*, 1988.3.7, morning issue.

Japanese couples choosing church weddings. "It seems they are attracted to Christianity naturally. The increase of church weddings of non-believers examplifies how Christianity took root in this country." To Neyrand, the indigenization of Christianity in Japan meant "using a Japanese point of view to understand Christianity and making it blossom." He also thought, "It is possible to have rituals, theological studies, and church management in a Japanese manner."[75]

Fig. 21, Neyrand celebrating the 50th anniversary of his ordination, from the Home Page of Épopée.

Neyrand strategically aimed his books written in Japanese at Japanese readers. It was with Japanese readers in mind that he wrote, "Among millions of creatures, human beings are the only ones who know that they all have to die...But humans were created to try to gain eternal life by transcending death. In this sense, there is no contradiction between knowing the destiny of death and trying to live long...Christ overcame death, therefore those who live with Christ can also overcome death. The so-called next world is to live eternally with Christ."[76]

In pronouncements such as this, Neyrand preached to his Japanese audience that relying on Christ can satisfy humans' desire for "living forever." He combined "faith" and "religion" for them. Using a propagation method very different from that of Xavier, adopting a clown-like style, engaging them over drinks at a bar, and writing many books and essays in their language, Neyrand appealed to the psychology and emotions of the Japanese people. His teaching succeeded in bringing Christianity into the daily lives of multitudes of Japanese.

---

75 Neyrand, *Obaka-san no jijoden hanbun: Seisho katate ni Nippon 36 nenkan*, 176.
76 Ibid., 192.

Chronology of G. Neyrand's Life[77]

Years	age	Activities
1920	0	2 February, born in Lyon, France.
1937	17	Graduated from high school.
1939	19	June, admitted to École Spéciale Militaire de Saint-Cyr. Graduated early because of World War II. Became second lieutenant and was sent to fight at Narbonne city in south France.
1940	20	Demobilized from the army as first lieutenant when France surrendered to Germany.
1943	23	September, entered the Grand Séminaire de Lyon.
1950	30	June, ordained a priest. July, welcomed Endō Shūsaku and the Mikumo brothers to Lyon.
1951	31	September, joined the Société des Auxiliaires des Missions in Belgium.
1952	32	9 December, arrived in Yokohama. Called the day "my second birthday."
1955	33	September, assigned to the Nagasaki diocese.
1957	37	Transferred to Tokyo and began twenty-year assignment as supervisor of students at Shinsei Kaikan. Became priest in charge of the Association of Catholic Research at the University of Tokyo, Tokyo University of Education, and Chūō University.
1959	39	Commenced publication of 13 volumes of *Rogosu: Kirisutokyō kenkyū sōsho* (Logos: Research Series on Christianity) which continued until 1964.
1960	40	Published *Anchioke no Igunachio shokan* (Correspondence of Ignatius in Antioch), co-translated with Kawazoe Toshiaki.
1962	42	April, opened Neran Juku; trained 1500 students until its closure in 1967.
1963	43	December, baptized Miura Shumon.
1969	49	Published *Warera jinsei o ronzu* (We Talk about Life)
1970	50	Became the chief director of Shinsei Kaikan; continued in that position until 1976.
1972	52	Published *Kami no ba: Tiyāru do Sharudan no Kirisutokyōkan* (The Space of God: Teilhard de Chardin's View of Christianity).
1974	54	Published *Shinzuru koto* (To Believe).
1976	56	Became priest for S. Mary's International School.
1979	59	December, published *Kirisuto ron* (On Christ).
1980	60	June, opened Épopée as an evangelization bar. July, *Sakariba shisai no mōgoroku* (Teachings by a Bar Priest) was published.
1982	62	Published *Le Palais des Fêtes* (translation of Mishima Yukio's *Rokumeikan*).
1983	63	16 February, was honored at a ceremony to commemorate Neyrand's thirty years in Japan at Shinsei Kaikan.
1988	68	Retired from Épopée and moved to "Home of Priests." Published *Obaka-san no jijoden hanbun: Seisho katate ni Nippon 36 nenkan* (Half-Autobiography of the Wonderful Fool: Thirty-six Years in Japan with the Bible in Hand).
1997	77	Published *Kirisuto no fukkatsu* (The Resurrection of Christ).

---

77 Based on Yamauchi, "Neran-san wa Nihonjin ni nani o katatta ka," 63, and Neyrand, *Obaka-san no jijoden hanbun: Seisho katate ni Nippon 36 nenkan.*

2000	80	Celebrated fifty years of priesthood at the hall of St. Mary's Cathedral in Tokyo. Published *Ma, nominagara demo, anata ni Kirisuto o go-shōkai shimasu* (Let Me Introduce You to Christ while Drinking).
2011	91	24 March, died.
2016		Neyrand's *Nani o oitemo Seisho o yominasai* (Read the Bible First) was published.

CONCLUSION

Missionary Contributions to Japanese Culture

This book substantiates that the influence of St. Francis Xavier on Japan did not end when the so-called Kirishitan century was forcibly terminated, but rather it was inherited and further developed by modern missionaries who mastered the Japanese language, acquired a deep comprehension of Japanese culture, and wrote copiously in Japanese.

This fact has attracted little attention from researchers of Japanese Studies, either inside or outside Japan. Overlooked has been the quantity and quality of books penned in Japanese by at least three hundred missionaries between the 1860s and the beginning of the twenty-first century; approximately three thousand books have been identified so far by a recent research project.[1]

Generally speaking, in addition to the selection and organization of content, authors always have to face decisions about which language and what

---

1 The author of this book led a team research project (funded by the National Institutes for the Humanities) titled "Literary Legacy of Kirishitan Culture: Missionary Writings in the Vernacular" from October 2014 till March 2019, with about thirty participating scholars from Britain, China, Italy, Japan, New Zealand, Portugal, Serbia, Spain, Taiwan, and the United States. This research project's website, located in the homepage of the International Research Center for Japanese Studies (with which the author was formerly affiliated), https://krishitan.rspace.nichibun.ac.jp, includes an extensive bibliography of books written in Japanese by modern missionaries.

style to employ for writing. The majority of authors use the language they have the best command of, usually their mother tongues. However, using a foreign language or a language acquired by education—for example, Latin in Europe and Chinese *kanbun* in East Asia—was a common practice among intellectuals until the early twentieth century.

There have been also numerous novelists and poets in the world who have chosen, for social, political, religious, or artistic reasons, to write literary works in what is for them a foreign language. In present-day Japan, it is not surprising that books are being written in Japanese by non-native speakers, yet the number of the non-Japanese writers and the quantity of their writings remain limited.

During the last thirty years, *Nihongo Bungaku* (literature in Japanese by non-native writers, or by authors from multilingual backgrounds) has emerged as a new research field, and its value and future potential are being assessed.[2] The writings by missionaries (mainly from Europe and North America) should not be ignored, for the number of authors is large, the quality of their works is high, and the quantity of their writings is vast. Eventually I believe this genre will become esteemed as one of the main streams within the field of *Nihongo Bungaku*.

Studying the Japanese language and immersing themselves in Japanese society is part of the work of missionaries. Not only oral communication, but written texts are also important tools of propagation. Writing in Japanese, often with Japanese assistants, is an essential task in their Japan life. Since the 1990s, the convenience of Japanese word processing software which has the capability to convert rōmaji into kanji and kana, has made it much easier for missionaries to perform this task.

This book investigated four Catholic missionaries who devoted their lives to the Japanese people: Aimé Villion who spent sixty-four years in Japan, Sauveur Candau, twenty-one years, Hermann Heuvers, fifty-four years, and Georges Neyrand, fifty-nine years. It is relatively easy to recognize the influence of their writings on Japan, but there are many more missionaries whose contributions to modern Japan still await research and evaluation.

Many of their publications have gone out of print, but some have enjoyed wide circulation, as they spoke in a timely manner to contemporary Japa-

---

2 See Guo/Kaku, ed., *Bailingaru na Nihongo Bungaku: Tagengo tabunka no aida* (2013), a collection of papers investigating literary works by non-native writers.

nese concerns. For instance, Fr. Alfons Deeken (b. 1932), a German-born Jesuit who taught *Ningengaku* (On Human Beings) and *Shi no tetsugaku* (Philosophy of Death) at Sophia University, and pioneered a research field *Shiseigaku* (Study of Death and Living) as a field for scholarly research, is a well-known figure in Japan. "Humans have to die," he once wrote, "because the genetic code of death is already built into their DNA. It is an inevitable natural phenomenon that humans, as organisms, age and die. Only when we know this, can we appreciate the preciousness of our life, and can spend our days more meaningfully."[3] This kind of advice is beneficial to anyone who takes life seriously. That is why Deeken's works enjoy wide and repeated circulation.

Most clergy were born and raised by pious families, so devotion, modesty, and charity were all part of their upbringing. These characteristics can be seen in their Japan missions as well. The most obvious feature shared by missionary authors is their commitment to learning the local tongue and culture, and to communicating with the Japanese people in the Japanese language.

The four missionaries treated in this book followed Xavier's steps. They helped Japanese communities to improve medical care, social welfare, and educational systems. Although their ultimate goal was to convey Christian messages and convert the people, they often opted not to try to impose Christianity, as the men and women they got to know seemed to be "Christian enough" already.

Candau's talents in the Japanese language were thought to be "a gift from God."[4] Not only Candau, but also many other missionaries spoke excellent Japanese, as if having been touched by the tongues of fire of the Holy Spirit described in the New Testament. In fact, they all tried to share the Spirit with the Japanese people, even though not so many converted to Christianity.

According to recent statistics, in 2016 about 1,914,196 people, 1.5 percent of the Japanese population (126,706,000 in 2017) are registered as Christians.[5] Many Japanese people today practice three religious faiths during their life cycle—Shinto for birth, Christianity for marriage, and

---

3 Deeken/Dēken, *Yūmoa wa oi to shi no myōyaku: Shiseigaku no susume*, 3.

4 Nomura, "Wareware no oyaji," 127.

5 Bunkachō, *Shūkyō nenkan Heisei 29 nen*, 35.

Buddhism for funerals—without committing to a single one. Moreover, half of the population is characterized as having "double faith" in Buddhism and Shinto. The total number of worshipers is 172,441,768, about 50 million more than the entire population (survey respondents were allowed to give multiple answers for their religious affiliation). Most Japanese have never gone through any ritual to formally establish their identity as a believer in any particular faith.

In a Japanese government survey conducted in 2015, two interesting points of data stand out. One is that about 72 percent of 1,591 survey respondents stated that they have no religious faith. The other is that 66 percent of those surveyed responded that religious faith is "important," 21 percent said "not important," and 10 percent "don't know."[6] The results of this survey support the proposition that the Japanese people treasure religious faith, even though most of them disavow belonging to any religious organization.

The "double faithful" will never claim to be Christian, because they know that Christianity requires worshipers to be baptized. Interestingly, many people who rarely visit a church are happy to celebrate their own weddings in a church. Just for several hours, they become "triple faithful." With more than half of the population opting for church weddings, it is evident that there is a strong trust in and respect for Christian culture in Japan.

This phenomenon would not be possible if missionaries had not propagated Christianity in Japan with a significant measure of success. Villion awakened Japan to its bloody history of Kirishitan persecution, Candau opened the eyes of the people with his superb Japanese and philosophical instruction, H. Heuvers enchanted Japanese readers with his poetic expression, and Neyrand successfully transformed a bar into a place for evangelization.

By writing in Japanese, these men introduced Christian religion, history, and literature to the Japanese people; they observed Japan insightfully and influenced a surprising number of important Japanese intellectuals. It is not an exaggeration to say that they contributed greatly, alongside the people of Japan, to the construction of modern Japanese culture. They materialized Xavier's dream of evangelizing Japan.

---

6 Bunkachō Bunkabu Sōmuka, *Shūkyō kanren tōkei ni kansuru shiryōshū*, 56.

This book has investigated the Japanese literary output of these missionaries in order to shine light on their outstanding achievements in observing and describing Japan from inside and outside. Their writings amplify our understanding of the five-century-long dialogue between Europe and Japan, heightening our appreciation of the important role Christianity played in shaping Japanese culture today.

BIBLIOGRAPHY

Abe, Toshiya. "From Prohibition to Toleration: Japanese Government Views Regarding Christianity, 1854–73." *Japanese Journal of Religious Studies* 5: 2/3 (1978): 107–38.

Allières, Jacques/Jakku Ariēru ジャック・アリエール. *Basukujin* バスク人. Translated by Hagio Shō 萩尾生. Hakusuisha, 1992.

Ama Tokumon 阿満得聞. *Ikyō taiwa: Ichimei, Inmyōjutsu* 異教対話：一名・因明術. Osaka: Yorozuya Kyūsaemon, 1897.

An Jon'on 安廷苑. *Hosokawa Garasha: Kirishitan shiryō kara mita shōgai* 細川ガラシャ：キリシタン史料から見た生涯. Chūō Kōron Shinsha, 2014.

Ando, Yasunori. "Doi Takeo and the Development of the 'Amae' Theory." In *Religion and Psychotherapy in Modern Japan*, edited by Christopher Harding, Iwata Fumiaki, and Yoshinaga Shin'ichi, 137–49. Abingdon and New York: Routledge, 2015.

Anesaki Masaharu 姉崎正治. "Zesusu-kai no jinbutsu: Nihonbun no tassha Nabaruro to sono jūsha sūnin" ゼスス会の人物・日本文の達者ナバルロとその従者数人. In *Kirishitan hakugai shi chū no jinbutsu jiseki* 切支丹迫害史中の人物事蹟, edited by Anesaki, 49–58. Dōbunkan, 1930.

Anouilh, Paul/Anui Pōru アヌイ・ポール. "Daishingakkōchō to shite no Sōvūru Dandō" 大神学校長としてのソーヴール・カンドウ師. *Seiki* 世紀 73 (1956): 106–10.

Aoki Fukiko 青木富貴子. *731*. Shinchōsha, 2005.

Arima Makiko 有馬眞喜子. "Shiratori Yoshirō-shi" 白鳥芳朗氏. *Kikan jinruigaku* 季刊人類学 9: 2 (1978): 144–52.

Arrupe, Pedro. *Este Japon Increible*. Bilbao: El siglo de las misiones, 1959; fourth edition, Bilbao: Mensajero, 1991.

Asahi Shinbunsha 朝日新聞社, ed. *Kaigai hōdō ni miru Shōwa tennō* 海外報道にみる昭和天皇. Asahi Shinbunsha, 1989.

Baekelmans, Peter/Bākerumansu Petero バーケルマンス・ペテロ. *Iesu to Kūkai: Fuji no sekai* イエスと空海：不二の世界. Kyoto: Nakanishiya Shuppan, 2012.

Barillas, Martin. "A Prayer for the Autumn Years of Life." *Spero News* (3 July 2011) https://www.speroforum.com/a/56477/A-Prayer-for-the-Autumn-Years-of-Life

Besineau, Jacques/Bejino Jakku ベジノ・ジャック, and Echizen Kiroku 越前喜六, eds. *Tsukaeru tameni: Iezusu kaishi no ayumi* 仕えるために: イエズス会士の歩み. Sanpauro, 2007.

Bitter, Bruno/Bittā Burūno ビッター・ブルーノ. "Shinpu no hito to shōgai" 神父の人と生涯. In *Hoiverusu shinpu: Shinkō to shisō* ホイヴェルス神父: 信仰と思想, edited by Doi Takeo 土居健郎 and Morita Akira 森田明, 8–20. Nagasaki: Seibo no Kishisha, 2003.

Boxer, Charles R. "Hosokawa Tadaoki and the Jesuits, 1587–1646." *Transactions and Proceedings of the Japan Society, London*, 32 (1935): 79–119.

Bunkachō 文化庁. *Shūkyō chōsa tōkei* 宗教調査統計. 2018, 2008. https://www.e-stat.go.jp/stat-search/files?page=1&toukei=00401101&tstat=000001018471&cycle=0&second2=1

Bunkachō Bunkabu Sōmuka 文化庁文化部総務課. *Shūkyō kanren tōkei ni kansuru shiryōshū*

宗教関連統計に関する資料集. Bunkachō, 2015.

Candau, Sauveur/Kandō S. カンドウ. "Nihonjin to Basukujin" 日本人とバスク人. *Koe* 声 612 (1927): 30–33.

Candau, Sauveur/Kandō S. カンドウ. "Oriori no mondai" 折々の問題. *Koe* 声 648 (1930): 14–20.

Candau, Sauveur/Kandō S. *Lexicon Latino-Japonicum* 羅和字典. Kōkyō Shingakkō, 1934; reprint, Nan'undō Fenikkusu, 1995.

Candau, Sauveur/Kandō S. and Kanayama Masahide 金山政英, trans. *Ai no tetsugaku: Kami no awase tamaishi mono* 愛の哲学：神の合せ給ひしもの. Kawade Shobō, 1949.

Candau, Sauveur/Kandō S. and Kanayama Masahide, trans. *Kirisuto to sono jidai* キリストとその時代, 3 vols. Sanseidō, 1949–1950.

Candau, Sauveur/Kandō S. *Shisō no tabi* 思想の旅. Sanseidō, 1952.

Candau, Sauveur 苅田澄, trans. *Kaimiroa* カイミロア. Hōsei Daigaku Shuppankyoku, 1953.

Candau, Sauveur 苅田澄. *Seijin jigoku e iku* 聖人地獄へ行く. Hōsei Daigaku Shuppankyoku, 1953.

Candau, Sauveur/Kandō S. *Sekai no ura omote* 世界のうらおもて. Asahi Shinbunsha, 1955.

Candau, Sauveur/Kandō S. *Eien no kessaku* 永遠の傑作. Tōhō Shobō, 1955.

Candau, Sauveur/Kandō S. *Basuku no hoshi* バスクの星. Tōhō Shobō, 1956.

Candau, Sauveur/Kandō S. S. *Kandō ikkan senshū* S・カンドウ一巻選集. Shunjūsha, 1969.

Candau, Sauveur/Kandō S. *Shisaku no yorokobi: Kandō shinpu no eien no kotoba* 思索のよろこび：カンドウ神父の永遠のことば. Shunjūsha, 1971.

Candau, Sauveur/Kandō S. "Shisō no eizokusei: Watashi no kangaku shugyō jidai" 思想の永続性：私の漢学修業時代. *Shibun* 斯文 13 (1955): 1–12.

Candau, Sauveur/Kandō S. "Furansugo to Nihongo" フランス語と日本語. In *Utsukushii kokugo, tadashii kokuji* 美しい国語・正しい国字, edited by Mutō Tatsuo 武藤辰男, 124–26. Kawade Shobō, 1954.

Candau, Sauveur/Kandō S. "Banshū bōkyō" 晩秋望郷. In *Kandō zenshū* カンドウ全集, edited by Ikeda Toshio 池田敏雄, vol. 1, 64–72. Chūō Shuppansha, 1970.

Candau, Sauveur/Kandō S.. "Shingan ni eijitaru Nihon" 心眼に映じたる日本. In *Kandō zenshū* カンドウ全集, edited by Ikeda Toshio, vol. 1, 15–30. Chūō Shuppansha, 1970.

Candau, Sauveur/Kandō S. "Tōzai no zadankai" 東西の座談会. In *Kandō zenshū* カンドウ全集, edited by Ikeda Toshio, vol. 1, 73–78. Chūō Shuppansha, 1970.

Candau, Sauveur/Kandō S. "Gendai Furansu no shisōkai" 現代フランスの思想界. In *Kandō zenshū* カンドウ全集, edited by Ikeda Toshio, vol. 3, 283–98. Chūō Shuppansha, 1970.

Candau, Sauveur/Kandō S. "Kuruma to kaze to jibiki to" 車と風邪と字引と. In *Kandō zenshū* カンドウ全集, edited by Ikeda Toshio, vol. 4, 15–17. Chūō Shuppansha, 1970.

Candau, Sauveur/Kandō S. "Takezukushi" 竹づくし. In *Kandō zenshū* カンドウ全集, edited by Ikeda Toshio, vol. 4, 41–43. Chūō Shuppansha, 1970.

Candau, Sauveur/Kandō S. *Kandō zenshū* カンドウ全集, edited by Ikeda Toshio, 7 vols. Chūō Shuppansha, 1970.

Candau, Sauveur/Kandō S. and Shishi Bunroku 獅子文六. "Nihon are kore 'Shishi Bunroku-shi to no taidan" 日本あれこれ〈獅子文六氏との対談〉. In *Shisaku no yorokobi: Kandō shinpu no eien no kotoba* 思索のよろこび：カンドウ神父の永遠のことば, edited by Miyamoto Saeko 宮本さえ子, 143–59. Shunjūsha, 1971.

Catret, Juan/Katoretto, Hoan カトレット・ホアンand Takahashi Atsuko 高橋敦子, trans. *Pedoro Arupe: Kibō o motarasu hito* ペドロ・アルペ：希望をもたらす人. Shinseisha, 1996.

Chikuma Shobō 筑摩書房. *Sōgyō 50 shūnen: Chikuma Shobō tosho sōmokuroku, 1949–1990,*

創業五〇周年 筑摩書房図書総目録 一九四九―一九九〇. Chikuma Shobō, 1991.

Choe Yongsoo 崔英修. "Gaikokujin josei senkyōshi no bunkateki eikyō" 外国人女性宣教師の文化的影響. In *Kirishitan ga hiraita Nihongo Bungaku: Tagengo tabunka kōryū no engen* キリシタンが拓いた日本語文学: 多言語多文化交流の淵源, edited by Kaku Nanen, 384–401. Akashi Shoten, 2017.

Cole, Ann Louise. "Becoming All Things to All Men: The Role of Jesuit Missions in Early Modern Globalization." PhD diss., University of Arkansas, 2015.

Coleridge, Henry James. *The Life and Letters of St. Francis Xavier*. London: Burns and Oates. 2 vols. 1872.

Compri, Gaetano/Konpuri Gaetano コンプリ・ガエタノ. "Opera 'Hosokawa Garashia' konshū jōen" オペラ『細川ガラシア』今秋上演. Amici Musica Don Cimatti, 2014. http://www.v-cimatti.com/opera/200406.pdf

Cooper, Michael. *They Came to Japan: An Anthology of European Reports on Japan, 1543–1640*. Berkeley, Los Angeles, London: University of California Press, 1981.

Crasset, Jean (aka. Mr l'abbé de T). *Histoire de l'Église du Japon*. Paris: Estienne Michallet, premier imprimeur du Roy, 1689.

Crasset, Jean (aka. Mr l'abbé de T). *The History of the Church of Japan*, 2 vols. Translated by N. N. London: s. n., 1705–1707.

Crasset, Jean (aka. Mr l'abbé de T). *Nihon seikyō shi* 日本西教史. Translated by Daijōkan Honyaku Kakari 太政官翻訳係. Tokyo: Sakagami Hanshichi, 1880.

Dandō Shigemitsu 団藤重光. "*Shikei haishi ron* o kaita Keihō Gakkai no jūchin"『死刑廃止論』を書いた刑法学会の重鎮. In *Shikei haishi: Nihon no shōgen* 死刑廃止・日本の証言, edited by Kikuta Kōichi 菊田幸一, 77–93. San-ichi Shobō, 1993.

Deeken, Alfonse/Arufonsu Dēken アルフォンス・デーケン. *Yūmoa wa oi to shi no myōyaku: Shiseigaku no susume* ユーモアは老いと死の妙薬: 死生学のすすめ. Kōdansha, 1995.

Diarusu ディアルス. *Jinrui ai no shito* 人類愛の使徒. In *Kandō zenshū* カンドウ全集, edited by Ikeda Toshio, supplement vol. 1. Chūō Shuppansha, 1970.

Doak, Kevin/Dōku Kebin ドーク・ケビン. "Kandō shinpu no Nihon bunka e no kōken" カンドウ神父の日本文化への貢献. In *Kirishitan ga hiraita Nihongo Bungaku* キリシタンが拓いた日本語文学, edited by Kaku Nanen, 218–32. Akashi Shoten, 2017.

Doi Tadao 土井忠生. *Kirishitan ronkō* 吉利支丹論攷. Sanseidō, 1982.

Doi Takeo 土居健郎 and Morita Akira 森田明, eds. *Hoiverusu shinpu: Shinkō to shisō* ホイヴェルス神父: 信仰と思想. Nagasaki: Seibo no Kishisha, 2003.

Dumoulin, Heinrich/Dumorin Hainrihi デュモリン・ハインリヒ. "'Sei Igunachio no yūbe' no Kandō-shi"「聖イグナチオの夕べ」のカンドー師. *Seiki* 世紀 73 (1956): 111–14.

Dumoulin, Heinrich/Dumorin Hainrihi. *Bukkyō to Kirisutokyō no kaikō* 仏教とキリスト教との邂逅. Translated by Nishimura Eshin 西村恵信. Shunjūsha, 1975.

Ebisawa Arimichi 海老沢有道. "Nihon nijūroku seijin kankei Nihon bunken" 日本二十六聖人関係日本文献. *Kirishitan kenkyū* キリシタン研究 8 (1963): 137–75.

Ebisawa Arimichi. "Kirishitan shi kenkyū kotohajime" キリシタン史研究事始め. In *Tanbō daikōkai jidai no Nihon 8: Kaisō to hakken* 探訪大航海時代の日本八 回想と発見, edited by Shōgakukan 小学館. Shōgakukan, 1969.

Ebisawa Arimichi. *Kirishitan Nanban bungaku nyūmon* キリシタン南蛮文学入門. Kyōbunkan, 1991.

Endō Junko 遠藤順子 and Suzuki Hideko 鈴木秀子. *Otto Endō Shūsaku o kataru* 夫・遠藤周作を語る. Bungei Shunjū, 1997.

Endō Junko. *Saikai: Otto no shukudai, sorekara* 再会：夫の宿題 それから. PHP Kenkyūjo, 2000.

Endō Shūsaku 遠藤周作. "Waga shōsetsu no moderu ni tsuite" わが小説のモデルについて. In G. Neran, *Obaka-san no jijoden hanbun: Seisho katate ni Nippon 36 nenkan* おバカさんの自叙伝半分：聖書片手にニッポン36年間, 1–3. Kōdansha, 1988.

Endō Shūsaku. *Kawaru mono to kawaranu mono* 変るものと変らぬもの. Bungei Shunjū, 1990.

Endō Shūsaku. "Shinpu tachi (sono 2)" 神父たち（その二）. In *Endō Shūsaku bungaku zenshū* 遠藤周作文学全集, vol. 13, 213–15. Shinchōsha, 2000.

Endō Shūsaku. *Watashi no rirekisho* 私の履歴書. In *Endō Shūsaku bungaku zenshū* 遠藤周作文学全集, vol. 14, 217–72. Shinchōsha, 2000.

Ewart, Paul. "The Physical Sciences and Natural Theology." In *Oxford Handbook of Natural Theology*, edited by Russell Re Manning, 419–33. Oxford: Oxford University Press, 2013.

Fróis, Luís/Furoisu Ruisu フロイス・ルイス and Matsuda Kiichi 松田毅一, trans. *Nihonshi 6, Bungo hen 1* 日本史6 豊後篇Ⅰ. Chūō Kōronsha, 1978, 1981.

Fróis, Luís/Furoisu Ruisu and Matsuda Kiichi, trans. *Nihonshi 2, Toyotomi Hideyoshi hen II* 日本史2 豊臣秀吉篇Ⅱ. Chūō Kōronsha, 1977, 1981.

Fróis, Luís/Furoisu Ruisu and Matsuda Kiichi, trans. *Nihonshi 5, Gokinnai hen 3* 日本史5 五畿内篇Ⅲ. Chūō Kōronsha, 1978, 1981.

Fróis, Luís/Furoisu Ruisu and Matsuda Kiichi, trans. *Nihonshi 9, Nishi Kyūshū hen 1* 日本史9 西九州篇Ⅰ. Chūō Kōronsha, 1979, 1982.

Fróis, Luís/Furoisu Ruisu and Matsuda Kiichi, trans. *Nihonshi 12, Nishi Kyūshū hen 4* 日本史12 西九州篇Ⅳ. Chūō Kōronsha, 1980, 1982.

Fujii Hakumin 藤井伯民. *Hosokawa Garashiya* 細川がらしや. Kōkyō Seinenkai, 1922.

Fujisawa Kosetsu 藤沢古雪. *Garashia: Shigeki* がらしあ：史劇. Dainihon Tosho, 1907.

Fukuda Kingetsu 福田琴月. "Hosokawa Garasha" 細川ガラシャ. *Nihon minzoku* 日本民族 1: 2 (1913): 86–90.

Fukuzawa Yukichi 福沢諭吉. *Fukuzawa Yukichi zenshū*, vol. 20. Iwanami Shoten, 1965; 2nd edition 1971.

Gakuen 学苑. "Gakusha junpōki 7: Shosai ni okeru Kandō shinpu" 学者巡訪記（7）：書斎におけるカンドウ神父. *Gakuen* 学苑 12: 4 (1950): 2–3.

Genyū Sōkyū 玄侑宗久 and Suzuki Hideko 鈴木秀子. *Bukkyō, Kirisutokyō shinikata ikikata* 仏教・キリスト教 死に方・生き方. PHP Kenkyūjo, 2013.

Goethe, Johann Wolfgang von/Gēte ゲーテ. "Sekai Bungaku ron" 世界文学, translated by Kogishi Akira 小岸昭. In *Gēte zenshū* ゲーテ全集, vol. 13. Shio Shuppansha, 1980; revised edition, 2003.

Gössmann, Elizabeth/ Gosuman Erizabēto ゴスマン・エリザベート. "Garasha Hosokawa Tama no jitsuzō to kyozō" ガラシャ細川玉の実像と虚像. In *Onna to otoko no jikū: Nihon joseishi saikō III: Onna to otoko no ran: Chūsei* 女と男の時空：日本女性史再考Ⅲ 女と男の乱：中世, edited by Okano Haruko 岡野治子, 116–34. Fujiwara Shoten, 1996.

Guo, Nanyan. "Discovering Traces of Humanity: Taking Individual Responsibility for Medical Atrocities." In *Japan's Wartime Medical Atrocities: Comparative Inquiries in Science, History and Ethics*, edited by Jing-Bao Nie, Nanyan Guo, Mark Selden, and Arthur Kleinman, 107–22. Abingdon, New York: Routledge, 2010.

Guo, Nanyan/Kaku Nanen 郭南燕. *Bairingaru na Nihongo Bungaku: Tagengo tabunka no aida* バイリンガルな日本語文学：多言語多文化のあいだ. Sangensha, 2013.

Guo, Nanyan/Kaku Nanen. *Shiga Naoya de "Sekai Bungaku" o yomitoku* 志賀直哉で「世界文学」を読み解く. Sakuhinsha, 2016.

Guo, Nanyan /Kaku Nanen. "Hoiverusu kyakuhon *Hosokawa Garashia Fujin*" ホイヴェルス脚本『細川ガラシア夫人』. In *Kirishitan ga hiraita Nihongo Bungaku: Tagengo tabunka kōryū no engen* キリシタンが拓いた日本語文学: 多言語多文化交流の淵源, edited by Kaku Nanen, 253–71. Akashi Shoten, 2017.

Guo, Nanyan. "Internationalization of the Japanese Language in Interwar Period Japan (1920–1940): Foreign Missionaries and Writers." *Japanese Studies Around the World* 世界の日本研究 (2017): 335–47.

Guo, Nanyan/Kaku Nanen. "Kindai Nihongo Bungaku no senkusha: Putijan shikyō to Do Ro shinpu" 近代日本語文学の先駆者：プティジャン司教とド・ロ神父. In *Do Ro hanga no tabi: Yōroppa kara Shanghai-Nagasaki e no tabunkateki yūgō* ド・ロ版画の旅：ヨーロッパから上海〜長崎への多文化的融合, edited by Kaku Nanen, 165–87. Sōjusha Bijutsu Shuppan, 2019.

Guo, Nanyan/Kaku Nanen. "Do Ro hanga no zensōkyoku: Sekiban insatsu kara saishiki mokuhanga e" ド・ロ版画の前奏曲：石版印刷から彩色木版画へ. In *Do Ro hanga no tabi: Yōroppa kara Shanghai-Nagasaki e no tabunkateki yūgō* ド・ロ版画の旅：ヨーロッパから上海〜長崎への多文化的融合, edited by Kaku Nanen, 11–54. Sōjusha Bijutsu Shuppan, 2019.

Guo, Nanyan/Kaku Nanen. "Do Ro hanga no rūtsu: Konsutantsu kara Shanghai, Nagasaki e" ド・ロ版画のルーツ：コンスタンツから上海〜長崎へ. In *Do Ro hanga no tabi: Yōroppa kara Shanghai-Nagasaki e no tabunkateki yūgō* ド・ロ版画の旅：ヨーロッパから上海〜長崎への多文化的融合, edited by Kaku Nanen, 61–82. Sōjusha Bijutsu Shuppan, 2019.

Guzman, Luis de. *Historia de las missiones que han hecho los religiosos de la Compañia de Iesus: Para predicar el sancto Evangelio en la India oriental, y en los reynos de la China y Iapon*, 2 vols. En Alcalá: Por la Biuda de luan Gracian, 1601.

Guzman, Luis de/De Gusuman Ruisu デ・グスマン・ルイス. *Tōhō dendōshi* 東方伝道史, vol. 2. Translated by Arai Toshi 新井トシ. Tanba: Yōtokusha, 1945.

Habito, Ruben/Abito Ruben アビト・ルベン. *Mikkyō ni okeru Hōshinkan no haikei* 密教における法身観の背景. Nihon Indogaku Bukkyō Gakkai, 1987.

Habito, Ruben/Abito Ruben. *Shinran to Kirisutokyō no deai kara: Nihonteki kaihō no reisei* 親鸞とキリスト教の出会いから：日本的解放の霊性. Akashi Shoten, 1989.

Habito, Ruben/Abito Ruben. *Seisho to Shinran no yomikata: Kaihō no shingaku to undō no Kyōgaku* 聖書と親鸞の読み方：解放の神学と運動の教学. Akashi Shoten, 1990.

Habito, Ruben/Abito Ruben. *Shūkyō to sekai no itami: Bukkyō, Kirisutokyō no shinzui o motomete* 宗教と世界の痛み:仏教・キリスト教の心髄を求めて. Akashi Shoten, 1991.

Hagio Shō 萩尾生 and Yoshida Hiromi 吉田浩美, eds. *Gendai Basuku o shiru tame no 50 shō* 現代バスクを知るための50章. Akashi Shoten, 2012.

Hagiwara Shinsei 萩原新生. *Seishun no yume* 青春の夢. Takamatsu Shobō, 1943.

Hayashi Kōji 林浩治. *Zainichi Chōsenjin Nihongo Bungaku ron* 在日朝鮮人日本語文学論. Shinkansha, 1991.

Hayashi Masami 林正躬, ed. *Daitō retsujo den* 大東列女伝. Osaka: Naniwa Bunkai, 1884.

Heuvers, Hermann/Hoiverusu Heruman ホイヴェルス・ヘルマン. *Kami e no michi*. 神への道. Shunjūsha, 1928.

Heuvers, Hermann/Hoiverusu Heruman and Kogure Namio 木暮浪夫, trans. *Kirisuto no shōgai* キリストの生涯. Shibun Shoin, 1935.

Heuvers, Hermann/Hoiverusu Heruman. *Hosokawa Garashia fujin* 細川ガラシア夫人. Katorikku Chūō Shoin, 1939.

Heuvers, Hermann/Hoiverusu Heruman. *Uguisu to shijin* 鶯と詩人. Enderure Shoten, 1948.

Heuvers, Hermann/Hoiverusu Heruman. *Sanjō yori no mikoe: Seisho o yomite* 山上よりの御声：聖書を読みて, trans. Togawa Keiichi 戸川敬一. Enderure Shoten, 1950.

Heuvers, Hermann/Hoiverusu Heruman. *Toki no nagare ni* 時間の流れに. Chūō Shuppansha, 1953.

Heuvers, Hermann/Hoiverusu Heruman. *Kobune yori no koe: Kirisuto no tatoe* こぶねよりの御声：キリストの喩. Chūō Shuppansha, 1956.

Heuvers, Hermann/Hoiverusu Heruman. *Kirisuto no kotoba* キリストのことば. Shunjūsha, 1963.

Heuvers, Hermann/Hoiverusu Heruman. *Nihon de yonjūnen* 日本で四十年. Shunjūsha, 1964.

Heuvers, Hermann. *Vierzig Jahre in Japan, 1923–1963*. Tokyo: Die Japanisch-Deutsche Gesellschaft, 1965.

Heuvers, Hermann/Hoiverusu Heruman. *Waga furusato* わがふるさと. Chūō Shuppansha, 1968.

Heuvers, Hermann/Hoiverusu Heruman. *Jinsei no aki ni: Heruman Hoiverusu zuisōshū* 人生の秋に: ヘルマン・ホイヴェルス随想集. Shunjūsha, 1969; reprint, 2nd edition, 2012.

Heuvers, Hermann/Hoiverusu Heruman. *Jinsei sanka: 12 no seika ni yoru kami e no michi* 人生讃歌: 12の聖歌による神への道. Shunjūsha, 1971.

Heuvers, Hermann/Hoiverusu Heruman. *Gikyoku senshū* 戯曲選集. Chūō Shuppansha, 1973.

Heuvers, Hermann/Hoiverusu Heruman. *Hoiverusu shinpu sekkyōshū* ホイヴェルス神父説教集. Chūō Shuppansha, 1973.

Heuvers, Hermann/Hoiverusu Heruman. *Watashi no sukina kotoba: Shisōka to shijin no kotoba* 私の好きな言葉: 思想家と詩人の言葉, trans. Doi Takeo 土居健郎. Enderure Shoten, 1974.

Heuvers, Hermann/Hoiverusu Heruman. *Shi to sono deshi: Timoteo sho kaisetsu* 師とその弟子: ティモテオ書解説. Chūō Shuppansha, 1975.

Heuvers, Hermann/Hoiverusu Heruman. *Toki no magarikado* 時の曲り角, trans. Doi Takeo. Chūō Shuppansha, 1976.

Heuvers, Hermann/Hoiverusu Heruman. *Hoiverusu shinpu no kotoba: Kirisutokyō to Nihon no hitotsu no deai* ホイヴェルス神父のことば: キリスト教と日本の一つの出会い, edited by Togawa Keiichi and Doi Takeo. Kōbundō, 1986.

Heuvers, Hermann/Hoiverusu Heruman. *Hoiverusu shinpu: Nihonjin e no okurimono* ホイヴェルス神父: 日本人への贈り物, edited by Doi Takeo and Morita Akira 森田明. Shunjūsha, 1996.

Heuvers, Hermann/Hoiverusu Heruman. *Hoiverusu shinpu: Shinkō to shisō* ホイヴェルス神父: 信仰と思想, edited by Doi Takeo and Morita Akira. Nagasaki: Seibo no Kishi Sha, 2003.

Heuvers, Hermann/Hoiverusu Heruman. *Kokoro dake wa eien: Heruman Hoiverusu shinpu no kotoba* 心だけは永遠: ヘルマン・ホイヴェルス神父の言葉, edited by Doi Takeo and Morita Akira. Don Bosuko Sha, 2009.

Hibi Yoshitaka 日比嘉高. *Japanīzu Amerika: Imin bungaku, shuppan bunka, shūyōjo* ジャパニーズ・アメリカ: 移民文学・出版文化・収容所. Shinyōsha, 2014.

Hidaka Shinrokurō 日高信六郎. "Itaria ni okeru Kandō shinpu no omoide" イタリアに於るカンドウ神父の思い出. *Seiki* 世紀 73 (1956): 82–84.

Hino Hiroshi 日埜博司, ed. *Koryādo Zangeroku* コリャード 懺悔録. Yagi Shoten, 2016.

Hirakawa Sukehiro 平川祐弘. *Higashi no tachibana, Nishi no orenji* 東の橘西のオレンジ. Bungei Shunjū, 1981.

Hirakawa Sukehiro. *Shomotsu no koe, rekishi no koe* 書物の声 歴史の声. Gen Shobō, 2009.

Hiramatsu Guntarō 平松郡太郎. "Mikan to egao" ミカンと笑顔. In *Shōwa Nihon no onjin: S. Kandō-shi* 昭和日本の恩人: S・カンドウ師, edited by Ikeda Toshio 池田敏雄, 60–82. Chūō Shuppansha, 1966.

Hoesel-Uhlig, Stefan. "Changing Field: The Directions of Goethe's *Weltliteratur*" In *Debating World Literature*, edited by Christopher Prendergast, 26–53. London, New York: Verso, 2004.

Horie Shigeo 堀江薫雄. "Ikebuchi-san to Kandō shinpu no tsudoi" 池淵さんとカンドウ神父の集い. In *Fūrai: Ikebuchi Shōjirō tsuitōroku*, 風籟: 池淵祥次郎追悼録, edited by Ikebuchi Suzue 池淵鈴江. Tokyo: Ikebuchi Suzue, 1964.

Horikawa Keiko 堀川惠子. *Shikei no kijun: "Nagayama saiban" ga nokoshita mono* 死刑の基準:「永山裁判」が遺したもの. Nihon Hyōronsha, 2009.

Hosokawa Shūhei 細川周平. *Nikkei Burajiru imin bungaku* 日系ブラジル移民文学. 2 vols. Misuzu Shobō, 2012–2013.

Iemoto Tarō 家本太郎. "Tamirugo"タミル語. In *Sekai no kotoba shōjiten* 世界のことば小事典, edited by Shibata Takashi 柴田武. Taishūkan Shoten, 1993.

Ii Matsuzō 井伊松蔵. "Garashiya fujin o omou" ガラシャ夫人を懐ふ. *Jindō* 人道 195 (1921): 13.

Iida Tadahiko 飯田忠彦. "Hosokawa Tadaoki fujin" 細川忠興夫人. In *Chūgaku kanbun* 中学漢文, edited by Fukai Kan'ichirō 深井鑑一郎, vol. 2b, 20–21. Keigyōsha, 1894–1896.

Ikeda Toshio 池田敏雄. *Birion shinpu: Gendai Nihon Katorikku no chūseki, Keiō, Meiji, Taishō, Shōwa shi o haikei ni* ビリオン神父：現代日本カトリックの柱石　慶応、明治、大正、昭和史を背景に. Chūō Shuppansha, 1965.

Ikeda Toshio, ed. *Shōwa Nihon no onjin: S. Kandō-shi* 昭和日本の恩人：S・カンドウ師. Chūō Shuppansha, 1966.

Imamichi Tomonobu 今道友信. "Tōku kara no inori" 遠くからの祈り. In *Kuki Shūzō zenshū* 九鬼周造全集, vol. 10, *Geppō* 月報, no. 11. Iwanami Shoten, 1982.

Imamiya Shin 今宮新. "Kirishitan daimyō ki, Shutain cho, Yoshida Kogorō yaku, Ōokayama Shoten hakkō" 切支丹大名記、シュタイシェン著、吉田小五郎訳、大岡山書店発行. *Shigaku* 史学 9:4 (1930): 164–65.

Inoue Hisashi 井上ひさし and Shiba Ryōtarō 司馬遼太郎. "Shūkyō to Nihonjin" 宗教と日本人. In Shiba Ryōtarō, et al. *Gunzō Nihon no sakka: Shiba Ryōtarō* 群像日本の作家　司馬遼太郎, 261–74. Shōgakukan, 1998.

Inoue Shōichi, Guo Nanyan/Kaku Nanen, and Kawamura Shinzō 井上章一、郭南燕、川村信三. *Misshion sukūru ni naze bijin ga ōi no ka: Nihon joshi to Kirisutokyō* ミッションスクールになぜ美人が多いのか：日本女子とキリスト教. Asahi Shinbun Shuppankai, 2018.

Inukai Michiko 犬養道子. *Seiō no kao o motomete* 西欧の顔を求めて. Bungei Shunjū, 1974.

Irie Kiyoshi 入江滑. "Koryādo kan *Zangeroku* zakkō (No. 2)" コリヤード刊 懺悔録雑考（下）. *Kokugo kokubun* 国語国文32: 3 (1963): 39–57.

Ishimure Michiko 石牟礼道子. *Ishimure Michiko zenshū: Shiranui* 石牟礼道子全集・不知火, vol. 13. Fujiwara Shoten, 2007.

Isoda Michifumi 磯田道史. *"Shiba Ryōtarō" de manabu Nihonshi*「司馬遼太郎」で学ぶ日本史. NHK Shuppan, 2017.

Isogo Jinjō Kōtō Shōgakkō 磯子尋常高等小学校, ed. *Kokushi kyōju ni hitsuyō naru Nihon joseishi* 国史教授に必要なる日本女性史. Yokohama: Isogo Jinjō Kōtō Shōgakkō, 1931.

Iwase Kō 岩瀬孝. "Kandō-shi no ikun"カンドウ師の遺訓. *Seiki* 世紀 73 (1956): 133–35.

Junshin Joshi Tanki Daigaku Nagasaki Chihō Bunkashi Kenkyūjo 純心女子短期大学長崎地方文化史研究所, ed. *Puchijan shikyō shokanshū* プチジャン司教書簡集. Nagasaki: Junshin Joshi Tanki Daigaku, 1986.

Kaga Otohiko 加賀乙彦. *Shikeishū no kiroku* 死刑囚の記録. Chūō Kōron Shinsha, 1980; 33rd edition, 2002.

Kaga Otohiko. *Senkoku* 宣告, 3 vols. Shinchōsha, 2013.

Kaji Ryūichi 嘉治隆一. "Dōtokuteki shinsei ni okeru Tōyō to Seiyō" 道徳的心性における東洋と西洋. In vol. 2 of *Gendai dōtoku kōza: Gaikokujin no dōtokuteki shinsei* 現代道徳講座 第2巻 (外国人の道徳的心性), edited by Furukawa Tetsushi 古川哲史. Kawade Shobō, 1955.

Kanai Kiyomitsu 金井清光. "Kirishitan senkyōshi no Nihongo kenkyū" キリシタン宣教師の日本語研究. *Kokugakuin zasshi* 國學院雑誌 92: 6 (1991): 1–13.

Kanayama Masahide 金山政英. *Daremo kakanakatta Bachikan* 誰も書かなかったバチカン. Sankei Shuppan, 1980.

Kanbayashi Akatsuki 上林暁. "Sekkyō chōmon" 説教聴聞. In *Kanbayashi Akatsuki zenshū* 上林暁全集, vol. 10, 228–56. Chikuma Shobō, 1966.

Kanbayashi Akatsuki. "Byōchū dokusho" 病中読書. In *Kanbayashi Akatsuki zenshū* 上林暁全集, vol. 14, 49–54. Chikuma Shobō, 1967.

Kanō Michiko 狩野美智子. *Basuku monogatari: Chizu ni nai kuni no hitobito* バスク物語：地図にない国の人びと. Sairyūsha, 1992.

Kariya Heiji 狩谷平司. *Viriyon shinpu no shōgai* ヴィリヨン神父の生涯. Osaka: Inabata Kōryōten, 1938.

Kataoka Yakichi 片岡弥吉. *Aru Meiji no fukushizō: Do Ro shinpu no shōgai* ある明治の福祉像：ド・ロ神父の生涯. Nippon Hōsō Shuppann Kyōkai, 1977.

Kataoka Yakichi. *Nihon Kirishitan junkyō shi* 日本キリシタン殉教史. Jiji Tsūshinsha, 1979.

Kawakami Tetsutarō 河上徹太郎. "Nihon no autosaidā" 日本のアウトサイダー. In *Kawakami Tetsutarō zenshū* 河上徹太郎全集, vol. 3. Keisō Shobō 1969.

Kawamoto Yumiko 河元由美子. "Medohāsuto no *Eiwa Waei goishū*: Sono riyō no sarekata" メドハーストの『英和和英語彙集』：その利用のされ方. *Eigakushi kenkyū* 英学史研究 2004: 36 (2003): 13–27.

Kindaichi Haruhiko 金田一春彦. *Nihongo no tokushitsu* 日本語の特質. Nihon Hōsō Shuppan Kyōkai, 1981.

Kindaichi Haruhiko. "Giongo, gitaigo" 擬音語・擬態語. *Gekkan Nihongo* 月刊日本語 2: 3 (1989): 50–55.

Kirisutokyō Nenkan Henshūbu キリスト教年鑑編集部, ed. *Kirisutokyō nenkan* キリスト教年鑑, vol. 27. Kirisuto Shinbunsha, 1984.

Kishino Hisashi 岸野久. *Seiōjin no Nihon hakken, Zabieru rainichizen Nihon jōhō no kenkyū* 西欧人の日本発見：ザビエル来日前日本情報の研究. Yoshikawa Kōbunkan, 1989.

Kishino Hisashi. *Zabieru to Nihon* ザビエルと日本. Yoshikawa Kōbunkan, 1998.

Kishino Hisashi. "Furanshisuko Zabieru to 'Dainichi'" フランシスコ・ザビエルと「大日」. In *Supein to Nihon: Zabieru kara Nissei kōyū no shinjidai e* スペインと日本：ザビエルから日西交流の新時代へ, edited by Bandō Shōji 坂東省次 and Kawanari Yō 川成洋, 73–86. Ōtsu: Kohrosha, 2000.

Kishino Hisashi. *Zabieru to Higashi Ajia: Paionia to shite no ninmu to kiseki* ザビエルと東アジア：パイオニアとしての任務と軌跡. Yoshikawa Kōbunkan, 2015.

Kobayashi Yoshio 小林珍雄. "Kirisuto no yoki heishi" キリストのよき兵士. *Seiki* 世紀 73 (1956): 102–105.

Kobori Annu 小堀杏奴. *Jinsei butai: Kobori Annu zuihitsushū* 人生舞台：小堀杏奴随筆集. Hōbunkan, 1958.

Kobori Annu. *Fugū no hito Ōgai: Nihongo no moraru to bi* 不遇の人鷗外：日本語のモラルと美. Kyūryūdō, 1982.

Koe 声. "Meiji Tennō no gyosei o kinyaku suru Hoiverusu Jōchi Daigaku gakuchō" 明治天皇の御製を謹訳するホイヴェルス上智大学学長. *Koe* 声 754 (1938).

Kohira Takubo 小平卓保. *Kagoshima ni kita Zabieru* 鹿児島に来たザビエル. Kagoshima: Shunendō, 1998.

Kojima Genju 小島玄寿, ed. *Nihon retsujo den* 日本列女伝, vol. 2. Otomemura, Tochigi prefecture: Yamanaka Hachirō, 1878.

Kojima Yukie 小島幸枝. "Koryādo no akusento: *Seinichi jisho* no jihitsu kōbon o megutte" コリャードのアクセント：西日辞書の自筆稿本をめぐって. *Kokugo kokubun* 国語国文 41: 11 (1972): 33–46.

Kōno Yoshinori 河野純徳. *Kagoshima ni okeru Seisho hon'yaku: Rage shinpu to Daishichi Kōtōgakkō Zōshikan kyōju tachi* 鹿児島における聖書翻訳：ラゲ神父と第七高等学校造士館教授たち. Kirishitan Bunka Kenkyūkai, 1981.

Kōso Toshiaki 高祖敏明. *Putijan-ban shūsei: Honpō Kirishitan fukyō kankei shiryō: Kaisetsu 1865–1873 nen* プティジャン版集成：本邦キリシタン布教関係資料　解説：1865–1873年. Yūshōdō Shoten, 2011.

Kotera Kenji 小寺健二. "Papa sama to Virion shinpu" パパ様とヴィリオン神父. *Koe* 声 758 (1939): 66–68.

Kōtō Otogi Kai 高等お伽会, ed. *Sekai Nihon shin otogi jusshu* 世界日本新お伽十種. Osaka: Higuchi Seikidō, 1909.

Kracht, Klaus/Kurausu Kurahato クラウス・クラハト and Katsumi Kracht-Tateno 克美・タテノ ＝クラハト. *Ōgai no Kōtansai (Kurisumasu): Mori-ke o meguru nendaiki* 鴎外の降誕祭（クリスマス）：森家をめぐる年代記. NTT Shuppan, 2012.

Kumura Toshio 玖村敏雄. "Viriyon-san no itsuwa" ヴィリヨンさんの逸話. *Zenjin kyōiku* 全人教育 34:8 (1960): 20–24.

Kurata Yoshihiro 倉田喜弘 and Rin Shukuki 林淑姫. *Kindai Nihon geinō nenpyō* 近代日本芸能年表, vol. 1. Yumani Shobō, 2013.

Labarthe, Laurent/Rabaruto Rōran ラバルト・ローラン. *Senkyōshi no jigazō* 宣教師の自画像, edited by Rabaruto Shinpu Kinshuku Jikkō Iinkai ラバルト神父金祝実行委員会. Furīpuresu, 1998.

Laures, Johannes ラウレス・ヨハネス. *Sei Furanshisuko Zabieru no shōgai* 聖フランシスコ・ザヴィエルの生涯. Translated by Matsuda Kiichi 松田毅一. Enderure Shoten, 1948.

Lee Yongsang 李容相. "Gaikokujin senkyōshi no Hantō dendō to chojutsu katsudō" 外国人宣教師の半島伝道と著述活動; In *Kirishitan ga hiraita Nihongo Bungaku: Tagengo tabunka kōryū no engen* キリシタンが拓いた日本語文学：多言語多文化交流の淵源, edited by Kaku Nanen, 370–83. Akashi Shoten, 2017.

Leiter, Samuel L. *Kabuki at the Crossroads: Years of Crisis 1952–1965*. Leiden/Boston: Global Oriental, 2013.

Lemaître, Georges. "The Beginning of the World from the Point of View of Quantum Theory." *Nature* 127: 3210 (9 May 1931): 706.

MacArthur, Douglas/Makkāsā・Dagurasu マッカーサー・ダグラス. "Seijin no kokoro de heiwa o: Ma gensui kinō seimei" 聖人の心で平和を：マ元帥きのう声明. *Asahi shinbun* 朝日新聞, 1949. 5. 26, morning issue, 2. The original English version is "Statement by General MacArthur on Four Hundredth Anniversary of St. Francis Xavier" on 25 May 1949, in Press Release: Far East Command, 1945/05–1949/07, GHQ / SCAP Records, Government Section.

Marnas, Francisque. *La "Religion de Jésus" (Iaso ja-kyo) ressuscitée au Japon dans la seconde moitié du XIXe siècle*, 2 vols. Paris: Delhomme et Briguet, [1897?]

Marnas, Francisque/Marunasu Furanshisuku マルナス・フランシスク. *Nihon Kirisutokyō fukkatsu shi* 日本キリスト教復活史. Translated by Kuno Keiichirō 久野桂一郎. Misuzu Shobō, 1985.

Maruta Mura 丸田むら. "Kandō shinpu-sama no mitama ni" カンドウ神父様の御魂に. *Koe* 声 938 (1956): 49–50.

Mathy, Francis/Mashī Furanshisu マシー・フランシス. "Ippiki no daken ga tsukuru dorama: Kaisetsu" 一匹の駄犬がつくるドラマ：解説. In Endō Shūsaku, *Obaka-san*, 324–30. Kōdansha, 1974.

Matsuda Kiichi 松田毅一. *Kinsei shoki Nihon kankei Nanban shiryō kenkyū* 近世初期日本関係南蛮史料の研究. Kazama Shobō, 1967.

Miki Rofū 三木露風. "Chishio no kakioki kō" 鮮血遺書考. *Shomotsu tenbō* 書物展望 61 (1936): 14–15.

Mishima Yukio 三島由紀夫. *Le Palais des Fêtes: Drame en quatre actes*. Translated by Georges Neyrand. Paris: Gallimard, 1983.

Mitsue Iwao 満江巌. *Hosokawa Garasha fujin* 細川ガラシャ夫人. Tōkō Shoin, 1937.

Miura Shumon 三浦朱門. "Miura Shumon nenpu" 三浦朱門年譜. In *Fukazawa Shichirō, Ariyoshi Sawako, Miura Shumon, Minakami Tsutomu shū* 現代日本文学大系　深沢七郎、有吉佐和子、三浦朱門、水上勉集, 407–409. Chikuma Shobō, 1982.

Miyake Setsurei 三宅雪嶺. *Setsurei zeppitsu* 雪嶺絶筆. Jitsugyō no Sekaisha, 1955.

Miyamoto Toshiyuki 宮本敏行. "Kandō shinpu-sama no koto" カンドウ神父様のこと. *Koe* 声 935 (1955): 51–53.

Miyamoto Toshiyuki. "Kyoju no kage ni: Kandō shinpu o mishiranu hitobito no koe" 巨樹の蔭に：カンドウ神父を見知らぬ人々の声. *Seiki* 世紀 73 (1956): 95–99.

Miyamoto Toshiyuki. "Nihon to sekaiteki yūjō no shito: S. Kandō shinpu shōden" 日本と世界的友情の使徒：S・カンドウ神父小伝. In *S. Kandō ikkan senshū* S・カンドウ一巻選集, edited by Miyamoto Toshiyuki 宮本敏行, 273–81. Shunjūsha, 1969.

Miyashita Sei 宮下生. "Urawa Kōtōgakkō Katorikku Kenkyūkai sōritsu" 浦和高等学校カトリック研究会創立. *Koe* 声 635 (1928): 40–44.

Mochizuki Yōko 望月洋子. *Hebon no shōgai to Nihongo* ヘボンの生涯と日本語. Shinchōsha, 1987.

Moran, Joseph. "The Well of Japanese Undefiled, Joan Rodrigues' Advice on How to Study Japanese." *Monumenta Nipponica* 30: 3 (Autumn, 1975) : 277–89.

Mori Arimasa 森有正. "Omoide sonota" 思い出 その他 (1970). In *Mori Arimasa zenshū* 森有正全集, supplementary vol. Chikuma Shobō, 1982.

Murotani Kōkichi 室谷幸吉 and Tomiga Masatoshi 富賀正俊. *Kandō shinpu: Nihonjin no kokoro no tomo* カンドウ神父：日本人の心の友. Joshi Paurokai, 1979.

Nada Inada なだいなだ. *Minzoku to iu na no shūkyō* 民族という名の宗教. Iwanami Shoten, 1992.

Nadehara, Hanako. "The Emergence of a New Woman: The History of the Transformation of Gracia." *Tōkyō Joshi Daigaku kiyō ronshū* 東京女子大学紀要論集 64 (2014): 107–19.

Nagashima Kan'ichi 永島寛一. "Kandō-shi to 'toriko'" カンドウ師と"虜". *Seiki* 世紀 73 (1956): 92–94.

Nagata Mikihiko 長田幹彦. *Ryokui no seibo* 緑衣の聖母. In *Nagata Mikihiko zenshū* 長田幹彦全集, vol. 11, 1–547. Nihon Tosho Sentā, 1998.

Nagatomi Masaji 長富雅二, ed. *Zaberiyo to Yamaguchi* ザベリヨと山口. Yamaguchi: Hakugin Nisshindō, 1923.

Nakahara Fuku 中原フク and Murakami Mamoru 村上護. *Watashi no ue ni furu yuki wa: Waga ko Nakahara Chūya o kataru* 私の上に降る雪は：わが子中原中也を語る. Kōdansha, 1998.

Nakahara Shirō 中原思郎. *Ani Nakahara Chūya to sosen tachi* 兄中原中也と祖先たち. Shinbisha, 1970.

Nakahara Shirō. *Nakahara Chūya nōto* 中原中也ノート. Shinbisha, 1978.

Nakano Osamu 中野収. *Kī shinboru: Kotoba no shakai tanken* キー・シンボル：ことばの社会探険. Kirihara Shoten, 1989.

Nakata Tōtarō 中田藤太郎. "Kandō kōchō no omoide" カンドウ校長の思い出. *Koe* 声 938 (1956): 47–49.

Neill, Stephen. *A History of Christianity in India: The Beginnings to AD 1707*. Cambridge: Cambridge University Press, 1984.

Neyrand, Georges/Neran G. ネラン・G. "Yabakei kara Higi Oguni e: Nebukuro motte shinwa no Kyūshū o tabi suru" 邪馬渓から肥後小国へ：寝袋もって神話の九州を旅する. *Tabi* 旅 31: 6 (1957): 70–71.

Neyrand, Georges/Neran G. *Rogosu: Kirisutokyō kenkyū sōsho, Fukkatsu* ロゴス：キリスト教研究叢書 復活, vol. 1. Tokyo: G. Neran, 1959.

Neyrand, Georges/Neran G. *Rogosu: Kirisutokyō kenkyū sōsho, Kirisuto no karada* ロゴス：キリスト教研究叢書 キリストの体, vol. 2. Tokyo: G. Neran, 1960.

Neyrand, Georges/Neran G. *Rogosu: Kirisutokyō kenkyū sōsho, Eremia* ロゴス：キリスト教研究叢書 エレミア, vol. 3. Tokyo: G. Neran, 1960.

Neyrand, Georges/Neran G. *Rogosu: Kirisutokyō kenkyū sōsho, Kekkon, dokushin* ロゴス：キリスト教研究叢書 結婚・独身, vol. 4. Tokyo: G. Neran, 1960.

Neyrand, Georges/Neran G. and Kawazoe Toshiaki 川添利秋, trans. *Anchioke no Igunachio shokan* アンチオケのイグナチオ書簡. Misuzu Shobō, 1960.

Neyrand, Georges/Neran G. *Rogosu: Kirisutokyō kenkyū sōsho, Inori* ロゴス：キリスト教研究叢書 祈り, vol. 5. Tokyo: G. Neran, 1961.

Neyrand, Georges/Neran G. *Rogosu: Kirisutokyō kenkyū sōsho, Seisho no yomikata* ロゴス：キリスト教研究叢書 聖書の読み方, vol. 6. Tokyo: G. Neran, 1961.

Neyrand, Georges/Neran G. *Rogosu: Kirisutokyō kenkyū sōsho, Kami no kiseki* ロゴス：キリスト教研究叢書 神の軌跡, vol. 7. Tokyo: G. Neran, 1961.

Neyrand, Georges/Neran G. *Rogosu: Kirisutokyō kenkyū sōsho, Keizai shakai to ningen* ロゴス：キリスト教研究叢書 経済社会と人間, vol. 8. Tokyo: G. Neran, 1962.

Neyrand, Georges/Neran G. *Rogosu: Kirisutokyō kenkyū sōsho, Hito to natta kami* ロゴス：キリスト教研究叢書 人となった神, vol. 9. Tokyo: G. Neran, 1962.

Neyrand, Georges/Neran G. *Rogosu: Kirisutokyō kenkyū sōsho, Kami no kuni* ロゴス：キリスト教研究叢書 神の国, vol. 10. Tokyo: G. Neran, 1962.

Neyrand, Georges/Neran G. *Rogosu: Kirisutokyō kenkyū sōsho, Saishi to shisai* ロゴス：キリスト教研究叢書 祭祀と司祭, vol. 11. Tokyo: G. Neran, 1963.

Neyrand, Georges/Neran G. *Rogosu: Kirisutokyō kenkyū sōsho, Senreishiki* ロゴス：キリスト教研究叢書 洗礼式, vol. 12. Tokyo: G. Neran, 1963.

Neyrand, Georges/Neran G. *Rogosu: Kirisutokyō kenkyū sōsho, Senkyō ron* ロゴス：キリスト教研究叢書 宣教論, vol. 13. Tokyo: G. Neran, 1964.

Neyrand, Georges/Neran G. "Kaisetsu" 解説. In *Gendai no bungaku*, vol. 37: *Endō Shūsaku shū* 現代の文学37 遠藤周作集, 383–91. Kawade Shobō Shinsha, 1966.

Neyrand, Georges/Neran G. *Warera jinsei o ronzu* われら人生を論ず. Shunjūsha, 1969.

Neyrand, Georges/Neran G. *Kami no ba: Tiyāru do Sharudan no Kirisutokyōkan* 神の場：ティヤール・ド・シャルダンのキリスト教観. Shinkyō Shuppansha, 1972.

Neyrand, Georges/Neran G. *Shinzuru koto* 信ずること. Shinkyō Shuppansha, 1974.

Neyrand, Georges/Neran G. *Kirisuto ron* キリスト論. Sōbunsha, 1979.

Neyrand, Georges/Neran G. *Sakariba shisai no mōgoroku* 盛り場司祭の猛語録. Korube Shuppansha, 1980.

Neyrand, Georges/Neran G. *Obaka-san no jijoden hanbun: Seisho katate ni Nippon 36 nenkan* おバカさんの自叙伝半分：聖書片手にニッポン36年間. Kōdansha, 1988.

Neyrand, Georges/Neran G. *Obaka-san no jijoden hanbun: Seisho katate ni Nippon 40 nenkan* おバカさんの自叙伝半分：聖書片手にニッポン40年間. Kōdansha, 1992.

Neyrand, Georges/Neran G. *Kirisuto no fukkatsu* キリストの復活. Shinkyō Shuppansha, 1997.

Neyrand, Georges/Neran G. "Gendai ni okeru Kirisuto ron to wa" 現代におけるキリスト論とは. *Shingaku daijesuto* 神学ダイジェスト 84 (1998): 2–5.

Neyrand, Georges/Neran G. *Ma, nominagara demo, anata ni Kirisuto o go-shōkai shimasu* ま、飲みながらでも：貴方にキリストをご紹介します. Furī Puresu, 2000.

Neyrand, Georges/Neran G. "Iesu wa ikiteiru," イエスは生きている. In *Watashi ni totte 'Fukkatsu' towa* 私にとって「復活」とは, edited by Hayashi Amari, et al. Nihon Kirisutokyōdan Shuppankyoku, 2004.

Neyrand, Georges Neran G. *Nani o oitemo Seisho o yominasai* 何をおいても聖書を読みなさい. Nansōsha, 2016.

NHK Kaidō o Yuku Purojekuto 「街道をゆく」プロジェクト. *Shiba Ryōtarō no fūkei 3: Kita no mahoroba, Nanban no michi* 司馬遼太郎の風景３、北のまほろば／南蛮のみち. Nihon Hōsō Shuppan Kyōkai, 1998.

Nihon Kirisutokyō Rekishi Daijiten Henshū Iinkai. *Nihon Kirisutokyō rekishi daijiten* 日本キリスト教歴史大辞典. Kyōbunkan, 1988.

Niiyama Karitsuki Fumiko 新山カリツキ富美子, trans. *Kijō na kifujin: Hosokawa Garasha* 気丈な貴婦人: 細川ガラシャ. Niiyama Karitsuki Fumiko, 2016.

Niiyama Karitsuki Fumiko. "Yōroppa ni okeru Nihon junkyōsha geki: Hosokawa Garasha ni tsuite no Ongakugeki Uīn Iezusukai dorama" ヨーロッパにおける日本殉教者劇：細川ガラシャについてのウィーン・イエズス会ドラマ. *Sekai no Nihon kenkyū* 世界の日本研究 (2017): 284–94.

Niki Harumi 二木晴美. "*Hakuchi gun to sono shūhen ni tsuite*"『白痴群』とその周辺に就いて. In vol. 28 of *Nihon bungaku kenkyū shiryō shinshū: Nakahara Chūya: Tamashii to rizumu* 日本文学研究資料新集28 中原中也：魂とリズム, edited by Nagano Takashi 長野隆. Yūseidō, 1992.

Nishimura Shigeki 西村茂樹, ed. *Fujo kagami* 婦女鑑, vol. 6. Kunaishō, 1887.

Nogami Yaeko 野上弥生子. "Omoi dasu koto" 思ひ出すこと. In *Nogami Yaeko zenshū* 野上弥生子全集, vol. 29. Iwanami Shoten, 1991.

Nomura Yoshio 野村良雄. "Wareware no oyaji" われわれの親仁. *Seiki* 世紀 73 (1956): 124–28.

Nomura Yoshio. *Wakai hi no deai* 若い日の出会い. Shinjidaisha, 1971.

Obara Satoru 尾原悟. "Kirishitan jidai no Iezusukai kyōiku: Zabieru no shukugan 'Miyako ni daigaku o'" キリシタン時代のイエズス会教育：ザビエルの宿願「都に大学を」. *Shingaku daijesuto* 神学ダイジェスト 114 (2013): 16–24.

Ogawa, Kiyoko and Tadashi Ogawa. "A Short Study of *Jisei* (Swan Songs): Death, Cosmos and Its Transmigration." In *The Cosmos and the Creative Imagination*, edited by Anna-Teresa Tymieniecka and Patricia Trutty-Coohill, 321–34. Cham: Springer, 2016.

Ōhira Ken 大平健. "'Saijō no waza' ni tsuite"〈最上のわざ〉について. In Heuvers, *Jinsei no aki ni: Heruman Hoiverusu zuisōshū* 人生の秋に：ヘルマン・ホイヴェルス随想集, i–v. Shunjūsha, 1969; reprint, 2nd edition, 2012.

Ōi Sōgo 大井蒼梧. *Hosokawa Tadaoki fujin* 細川忠興夫人. Takemiya Shuppanbu, 1936.

Okada Hiroko 岡田弘子. *Kokyō no Shibakusa* 古京の芝草. Kyoto: Ritsumeikan Shuppanbu, 1941.

Okada Jun'ichi 岡田純一. "Kandō-shi no kanshikigan" カンドウ師の鑑識眼. *Seiki* 世紀 73 (1956): 136–38.

Okada Kishū 岡田喜秋. *Tabi no ki no mi* 旅の木の実. Bunka Shuppankyoku, 1981.

Okada Yachiyo 岡田八千代. "Yūrakuza no 'Hosokawa Garashiya'" 有楽座の「細川がらしや」. *Katorikku* 2: 8 (1922): 64–65.

Okamoto Kidō 岡本綺堂. "Hosokawa Tadaoki no tsuma" 細川忠興の妻. In *Kidō gikyoku shū* 綺堂戯曲集, vol. 7, 361–98. Shunyōdō, 1928–1929.

Okazaki Kaheita 岡崎嘉平太. *Watashi wa omou: Nihon no kadai* 私は思う：日本の課題. Yomiuri Shinbunsha, 1972.

Okimoto Tsunekichi 沖本常吉. *Otome-tōge to Kirishitan* 乙女峠とキリシタン. Tsuwano: Tsuwano Rekishi Shirīzu Kankōkai, 1971; 6th edition, 1993.

Okuno Kumiko 奥野久美子. "'Itojo oboegaki': Retsujo o koete"「糸女覚え書」：〈烈女〉を超えて. In *Akuragawa Ryūnosuke to Kirishitan mono: Tasei, kōsa, ekkyō* 芥川龍之介と切支丹物：多声・交差・越境, edited by Miyazaka Satoru 宮坂覚, 318–29. Kanrin Shobō, 2014.

Ōmura Hikojirō 大村彦次郎. *Bundan eiga monogatari* 文壇栄華物語. Chikuma Shobō, 1998.

Ōno Susumu 大野晋. *Nihongo no kigen* 日本語の起源. Iwanami Shoten, 1957.

Ōno Susumu. *Nihongo to Tamirugo* 日本語とタミル語. Shinchōsha, 1981.

Ōno Susumu. *Nihongo izen* 日本語以前. Iwanami Shoten, 1987.

Ōno Susumu. *Nihongo no genryū o motomete* 日本語の源流を求めて. Iwanami Shoten, 2007.

Ono Toyoaki 小野豊明. "Hitō shūkyōhan no katsudō" 比島宗教班の活動. In *Nihon no Firipin senryō: Intabyū kiroku* 日本のフィリピン占領：インタビュー記録, edited by Nihon no Firipin Senryōki ni Kansuru Shiryō Chōsa Fōramu 日本のフィリピン占領期に関する史料調査フォーラム. Ryūkei Shosha, 1994.

Ōoka Shōhei 大岡昇平. "Nakahara Chūya den: Yōran" 中原中也伝：揺籃. In *Gunzō Nihon no sakka 15 Nakahara Chūya* 群像日本の作家一五 中原中也, edited by Ōoko Makoto 大岡信. Shōgakukan, 1991.

Orita Hiroharu 折田洋晴. "Nihon kankei Yōkosho no wagakuni de no juyō ni tsuite" 日本関係洋古書の我が国での受容について. *Sankō shoshi kenkyū* 参考書誌研究 68 (2008).

Osanai Kaoru 小山内薫. "'Hosokawa Garashiya' o mite" 「細川がらしや」を見て. *Katorikku* カトリック 2: 8 (1922): 62–63.

Osaragi Jirō 大佛次郎. *Tennō no seiki 15: Shinsei no fu* 天皇の世紀（15）新政の府. Asahi Shinbunsha, 1978.

Osaragi Jirō. *Tennō no seiki 16: Bushi no shiro* 天皇の世紀（16）武士の城. Asahi Shinbunsha, 1979.

Ozawa Ken'ichi 小澤謙一. "Kandō-shi o itamu" カンドウ師を悼む. *Shintaiiku* 新体育 25: 11 (1955): 15.

Pagès, Léon. *Lettres de saint François-Xavier de la Compagnie de Jésus, apotre des Indes et du Japon: traduites sur l'édition Latine de Bologne*, 2 vols. Paris: Libr. de Mme Ve Poussielgue-Rusand, 1855.

Pagès, Léon. *Histoire des vingt-six martyrs japonais: dont la canonisation doit avoir lieu à Rome, le jour de la Pentecôte*. Paris: Benjamin Duprat, 1862.

Pagès, Léon. *Histoire de la religion chrétienne au Japon depuis 1598 jusqu'à 1651, comprenant les faits relatifs aux deux cent cinq martyrs, béatifiés le 7 juillet 1867*. Paris: C. Douniol, 1869–1870.

Pagès, Léon/Reon Pajesu レオン・パジェス. *Nihon Kirishitan shūmonshi* 日本切支丹宗門史, 3 vols. Translated by Yoshida Kogorō 吉田小五郎. Iwanami Shoten, 1938; 1991.

Palacios, José/Parashiosu Hose パラシオス・ホセ. *Ima Birion shinpu o ou: Bakumatsu kara Shōwa made* 今、ビリオン神父を追う：幕末から昭和まで. Hagi: Agari Sōgō Kenkyūjo, 2003.

Polak, Christian/Porakku Kurisuchan ポラック・クリスチャン. "Nichi-futsu kōryū ryakushi" 日仏交流略史. In *Ishin to Furansu: Nichifutsu gakujutsu kōryū no reimei* 維新とフランス：日仏学術交流の黎明, edited by Nishino Yoshiaki 西野嘉章 and Porakku, pp. 49–206. Tōkyō Daigaku Sōgōkenkyū Hakubutsukan, 2009.

Rausch, Franklin ラウシュ・フランクリン. "Hanguru ni yoru Katorikku no shomotsu" ハングルによるカトリックの書物. In *Kirishitan ga hiraita Nihongo Bungaku: Tagengo tabunka kōryū no engen* キリシタンが拓いた日本語文学：多言語多文化交流の淵源, edited by Kaku Nanen, 354–69. Akashi Shoten, 2017.

Rodrigues, João/Rodorigesu Joan ロドリゲス・ジョアン. *Nihon daibunken* 日本大文典. Translated by Doi Tadao 土井忠生. Sanseidō, 1955.

Rodrigues, João/Rodorigesu Joan. *Nihongo shōbunten* 日本語小文典. Translated by Ikegami Mineo 池上岑夫. Iwanami Shoten, 1993.

Roggendorf, Joseph/Rogendorufu Yozefu ロゲンドルフ・ヨゼフ. *Ibunka no hazama made* 異文化のはざまで. Bungei Shunjū, 1983.

Roy, Jean-René. *Unveiling Galaxies: The Role of Images in Astronomical Discovery.* Cambridge: Cambridge University Press, 2018.

Ryūmonsha 龍門社, ed. *Shibusawa Eiichi denki shiryō* 渋沢栄一伝記資料, 58 vols. Shibusawa Eiichi Denki Shiryō Kankōkai, 1944–1965.

Sancti Francisci Xaverii: Epistolas aliaque scripta complectens (Monumenta historica Societatis Jesu, Monumenta Xaveriana ex autographis vel ex antiquioribus exemplis collecta; t. 1). Matriti: Typis Agustinin Avrial, 1899–1900 (?).

Santō Osamu 山東功. *Nihongo no kansatsusha tachi: Senkyōshi kara oyatoi gaikokujin made* 日本語の観察者たち：宣教師からお雇い外国人まで. Iwanami Shoten, 2013.

Schamoni, Wolfgang ヴォルフガング・シャモニ. "'Sekai Bungaku': Gēte yori hanseiki mo mae ni shoshutsu shite ita go"「世界文学」：ゲーテより半世紀も前に初出していた語. *Bungaku* 文学 11: 3 (2010): 173–82.

Schurhammer, Georg. *Das kirchliche Sprachproblem in der japanischen Jesuitenmission des 16. und 17. Jahrhunderts; ein Stück Ritenfrage in Japan.* Tokyo: Deutsche Gesellschaft für Natur- und Völkerkunde Ostasiens, 1928.

Schurhammer, Georg and Josef Wicki, eds. *Epistolae S. Francisci Xaverii aliaque eius scripta*, 15 vols. Romae: Monumenta Historica Soc. Jesu, 1944–1945.

Seibo no Kishisha 聖母の騎士社. "Kono hito 2000: Neran shinpu" この人2000　ナラン神父. *Seibo no kishi* 聖母の騎士 65: 9 (2000): unpaginated.

Seki Nozomu 関望. "Onshi no ningenmi" 恩師の人間味. In *Shōwa Nihon no onjin: S. Kandō-shi* 昭和日本の恩人：Ｓ・カンドウ師, edited by Ikeda Toshio 池田敏雄, 69–71. Chūō Shuppansha, 1966.

Sekine Reiko 関根礼子. *Nihon opera shi* 日本オペラ史, vol. 1. Edited by Shōwa Ongaku Daigaku Opera Kenkyūjo 昭和音楽大学オペラ研究所. Suiyōsha, 2011.

Seya Yukio 瀬谷幸男. "Fukkokuban ni tsuite" 復刻版について. In *Lexicon Latino-Japonicum* 羅和字, 1–12. Kōkyō Shingakkō, 1934; reprint, Nanundō Fenikkusu, 1995.

Shiba Ryōtarō 司馬遼太郎. *Shiba Ryōtarō zenshū 59: Kaidō o yuku 8, Nanban no michi* 司馬遼太郎全集 59：街道をゆく 8 南蛮のみち. Bungei Shunjū, 1999.

Shimatani Toshizō 島谷俊三. "Kandō shinpu to Minhō Yuian rōshi" カンドウ神父と眠芳惟安老師. *Bunka to kyōiku* 文化と教育 7: 1 (1955): 13–14.

Shimatani Toshizō. *Rōbaiju* 老梅樹. Sōzōsha, 1971.

Shimomiya Tadao 下宮忠雄. *Basukugo nyūmon: Gengo, minzoku, bunka* バスク語入門：言語・民族・文化. Taishūkan Shoten, 1979.

Shinmura Izuru 新村出. "Kaitei Jobun" 改版序文. In *Kirishitan chishio no kakioki* 切支丹鮮血遺書, edited by Matsuzaki Minoru 松崎実考註, 1–4. Kaizōsha, 1926.

Shinmura Izuru. "Kirishitan josei no hanashi" 吉利支丹女性の話 (1929). In *Shinmura Izuru zenshū* 新村出全集, vol. 7, 216–23. Chikuma Shobō, 1973.

Shinoda Kōichirō 篠田浩一郎. *Shura to chinkon: Nihon bunka shiron* 修羅と鎮魂：日本文化試論. Ozawa Shoten, 1990.

Shirai Takako 白井堯子. *Fukuzawa Yukichi to senkyōshi tachi: Shirarezaru Meijiki no Nichi-Ei kankei* 福沢諭吉と宣教師たち：知られざる明治期の日英関係. Miraisha, 1999.

Shishi Bunroku 獅子文六. *Musume to watashi* 娘と私. In *Shishi Fumiroku zenshū* 獅子文六全集, vol. 6, 217–555. Asahi Shinbunsha, 1968.

Shōgakukan 小学館. *Nihon daihyakka zensho* 日本大百科全書, vol. 6. Shōgakukan, 1985.

Soden, Aloysius/Sōden A. ソーデン・Ａand Fukai Keiichi 深井敬一, trans. *Seibo Maria to Nihon* 聖母マリアと日本. Chūō Shuppansha, 1954.

Song Lihua 宋莉華. *Chuanjiaoshi hanwen xiaoshuo yanjiu* 傳教士漢文小説研究. Shanghai: Shanghai Guji Chubanshe, 2010.

Song Lihua/Sō Rika. *Senkyōshi kanbun shōsetsu no kenkyū* 宣教師漢文小説の研究. Tōhō Shoten, 2017.

Steichen, Michael/Shutaishien Mikaeru シュタイシェン・ミカエル and Villion, Aimé/Biriyon Eme ビリヨン・エメ, trans. *Kirishitan daimyō shi* 切支丹大名史. Nara: Viriyon, 1929.

Steichen, Michael/Shutaishien Mikaeru and Yoshida Kogorō 吉田小五郎, trans. *Kirishitan daimyō ki* 切支丹大名記. Ōokayama Shoten, 1930.

Suga Atsuko 須賀敦子. *Suga Atsuko zenshū* 須賀敦子全集, vol. 7. Kawade Shobō Shinsha, 2000.

Sugimoto Tsutomu 杉本つとむ. *Kirishitan to Nihongo kenkyū* 吉利支丹と日本語研究. Vol. 10 of *Sugimoto Tsutomu chosaku senshū: Seiyōjin no Nihongo kenkyū* 杉本つとむ著作選集　西洋人の日本語研究. Yasaka Shobō, 1999.

Suzuki Hideko 鈴木秀子. "'Gendai shisō hihan' no kurasu"「現代思想批判」のクラス. *Seiki* 世紀 73 (1956): 139–40.

Suzuki Sumako 鈴木須磨子. "Kandō-shi no omoide"カンドウ師の思出. *Koe* 声 938 (1956): 42–47.

Tabata Yasuko 田端泰子. *Hosokawa Garasha: Chirinu beki toki shirite koso* 細川ガラシャ: 散りぬべき時知りてこそ. Mineruva Shobō, 2010.

Takagi Masafumi 高木昌史. *Yanagita Kunio to Yōroppa: Kōshō bungei no tōzai* 柳田國男とヨーロッパ: 口承文芸の東西. Sankōsha, 2006.

Takahashi Akira 高橋章. "Shohyō G. Neran cho 'Kirisuto ron' Sōbunsha, 1979" 書評　G・ネラン著『キリスト論』創文社、昭和五四年. *Aren Kokusai Tanki Daigaku kiyō* アレン国際短期大学紀要 15 (1997): 33–35.

Takahashi Kunisuke 高橋邦輔. "Kirishitan chishio no kakioki o yomu" 切支丹鮮血遺書を読む. *Seikyō jihō* 正教時報 15: 9 (1926): 14–20.

Takama Naomichi 高間直道. *Tetsugaku yōgo no kiso chishiki* 哲学用語の基礎知識. Seishun Shuppansha, 1961.

Takami Jun 高見順. "Kinō kyō" きのうきょう. In *Takami Jun zenshū* 高見順全集, vol. 18, 35–55. Keisō Shobō, 1970.

Takami Jun. "Daiyonsha no shutsugen: Gendai bunshi ron danpen" 第四者の出現：現代文士論断片. In *Takami Jun zenshū* 高見順全集, vol. 13, 593–600. Keisō Shobō, 1971.

Takamura Kōtarō 高村光太郎. "Jo" 序. In Mori Eisuke 森英介, *Hi no seijo* 火の聖女, unpaginated. Yonezawa: Hi no Kai, 1951.

Takao, Makoto Harris. "'In what storms of blood from Christ's flock is Japan swimming?': Gratia Hosokawa and the Performative Representation of Japanese Martyrdom in *Mulier fortis* (1698)." In *Changing Hearts: Performing Jesuit Emotions between Europe, Asia, and the Americas,* edited by Yasmin Haskell and Raphaële Garrod, 87–120. Leiden/Boston: Brill, 2019.

Takeda Tomoju 武田友寿. *Shūkyō to bungaku no setten* 宗教と文学の接点. Chūō Shuppansha, 1970.

Tamura Jōji 田村襄次. *Waga Heruman Hoiverusu shinpu* わがヘルマン・ホイヴェルス神父. Chūō Shuppansha, 1987.

Tanaka Kōtarō 田中耕太郎. *Gendai seikatsu no ronri* 現代生活の論理. Shunjūsha, 1957.

Tanaka Mineko 田中峰子. "Chinmoku no Seibo" 沈黙の聖母. *Seiki* 世紀 73 (1956): 115–17.

Taniguchi Sachiyo 谷口幸代. "Nihongo no kakite to shite no Hoiverusu: 'Saijō no waza' o chūshin ni" 日本語の書き手としてのホイヴェルス：『最上のわざ』を中心に. In *Kirishitan ga hiraita Nihongo Bungaku: Tagengo tabunka kōryū no engen* キリシタンが拓いた日本語文学: 多言語多文化交流の淵源, edited by Kaku Nanen, 339–52. Akashi Shoten, 2017.

Tarumi Chie 垂水千恵. *Taiwan no Nihongo Bungaku* 台湾の日本語文学. Goryū Shoin, 1995.

Tatsui Matsunosuke 龍居松之助. *Nihon meifu den* 日本名婦伝. Kyoto: Hokuto Shobō, 1937.

Tatsuno Yutaka 辰野隆. *Bongu mondō* 凡愚問答. Kadokawa Shoten, 1955.

Tatsuno Yutaka. "Basuku no hoshi: Jo ni kaete" バスクの星: 序にかえて. In Candau/Kandō, *Basuku no hoshi* バスクの星, 1–3. Tōhō Shobō, 1956.

Tatsuno Yutaka. *Bongu shunjū* 凡愚春秋. Kadokawa Shoten, 1957.

Tazaki Yūzō 田崎勇三. "Wasurenu hito" 忘れえぬ人. *Seiki* 世紀 73 (1956): 88–91.

Tehelle, Notto R. *Buddhism and Christianity in Japan: From Conflict to Dialogue, 1854–1899.* Honolulu: University of Hawai'i Press, 1987.

Tobari Tomoo 戸張智雄. "Kabukichō no kaisō Neran shinpu" 歌舞伎町の快僧ネラン神父. *Bungei shunjū* 文藝春秋 59: 6 (1981): 392–99.

Tobe Miyuki 戸部実之. *Basukugo jiten: Basukugo, Eigo, Nihongo* バスク語辞典：バスク語・英語・日本語. Tairyūsha, 1996.

Togawa Keiichi 戸川敬一 and Doi Takeo 土居健郎, eds. *Hoiverusu shinpu no kotoba* ホイヴェルス神父のことば. Kōbundō, 1986.

Tokutomi I'ichirō 德富猪一郎. *Kinsei Nihon kokuminshi, Toyotomi-shi jidai hei hen* 近世日本国民史、豊臣氏時代丙篇. Minyūsha, 1921.

Tokutomi I'ichirō. *Kinsei Nihon kokuminshi, Ieyasu jidai jōkan Sekigahara eki* 近世日本国民史、家康時代上巻関原役. Minyūsha, 1925.

Tokutomi I'ichirō. *Jinbutsu keikan* 人物景観. Minyūsha, 1939.

Tomizawa Takahiko 冨澤隆彦. "Onshi no omokage" 恩師のおもかげ. *Koe* 声 938 (1956): 22–25.

Tomoda Juichirō 友田寿一郎, ed. *Ayukawa Yoshisuje jūōdan* 鮎川義介縦横談. Sōgesha, 1953.

Torcivia, Mario. *Giovanni Battista Sidoti: (Palermo, 22 agosto 1667 – Tokyo, 27 novembre 1715) missionario martire in Giappone.* Soveria Mannelli: Rubbettino, 2017.

Toyabe Yōnosuke 鳥谷部陽之助. *Shin Towada-ko monogatari: Shinpi no mizuumi ni tsukareta hitobito* 新十和田湖物語：神秘の湖に憑かれた人びと. Sairyūsha, 1983.

Tsuchiya Motosaku 土屋元作. "Garashiya" ガラシヤ. In Tsuchiya Motosaku, *Muchūgo: Tsuchiya Taimu bunshū* 夢中語：土屋大夢文集, 788–91. Osaka: Tsuchiya Bunshū Kankōkai, 1931.

Tsuge Teruhiko 柏植光彦 and Kojima Yōsuke 小嶋洋輔. "Intabyū, Endō Junko fujin ni kiku: Hanseiki no kioku, Shōsetsu wa dono yō ni kakareta ka" インタビュー・遠藤順子夫人に聞く：半世紀の記憶：小説はどのように書かれたか. In *Endō Shūsaku: Chōhatsu suru sakka* 遠藤周作：挑発する作家, edited by Tsuge Teruhiko, 1–18. Shibundō, 2008.

Tsurumi Shunsuke 鶴見俊輔. "Basuku made kita nagai nagai michi" バスクまで来た長い長い道. In *Tsurumi Shunsuke shohyō shūsei*, vol. 2. Misuzu Shobō, 2007.

Uchida Roan 内田魯庵. "Fujin ni yomasetai yōsho" 婦人に読ませたい洋書 (1922). In *Uchida Roan zenshū* 内田魯庵全集, supplementary vol. 3. Yumani Shobō, 1987.

Uchida Roan. *Shimi no jiden* 蠹魚之自伝 (1923). In *Uchida Roan zenshū* 内田魯庵全集, vol. 8. Yumani Shobō, 1987.

Urakawa Wasaburō 浦川和三郎. *Nihon ni okeru Kōkyōkai no fukkatsu* 日本に於ける公教会の復活. Nagasaki: Tenshudō, 1915.

Valignano, Alejandro. *Sumario de las cosas de Japón (1583); Adiciones del Sumario de Japón (1592). Monumenta Nipponica monographs*, no. 9, vol. 1, edited by José Luis Alvarez-Taladriz. Tokyo: Sophia University, 1954.

Verwilghen, Albert Felix. "The Buddhist Studies of Father A. Villion." *Fukyō* 布教: *Japan Missionary Bulletin* 25 (1971), 251–55.

Villion, Aimé/Biriyon A. ビリヨン・ア and Kako Giichi 加古義一. "Fukusha Pōro Naboro oyobi tsure no chimei" 福者ポーロナバロ及び連の致命, 309–22. In Biriyon and Kako, *Nihon hijiri chishio no kakioki* 日本聖人鮮血遺書. Kyoto: Murakami Kanbei, 1887.

Villion, Aimé/Biriyon A. ビリヨン・ア. *Yamato hijiri chishio no kakioki* 日本聖人鮮血遺書, edited by Kako Giichi 加古義一. 1st edition. Kyoto: Murakami Kanbei, 1887; 2nd edition, 1888; 4th edition, 1893; revised 5th edition, Osaka: Sei Joseph Kyōikuin, 1911; revised 6th edition, Katorikku Kankōkai, 1926; 7th edition, Nishinomiya: Nihon Junkyō Sendenkai, 1931.

Villion, Aimé/Biriyon A. *Baramon-kyō ron: Bukkyō kigen* 婆羅門教論: 仏教起原, edited by Kako Giichi. Kyoto: Shimizu Kyūjirō, 1889.

Villion, Aimé/Biriyon A. *Yamaguchi Kōkyōshi* 山口公教史, edited by Kako Giichi. Kyoto: Kako Giichi, 1897.

Villion, Aimé/Biriyon A. *Nagato Kōkyōshi* 長門公教史, edited by Kako Giichi. Hagi: Tenshu Kōkyōkai, 1918.

Villion, Aimé/ Biriyon A. *Yamaguchi Daidōji ato no hakken to saikyojō ni tsuite* 山口大道寺跡の発見と裁許状に就て. Nara: A Villiyon, 1926; Osaka: Taiyōsha, 1926.

Villion, Aimé/ Biriyon A. and Matsuzaki Minoru 松崎実. *Kirishitan chishio no kakioki* 切支丹鮮血遺書. Kaizōsha, 1926.

Villion, Aimé. *Cinquante ans d'apostolat au Japon*, Hong Kong: Imprimerie de la Société des Missions Étrangères, 1923.

Villion, Aimé/Biriyon A. "Yoshida Shōin o omou (Taishō 10 nen 12 gatsu)" 吉田松陰を懐ふ (大正十年十二月). Translated by Takenaka Toshikazu 竹中利一. In *Yoshida Shōin zenshū* 吉田松陰全集, edited by Yamaguchi-ken Kyōiku Iinkai 山口県教育委員会, 11 vols. Iwanami Shoten, 1986.

Villion, Aimé. *Pourquoi j'aime les Japonais?* Louvain: Xaveriana, 1929.

Wada Makoto 和田誠. *Sōtei monogatari* 装丁物語. Hakusuisha, 2006.

Wada Sei 和田清. *Tōyō shijō yori mitaru kodai no Nihon* 東洋史上より観たる古代の日本. Harvard/Yenching/Dōshisha Tōhō Bunka Kōza Iinkai, 1956.

Wada Yūichi 和田祐一. *Tōji ruikei ron: Nihongo no ichizuke ni tsuite* 統辞類型論:日本語の位置づけについて. *Kikan jinruigaku* 季刊人類学 1: 4 (1970): 3–23.

Wakaba Sei 若葉生. "Hosokawa Tadaoki fujin" 細川忠興夫人. *Koe* 声(1907–1908), 383–87.

Ward, Haruko Nawata. *Women Religious Leaders in Japan's Christian Century, 1549–1650.* Surrey and Burlington: Ashgate Publishing Company, 2009.

Washio Ukō 鷲尾雨工. "Hideyoshi to Hosokawa" 秀吉と細川. *Ishin* 維新 3: 8 (1936): 85–97.

Williams, Peter and David Wallace. *Unit 731: The Japanese Army's Secret of Secrets.* London: Hodder & Stoughton, 1989.

Wycliff Bible Translators. https://www.wycliffe.org/about/why/Xavier, Francis and Orazio Torsellino, trans. *Francisci Xaverii Epistolarum libri quatuor.* Moguntiæ: Apud Balthasarum Lippium, 1600.

Xavier, Francis and un P. de la mesme compagnie. *Lettres du B. pere Saint Francois Xavier, de la Compagnie de Iesus, apostre du Iapon: divisees en quatre livres.* Paris: Chez Sebastien Cramoisy, 1628.

Xavier, Francis and Antoine Faivre, trans. *Lettres de S. François-Xavier, apôtre des Indes et du Japon*, 3 vols. Lyons: Sauvignet, 1828.

Xavier, Francis/Zaberiyo [Zabieru] Furanshisuko フランシスコデ・ザベリヨ. *Sei Furanshisuko Zabiriyo shokanki* 聖フランセスコザベリヨ書翰記, 3 vols. Translated by Asai Torachirō 浅井虎八郎. Tokyo: Asai Torachirō, 1891.

Xavier, Francisco/Zabieru. *Sei Furanshisuko Zabieru zenshokan* 聖フランシスコ・ザビエル全書簡. 4 vols. Translated by Kōno Yoshinori 河野純徳. Heibonsha, 1994.

Yamaji Aizan 山路愛山. *Gendai Nihon kyōkai shi ron* 現代日本教会史論 (1905). In *Kirisutosha hyōronshū: Shin Nihon koten bungaku taikei Meiji hen 26* キリスト者評論集　新日本古典文

学大系明治編二六, edited by Yabu Teiko 藪禎子, Yoshida Masanobu 吉田正信, and Izuhara Takatoshi 出原隆俊. Iwanami Shoten, 2002.

Yamanashi Atsushi 山梨淳. "Pari Gaikoku Senkyōkai no shuppanbutsu to kindai Nihon no bungakusha" パリ外国宣教会の出版物と近代日本の文学者. *Kirisutokyō Bunka Kenkyūjo kiyō* キリスト教文化研究所紀要 25:1 (2010): 79–106.

Yamanashi Atsushi. "Eiga *Junkyō ketsushi Nihon 26 Seijin* to Hirayama Masajū: 1930 nendai zenhanki Nihon Katorikku kyōkai no bunka jigyō" 映画『殉教血史　日本二十六聖人』と平山政十：一九三〇年代前半期日本カトリック教会の文化事業. *Nihon kenkyū* 日本研究 41 (2010): 179–217.

Yamanashi Atsushi. "Kindai Nihon ni okeru Rigyōru shinpu no shuppan katsudō to sono hankyō" 近代日本におけるリギョール神父の出版活動とその反響. *Katorikku kenkyū* カトリック研究 79 (2010): 39–73.

Yamanashi Atsushi. "Sōvūru Kandō shinpu to kindai Nihon no chishikijin" ソーヴール・カンドウ神父と近代日本の知識人. *Katorikku kenkyū* カトリック研究 81 (2012): 101–40.

Yamane Michihiro 山根道公. "Kaidai" 解題. In *Endō Shūsaku bungaku zenshū* 遠藤周作文学全集, vol. 5, 337–46. Shinchōsha, 1999.

Yamauchi Keisuke 山内継祐. "Neran-san wa Nihonjin ni nani o katatta ka" ネランさんは日本人に何を語ったか. *Fukuin to shakai* 福音と社会 258 (2011): 46–63.

Yamazaki Tadao 山崎忠雄. *Idai naru Viriyon shinpu: Viriyon shinpu ni manabite* 偉大なるヴィリヨン神父: ヴィリヨン神父にまねびて. Tokyo: Yamazaki Tadao, 1965.

Yanagiya Takeo 柳谷武夫. "Shohyō Hosokawa Garashia fujin" 書評　細川ガラシア夫人. *Katorikku kenkyū* カトリック研究 20: 1 (1940): 73–76.

Yano Michiko 矢野道子. *Do Ro shinpu sono ai no te* ド・ロ神父その愛の手. Nagasaki: Yano Michiko, 2004.

Yano Michiko. *Do Ro shinpu kurokawa no nichinichiroku* ド・ロ神父黒皮の日日録. Nagasaki: Nagasaki Bunkensha, 2006.

Yasuoka Shōtarō 安岡章太郎. "Daiseikimatsu sākasu" 大世紀末サーカス. *Asahi jānaru* 朝日ジャーナル 25: 41 (1983): 65–69.

Yokoyama Kendō 横山健堂. *Chōshū yūranki* 長周遊覧記. Kyōdo Kenkyūsha, 1930.

Yoneda Kaori 米田かおり. "Hosokawa Garasha to Iezusukai no Ongakugeki" 細川ガラシャとイエズス会の音楽劇. *Tōhō Gakuen Daigaku kenkyū kiyō* 桐朋学園大学研究紀要 28 (2002): 91–98.

Yoshida Hiromi 吉田弘美. "Basuku go" バスク語. In *Sekai no kotoba, jisho nojiten: Yōroppa hen* 世界のことば・辞書の辞典：ヨーロッパ編, edited by Ishii Yoneo 石井米雄, 272–82. Sanseidō, 2008.

Yoshimi Kaneko 吉見周子. "Masugi Shizue" 真杉静枝. In *Koi ni moe ai ni ikiru* 恋に燃え愛に生きる, edited by Enchi Fumiko 円地文子, 201–42. Shūeisha, 1980.

Yoshino Sakuzō 吉野作造. *Arai Hakuseki to Yowan Shirōte* 新井白石とヨワン・シローテ. Bunka Seikatsu Kenkyūkai, 1924.

Yoshiya Nobuko 吉屋信子. "Kozakana no kokoro" 小魚の心. In *Yoshiya Nobuko zenshū* 吉屋信子全集, vol. 11, 382–95. Asahi Shinbunsha, 1975.

Yūbunkan Henshūbu 祐文舘編集部, ed. *Shūshin no maki* 修身の巻. Ahūeidō Ōkawaya Shoten, 1905.

Yunesuko Higashi-Ajia Bunka Kenkyū Sentā ユネスコ東アジア文化研究センター, ed. *Shiryō oyatoi gaikokujin* 資料御雇外国人. Shōgakukan, 1975.

INDEX

ABOUT THE AUTHOR

Professor Nanyan Guo teaches in the Center for the Development of Global Leadership Education at the University of Tokyo. Born in Shanghai, she received both her MA and PhD degrees from Ochanomizu University (Tokyo), and taught for fifteen years at the University of Otago in New Zealand before returning to Japan to conduct research at the International Research Center for Japanese Studies (Kyoto) for ten years. She is a member of Academia Europaea.

Her research focuses on modern Japanese literature, Christianity in Japanese culture, and vernacular writings of Christian missionaries in East Asia. Her monographs include *Zabieru no yume o tsumugu: Kindai senkyōshi-tachi no Nihongo Bungaku* (Heibonsha, 2018), *Shiga Naoya de "Sekai Bungaku" o yomitoku* (Sakuhinsha, 2016), and *Refining Nature in Modern Japanese Literature: The Life and Art of Shiga Naoya* (Lexington Books, 2014).

Among her recent edited volumes are *Do Ro hanga no tabi (The Journey of the Woodblock Prints of Father Marc de Rotz: From Konstanz to Shanghai and Nagasaki*; Sōjusha Bijutsu Shuppan, 2019), and *Kirishitan ga hiraita Nihongo Bungaku: Tagengo tabunka kōryū no engen* (Akashi Shoten, 2017).

（英文版）ザビエルの夢を紡ぐ：近代宣教師たちの日本語文学

Making Xavier's Dream Real: Vernacular Writings of Catholic Missionaries in Modern Japan

2020年3月26日　第1刷発行

著　者　　郭　南燕

発行所　　一般財団法人出版文化産業振興財団
　　　　　〒101-0051 東京都千代田区神田神保町2-2-30
　　　　　電話　03-5211-7283
　　　　　ホームページ　　https://www.jpic.or.jp/

印刷・製本所　　大日本印刷株式会社